Telling Tragedy

Telling Tragedy

Narrative Technique in Aeschylus, Sophocles and Euripides

Barbara Goward

Duckworth

Paperback edition 2004
First published in 1999 by
Gerald Duckworth & Co. Ltd.
90-93 Cowcross Street, London EC1M 6BF
Tel: 020 7490 7300
Fax: 020 7490 0080
inquiries@duckworth-publishers.co.uk
www.ducknet.co.uk

A catalogue record for this book is available
from the British Library

ISBN 0 7156 3176 4

Printed and bound in Great Britain by
CPI Bath Ltd

Contents

Part III. Sophocles

Part IV. Euripides

To my parents, with love

Introduction

The two great epic poems, *Iliad* and *Odyssey*, have stunning narrative power and complexity. To read them is to be plunged headlong into pleasurable engagement with a variety of narrative strategies of a high order. Their influence on all subsequent genres of literature is manifest, but particularly so in tragedy. On a simple level, tragedy makes use of the same characters and the same story-lines as those in Homeric and Cyclic epic, dramatising, for example, many Odyssean *nostoi* tales, centred on a hero's problematic homecoming with its attendant plotting and deceits. At the most general level, it portrays a crisis in heroic lives lived out as in the *Iliad* (a poem rightly considered 'proto-tragic') in a context of enmity, stark choice, divine manipulation and, perhaps, inevitable death. But more significantly, many narrative techniques of epic, both large and small, obvious and less obvious, find their way into tragedy, richly adapted by their transformation into the challengingly different medium of drama. In Chapter 1, after validating the application of narrative theory to tragedy, I explore the different values of 'telling' and 'showing', the distinctive modes of communication of those two genres, narrative epic and dramatic tragedy.

Narrative time is an important area. Homer had deviated from a linear time-continuum and used foreshadowing techniques and flash-backs (prolepsis and analepsis) to make us aware of parameters beyond the timespan of the action covered in the poems. In the *Iliad* we know that after ten years Troy will fall and Achilles die (prolepsis); Odysseus' famous adventures are narrated in flashback at the court of the Phaeacians (analepsis, *Od.* 9-12.) The action of both poems, set against a larger frame, resonates with echoes from its outer boundaries. Adapting such temporal narrative strategies to tragedy so as to create shaping and perspective was particularly vital for the tragic dramatists, constrained to create both *desis* and *lusis* within the much briefer span of trilogy or single play: as I discuss in Chapter 2, ancient tragedies are structures typically built up by juxtaposing narratives of different temporal extent, and these constitute some of tragedy's most typical features. Long-range narratives in the form of oracles or dreams are present in virtually every surviving play by Aeschylus and Sophocles (portents and curses less commonly appear), while an almost 'standard' short-range narrative in Sophocles and Euripides is the messenger speech. Both these long and short-range narratives are features developed and adapted from pre-existing Homeric models.

However, by drawing on the resources of its own genre, tragedy's staged stories can be shaped by an even wider range of temporal narrative features. The chorus can be used to set out the past and hint at the future in its own distinctive lyric voice, creating, especially in Aeschylus, a suspenseful uncertainty and a strong religious dimension. At the opposite pole of this narrative suggestiveness, Euripides' formal prologues, especially if delivered by a god, appear to foretell the future course of the play in every exact detail. And at many of his endings a *deus ex machina* frequently prescribes the establishment of a cult to link mythical past of the play to historical present of the audience, quickly creating a shift in perspective and a sense of closure. (Sophocles makes more subtle future references; to cult also in *Ajax* and *Trachiniae* and, more blatantly, *Oedipus at Colonus*.) Then too, the concrete resources of the stage can be brilliantly exploited in occasional scenes of 'simultaneous' narrative – another distinct temporal narrative category in tragedy – when an off-stage event is simultaneously overheard, reported, and reacted to by those on-stage, as at *Agamemnon* 1331f.

Knowledge and lack of knowledge, whether the latter is simple ignorance or the product of another party's deliberate deceit, are, with time, another central feature of narrative (cf. the etymological links between *narrare*, **gnarare* and *gnarus*, 'knowing'). In Homer, *discrepant awareness* (disparate levels of knowledge) can be marked and engrossingly complex. For example we, the external audience, know that in *Iliad* 2 Zeus sends the 'deadly dream' deliberately to deceive Agamemnon; persuaded by Thetis, Zeus' motive is to make the Greeks realise how badly off they are without Achilles. We the audience know that the dream figure of Nestor, and his dream-narrative that Troy can be captured on that very day are false. But not predicted to us in Homer's narrative is Agamemnon's reaction to this false information – to conceal it from the army and instead, test out its loyalty. This test takes the form of a *second* false narrative whose sense runs in the opposite direction to the first: Agamemnon tells the army that Troy cannot, after all, be conquered and that they should sail home. The resultant splendid confusion is thus the product of *two* false narratives, one divine and one human, with contradictory import. All humans are deceived, though the heroes sharing Agamemnon's counsel are not doubly deceived like the army. And even we, the external audience are, if not deceived, at least surprised by the unexpected turn events take – even though they conform, if we think of it, to Zeus' overall scheme. This complex, ironic narrative strategy invites the audience to enjoy the effects of different levels of knowing and not knowing. Differently cast, the same might be said of Odysseus' four major deceitful narratives in the second half of the *Odyssey*. From these examples it is clear that false narrative, deliberately created to thwart knowledge, is a feature deeply inscribed within the narrative tradition. Tales within tales, lies within fiction: were it not for the guiding figure of Homer, authoritative external narrator, the audience itself would be at a loss to distinguish fictive truth from fictive falsehood.

Yet this is exactly the situation of tragedy, where the controlling external narrator is always suppressed. Chapter 3 discusses deceit, or *dolos*, as another of narrative's inherent properties, creating a model which seems particularly well suited to explore narrative operations in tragedy which, unmediated by epic's external narrator, has great inherent potential for discrepant awareness; each playwright creating his own idiosyncratic effects of grim or delicate irony, suspense or pathos, as his play makes its movement towards some apparent ultimate acquisition of knowledge. Manifest as a three-dimensional, enacted *dolos*, tragedy has, paradoxically, a frequently explicit concern for knowledge in the most profound religious or philosophical sense.

After this first, largely theoretical section, the rest of the book devotes a section each to Aeschylus, Sophocles and Euripides, in each case discussing their narrative strategy in general terms before making close readings of particular scenes, focusing in on narrative strategies particularly typical of each poet. Aeschylus' use of narrative time is an inexhaustible area for investigation: in Chapter 4 I discuss his creation of suspense, using delay and a kind of time-pendulum, and his rich use of predictive narratives in the form of dreams and oracles. His idiosyncratic use of narrative in three central scenes from *Septem*, *Agamemnon* and *Prometheus Bound*, each one highly specific and yet with many underlying similarities, is discussed in Chapter 5.

The section on Sophocles is exclusively concerned with 'narrative loops', sections of his tragedies where a deviation from a given story-line is created by the production of a false or ambiguous narrative, giving rise to new if temporary possibilities; the loop is later rejoined to the story-line at the point of exit. These narrative loops seem of overlooked significance to any understanding of Sophocles' narrative technique. To investigate the possible range of audience reactions aroused during their course, Rabinowitz's model of audience 'morphology' is helpful: Rabinowitz makes a theoretical distinction between authorial audience (sophisticates, capable of responding e.g. to metatheatrical or contemporary allusion) and narrative audience (temporarily assenting to believe in the fictive world and responding to the story as it unfolds, forgetting what they already know about the outcome). Any individual in the audience may be 'split' between these two functions. The model makes it possible to access the complex, disturbing and frequently contradictory range of emotions likely to have been aroused in the original audience by the events occuring in these loops. Chapter 6 looks at the loops *Ajax* 646-865, *Trachiniae* 180-496 and *Philoctetes* 541-627; chapter 7 at the stream of *doloi* – concealed, abortive, ambiguous or deceitful narratives – in the early part of *Electra*, leading up to and including the great false messenger speech, 680-787.

It seems impossible to tackle narrative techniques in Euripides' much more extensive and varied output without first acknowledging the possible effect of two external factors: the comparative crystallisation of the genre of tragedy, and the changed circumstances of the polis (factors which, of course, affected Sophocles too). In the attempt to answer the question, 'by what single strategy was Euripides able to create such novel dramas while still remaining within the tradition', Chapter 8 finds a solution in his use of *narrative*, positioned invariably at the beginning and, in fourteen out of the seventeen surviving tragedies, at the end; that is, the prologue-*rhêsis* and the closing narrative of the *deus*. Chapter 8 demonstrates how the presence of these narratives can function as a substitute for oracles and dreams to provide shaping to the structure while at the same time enabling a range of complex and idiosyncratic developments to take place within the narrative frame.

Chapter 9 takes two 'non-tragic' dramas – *Iphigeneia in Tauris* and *Helen* – and compares the functioning of one such complex development, recognition. An initial discussion of recognition as a figure for narrative as a whole (which reflects its continuing concern for knowledge) attempts to set tragic recognition within a wide frame.

Chapter 10 returns to serious tragedy and the topic of narrative at beginning and end, considering the prologue *rhêseis* delivered by gods in *Hippolytus* and *Bacchae*. Analysis shows that authoritative narrator, limpid narrative and lucidity of language mask a variable extent of unobtrusive *doloi* which ensure that, despite initial appearances, the plays will not only fulfil their predictions but also deliver profound shock and emotional release.

The fifth-century audience who heard the four-yearly competitive recital of the Homeric poems at the Great Panathenaia festival were the same people who watched the dramatic competition in the theatre of Dionysus. We lack their life-long exposure to the tellings and re-tellings of familiar stories and, with the vast proportion of tragedy lost, cannot begin to match the sophistication of their response as, year by year, they watched the reworking of tragedy's repertoire of typical narrative shapes, to be confirmed, subverted, capped or deleted in the poets' competitive attempt to make the limited body of story material once again suspenseful and relevant to the changing circumstances of the polis.

All the same, with the help of developments in narrative theory since the mid-seventies, it is possible to isolate some of tragedy's typical narrative procedures and describe something of the individual 'handprints' of each of the three tragic poets. The work of Roberts (1987, 1988, 1989), de Jong (1991) and now Dunn (1996) is important here. We can gain a better insight into the unfolding dynamics of individual plays, understanding them both in terms of their continuing debt to traditional narrative patterns and defining more closely the continuous exploration of the new. This book explores the interplay of narrative strategies between the tragic poet and his audience.

January 1998

Acknowledgements and thanks

I am hugely indebted to Pat Easterling, who supervised the thesis from which this book developed. Her special combination of scholarly sensitivity and benevolent encouragement galvanised my crude efforts. I would also like to thank Shirley Barlow, Irene de Jong, Chris Kraus, Nick Lowe, Deborah Roberts, Jenny March and Susan Woodford for their helpful suggestions and tactful editing. The two latter have kept me going. Remaining errors are certainly mine alone. Deborah Blake at Duckworth has been everything an editor could be. Friends and family, especially Chris, have also been tolerant and supportive over a long period. Finally, I have also benefited very much from studying tragedy over the last decade with students at the City Lit.

Part I

Narrative Theory and Tragedy

1

Theoretical Aspects

1.1 Can narrative theory be applied to drama?

Narrative theory views any text very simply as a communication between a narrator and a narratee. The external narrator of any text is its implied author, addressing the implied audience, the external narratee. However, inscribed within the narrative itself may be one or many figures who consistently or intermittently function as internal narrators or narratees.

Narrative theory has already been used to great effect with the novel and other more obviously narrative texts to investigate such areas as the sequential ordering of the plot in relation to the linear time-scale of the narrative overall; focalisation; and the whole subject of the narrator, his authority to narrate, and his complex relationship with his narratees.[1]

The question arises, to what extent narrative theory can be applied to drama when the narrator is always hidden behind his characters, and when the codes of communication available for the production of meaning are so much more complex than those involved in other models of narrative communication. We must begin by considering the different hermeneutic task that is entailed by each mode in theory – as well as observing how in fact drama meaningfully intermingles both dramatic and narrative codes, both of which originate in oral poetry.

It is clear that drama has a more intricate and paradoxical relationship to reality than narrative: while pure narrative relies on stimulation through language alone for its mimetic effect, drama, by the establishment of complex framing devices (see Goffman, 1974, ch. 5 and pp. 138ff.) creates a new onstage reality. What happens onstage is 'real' because it uses flesh-and-blood people with 'real' clothes on, who speak, gesture, react and interact in the present tense. The audience, aurally and visually stimulated, perceives ongoing, unfolding events taking place in a concrete reality. Yet of course, all but the youngest of audiences are at the same time well aware that what they see is a continuous deception.

It is the living figure of the actor which embodies the continuous tension between offstage and onstage reality.[2] Every stage figure has (at least) a double reference, first within the frame of the play as, for example, 'Agamemnon, King of Mycenae, stepping out of his chariot onto the tapestry in accordance with his wife's wishes', and secondly as the masked and robed actor cleverly impersonating Agamemnon with his own identity concealed.

In the dramatic mode, in theory the audience cannot interpret onstage events any better than those occurring outside the theatre (although framing mechanisms are likely to restrict the range of possible responses). That means, in terms of characterisation for example, that there is no possibility of making more than provisional assumptions about the on-stage characters. As in life, nothing is stable beyond basic definitions such as gender, status and age. Motivation can be only partially understood, giving rise to widely varying interpretations. Narrative and dramatic codes appear to differ here. Goffman (1974, 152) writes: 'Onstage, one character's interpretive response to another character's deeds, that is, one character's reading of another character, is presented to the audience and taken by them to be no less partial and fallible than a real individual's conduct in ordinary offstage interactions would be. But authors of novels and short stories assume and are granted definiteness; what they say about the meaning of a protagonist's action is accepted as fully adequate and true.'

The phrase 'granted definiteness' seems to create an important distinction between narrative and drama. The very plethora of codes at work in the theatre and the fact that the events of the play are variously interpreted as they occur by the stage figures as well as by the audience, seems to deny the possibility of incontrovertible meaning. In abstract, narratological terms, pure drama goes in for multiple focalisation at all times, without any narrative hierarchies to restrict the audience's reaction. Thus what might be interpreted as an advantage of a sort that drama possesses over narrative (i.e. 'concreteness'), is potentially a loss in terms of the 'definiteness' accorded pure narrative.

Ancient narrative epic partly acquires its overall definiteness or authority because focalisation is fixed at the outset on the poet, who is at the same time invoking the divine Muse. De Jong's discussion (1987, 52ff.) of the double presentation of the *Iliad* by both poet and Muse shows how a two-fold, overlapping authority is created. Perhaps it is also just as important that the events described take place in the *past* tense, so that they fall into the simple category of 'what happened', thus by tense alone acquiring a natural authority.[3] Epic narrative is the traditional channel of history, its truth indisputable, as long as the narrative focalisation remains with the external narrator. When the narrative of the *Iliad* moves from the Achaean to the Trojan side, or up to Olympus, we have no sense of doubt that 'Homer' can know all this. It is only because the narrative of the *Odyssey* has overall definiteness that the many false narratives issuing from Odysseus' lips are meaningful rather than creating total chaos.

All the same, even if drama and narrative have different tendencies that need to be taken into account, it is important to realise that these are not absolute differences. Like Odysseus in the *Odyssey*, the narrator may be unreliable. Nor is it easy to find texts sustaining 'pure' narrative or 'pure' drama throughout; the particular virtues inherent in each mode were from the outset exploited by placing them in conjunction with each other. Almost half the Homeric poems consist of character-speech as opposed to direct narration, and available evidence (surveyed by Herington, 1985, 10-15) indicates that the rhapsode of ancient Greece was highly 'dramatic', altering his voice to 'become' each character in turn.

Descriptive passages of the poem were no doubt also given a dramatic rendition.[4] Narrative, it seems, has always had the potential of performance, putting narrative texts into the same category as dramatic ones, in the sense that they would require a complex communication model to expound all their codes.[5] It is striking that narrative studies (consciously and unconsciously) make great use of theatrical models: 'in all the "grammars", "taxonomies" and "morphologies" of narratology, the metalinguistic signs are those which represent pointing, showing, displaying, acting, speaking, framing, décor, and *mise-en scène'* (Maclean, 1988, 15-16). Actantial theory also has clear dramatic roots which can be traced from Propp's decision to call his folk-tale figures *dramatis personae*, through Souriau's 'dramatic calculus' to Greimas' actants and their narrative dynamics.

Conversely, narrative elements are also a constant feature of drama, worked out in different ways at different epochs.[6] Ancient tragedy, a hybrid form in so many senses, is a particularly striking hybrid of narrative and dramatic codes. Ancient playwrights regularly alternate dialogic episodes with continuous narrative or with sung narratives from the chorus. While these are going on a 'definiteness' may temporarily be granted (sometimes ironic) and there may be little sense of theatre's synaesthetic 'concreteness'. Tragedy's markedly hybrid form is one of its great strengths, since at each juncture between different modes and different focalisations the audience are freshly re-engaged in their struggle to discover meaning.[7]

Drama has been defined as 'a fusion of a fixed and a fluid component' (Esslin, 1976, 33), where the fixed element is the text and the fluid one the performance. 'A dramatic text is a blueprint for ... mimetic action, it is not yet itself, in the full sense, drama' (ibid. 24). Writers on theatre and drama rightly insist on the importance of the performance element. Our limited understanding of the performance conventions of ancient drama is a real loss. Stage action is 'an inextricable element of his [the playwright's] communication and hence of his meaning' (Taplin, 1977, 2).[8] However, we have the competence to do at least some of the necessary reconstruction work, via the existing text. Given that since antiquity Attic tragedy has never been continuously available in performance, this has always been normal and necessary practice: to read the text, imagine the performance element, and develop one's interpretation of the whole. As well as 'narrative competence' we can also develop 'theatrical and dramatic competence'. The reader takes theatrical codes into account as far as he can in his reading.

At a fundamental level, narrative and drama are indistinguishable.

Sharing a common origin in epic, they are best understood as each other's *alter ego*. Both are culturally-shaped language communications, liable to the sort of literary hermeneutic activity analysed in detail by Ricoeur who uses the phrase 'helix of dynamic productivity' to describe the process of creation of meaning. Both forms derive their existence from life, and in this sense are equally mimetic. Unlike incoherent life, however, both are 'intensely and meaningfully shaped' (Easterling, 1990, 108). Both forms excite in the reader or audience what Barthes has called 'the passion to discover meaning'. Narrative theory may usefully be applied to dramatic texts.

1.2 Tragedy as narrative

Each tragic text is an intelligible communication, a narrative. It exhibits no overall narrator such as 'Homer', operating at a different narrative level from the heroes – although, especially in the plays of Euripides, divine prologue-speakers and gods from the machine may temporarily assume such a position. Instead, operating at the same narrative and temporal level as that in which the action of the play takes place, any of the *dramatis personae* may take it in turns to supply the function of narrator, or to be the internal audience or narratee. Just as we see happening with characters in Homer – most obviously Odysseus in the *Odyssey* but others too such as Nestor in the *Iliad* – the stage figures themselves are capable of delivering narratives of their own. Tragedy is not really different in kind from, for example, the debate scenes between heroes in the *Iliad*, except that there are no links such as 'Thus spoke x, but y ...'.

From this perspective, it is apparent that not only obvious narrative elements such as the 'messenger speech' may be investigated for their narratological properties, but all other elements in a tragedy also, such as prologue, *rhêsis*, stichomythia, choral ode, etc. Each of these formal elements communicates to the internal and external narratees in its own particular way, with different truth effects and emotional colouring developed within the tragic tradition. The poet has available to him at any point a variety of messengers and a variety of formal modes through which he can develop his theme.

The complicating factor is the chorus, which is essentially hybrid and fluctuating in nature; there are always exceptions to the generalisations one would like to make about it. Its apparent spatial separation from the actors (but see n. 9), its separate sections of singing and dancing during the play when the actors are not present or not actively developing their roles, its group memory and its overt moralising seem to put it, on the one hand, at a different diegetic and temporal level from the main action, giving the chorus a typological resemblance to a purely external narrator, witness rather than participant. On the other hand, there are notable occasions when the chorus itself is the major character in the play (e.g.

Aeschylus *Supplices*, *Eumenides*), or when the intervention of the chorus definitely contributes to the action (e.g. *Choephoroe, Ion*), as well as many subtler occasions when the chorus interact with the protagonist and his emotional state in a lyric exchange, offering words of consolation, encouragement, modification, suggestion, comparison, etc.[9] Frequently too it is the suffering victim of the action, threatened by Aegisthus in *Agamemnon*, afflicted by the plague in *Oedipus Tyrannus*, sold into slavery in *Trojan Women*. It cannot view the stage action from the distanced, temporal perspective with which Homer in the *Iliad* sees the war of Troy. The narrating occasion of Homer is always after the city has fallen; he knows the outcome of all the encounters between Greek and Trojan, the ultimate fates of Achilles, Hector, etc.. The chorus, on the other hand, despite their overviews and frequent attempts at prediction (sometimes derived from their role as repositories of the community's wisdom) belong to the same time-frame as the actors – unlike 'Homer'. They are often wrong about the future: they can be both wrong and right within the compass of a single ode.

Given these complexities, it seems only sensible to define the chorus in general as a potential narrator or narratee just as the other characters, while looking carefully at specific narrative functions the chorus of any one play may carry out.

1.3 Tragedy and knowledge

Compared with Shakespearian tragedy, it seems true to say that Greek tragedy distinctly encourages the audience (as external narratees working in parallel with the internal narratees) to involve themselves in the attempt to learn, interpret, understand. Ancient tragedies are often structured so that narrative information, whether proffered or withheld, is a firmly foregrounded topic, rather than an element that is buried as far as possible in favour (for example) of conversational naturalism or psychological realism. This is not to be accounted for by the restricted linear nature of drama (as opposed to painting, which presents all its information at the same time), or by a view that any of the surviving Greek tragedies are technically naive.

Rather, ancient tragedy displays an intermittent but continuing concern with the problem of gaining knowledge. At a superficial, technical level, entries and exits are frequently motivated by the need either to give or receive information. Especially in Euripides, the apparently random entry of a new character may be motivated by an opening speech in which the character says that he has heard voices and wishes to know more (for an earlier example of this see *Prometheus Bound* 133-5). More profoundly, many tragedies seem to thematise problems of communication and devote much of their extent to exploring the tensions and dangers of ignorance before certainty is acquired. This concern for knowledge shapes sections of tragedies or even entire plays. A common type of choral ode, from Aeschylus onwards, is sung in a state of tension while news is awaited. Plays with *nostos* plots (plots of homecoming) naturally give rise to a concern for intelligence, on the part both of the returning hero and of those waiting. Information-gathering can form the basis of the action. *Oedipus Tyrannus* is clearly a play with a plot structure based on acquiring and understanding information; in a different way the action of *Hippolytus* is made to turn on critical moments in which information is passed from one character to another. The difficulty of getting a reliable narrator is experienced harshly by many of Sophocles' heroes – Deianeira, Electra, Philoctetes.

The denial of knowledge by the creation of a false narrative is a common element in tragedy, which produces frequently fatal consequences. False narrative enmeshes and destroys Aegisthus in the tiny scene *Choephoroe* 838-54; this scene is itself only one peak of a sequence which begins at 652 and culminates in the two murders. The sequence contains an extraordinary build-up of suspense, surprise and speed, punctuated by the chorus. Tension is built almost entirely round the ability to exchange true and false messages in quick succession between one party and another.

At 838 Aegisthus enters, as he says, *hupangelos*, 'summoned by a messenger', but without his guards, since Clytemnestra's message (716-17) has been intercepted by the chorus, who have set up the Nurse Cilissa as their deceitful messenger. Aeschylus has taken pains to show us the set-up being created in an unusual earlier scene.[10] Aegisthus' dialogue with the chorus is significantly restricted to the need to verify the information he has received. It is clear to the audience that verification will entail going inside and being murdered, and indeed, after a brief choral interlude, his death cries are heard. In the logic of Attic drama, to be deceived by a false narrative into entering the stage building is very often the prelude to being killed (compare the carpet scene in *Agamemnon* of which this is a mirror, also Euripides *Hec.* 1011ff., *Her.* 701ff. A further discussion of such scenes follows at 2.2.3). The onstage scene of narrative deception virtually symbolises the offstage murder that will shortly take place. The discrepant awareness[11] between false narrator and victim-narratee creates great tension in the audience.

Different levels of knowledge and the obfuscating of truth by deliberate falsehood certainly produce suspense and turn revenge plots, but these are features characteristic of Shakespearian as much as of ancient tragedy. The original form early tragedy may have taken does not provide much insight to account for ancient tragedy's broader obsession with knowledge. In terms of 'the information' set out in a messenger speech, proto-tragedy doubtless consisted of a series of entrances by an actor who provided the permanently onstage chorus with information to which they reacted (sometimes with their own kind of narrative), while the single actor disappeared to change his identity. Michelini (1987, 21-2) considers how, as tragedy evolves, traditional forms might conflict with newer practices and thus create a focal point out of an element that was not previously in question at all. This may be the case with message narrative, which perhaps comprised a large part of early tragedy without being isolated as a feature in its own right: only when a greater naturalism has developed in conveying information[12] is message narrative perceived as a discrete structure available for development as a 'set piece'.[13] This consideration is useful if it helps banish the certainly mistaken view that overt sections of 'informing' are essentially an awkward legacy from tragedy's early history. However, it still leaves unanswered the reasons for tragedy's profound emotional investment in knowledge, a concern which shapes entire tragedies, not merely their messenger speeches.

Contemporary communication does not offer a satisfactory model either, beyond a certain point. Certainly, tragedy reflects the comparatively slow and face-to-face channels of communication available in the fifth-century Athenian world. In Herodotus and Thucydides, heralds, scouts, runners and more informal messengers play significant, sometimes critical roles.[14] In war time, the outcome of decisions made in a day's debate in the Assembly must often be awaited for many weeks, involving whole communities in the process of expectation. News came to the polis as we see it coming to the tragic stage, *viva voce*, from the mouth of an individual who had witnessed events or had been authorised to give a report (Longo, 1978, is excellent on the messenger's role in contemporary society and on the tragic stage). However, tragedy still seems to raise by a power what is already an inherent element of tension in the culture.

The concluding section of Burkert's fine discussion of *Oedipus Tyrannus* (1991, 24ff.) makes the point that in the Greek mind all knowledge is to be associated with divine knowledge. Greek religion is 'intellectualist in its character in the fact that it is through "knowing" that the divine asserts itself'. With no other, authorised form of religion (such as the Bible or an organised priesthood), it is left to oracles and prophets, with their divinely inspired fore-knowledge, to reassert divine omniscience. In many tragedies, the ultimate acquisition of knowledge, frequently presaged by oracle or divine prediction, leads to an understanding of human fate which is at the same time an understanding of divine will. Gaining knowledge in tragedy readily takes on the intensity of a religious revelation.[15]

1.4 Narrative versus action or 'telling' versus 'showing'

In this section narrative is considered in its more limited sense as a mode of expression which *contrasts* with the dramatic mode. Horace's crisp distinction is exactly right here: *aut agitur res in scenis aut acta refertur*, 'action either takes place on the stage or it is narrated' (*Ars Poetica*, 179). Modern definitions are more careful: drama is 'the scenic rendering of speech or thought and behaviour', while narrative is 'the representation of

real or fictive events and situations in a time sequence' (Prince, 1987).
Given the long and misleading tradition of comparing 'action' unfavour-
ably with 'narrative', I believe there is a case for attempting some kind of
rehabilitation for the place of narrative within drama. The following
discussion leaves lyric out of the picture for the moment.

Within the episodes of tragedy it is clear that major continuous narrative offers a marked contrast in mode from passages of dialogue or
dreigesprach. Unlike the concrete, visual, and essentially unfocalised
mode of dialogue, narrative offers to the audience a quite different mediated communication, entirely limited (in theory) by the narrator's
perspective.[16] Traditional comparisons between the two modes are made
in terms of the intrinsic mimetic qualities, in the sense of their ability to
be vivid, to imitate the stuff of real life. In making such a distinction, the
victory is invariably accorded to *showing* (by action or dialogue) rather
than to *telling* (by narrative).

Stage action certainly requires explanatory background information to
become intelligible to its audience. The narrative element, with its unlimited freedom to move offstage and through past and future time, can pick
out and give significance to certain elements so as to provide a distinct and
fresh reading of an old story. However, any view of narrative as separable
background orientation for the audience, an element tacked on to the 'real'
action is quite inadequate.

It helps here to consider Halliwell's range of definitions for Aristotle's
use of the terms *praxis* and *pragmata* (a play's 'action'), since they both
illustrate the perceived gap between narrative and dramatic forms, and
help to close it up. One the one hand, these terms mean acts or events
which are shown during the course of the play, approximating to the term
'plot' (see Halliwell, 1986, 141ff.). The narrative element of tragedy as we
mean it here would be largely excluded from a discussion of the play in
exclusively plot terms. However, *praxis* and *pragmata* also bear a more
generous meaning: Halliwell's phrases for this are 'overarching framework', 'essential design', and 'intelligible substance', bringing us back to
the broad definition of narrative argued for in 1.1.[17]

A distinction between art forms in terms of their different mimetic
qualities is not apparent in Aristotle. In *Poetics* ch. 1, tragedy, comedy, epic,
dithyramb and *aulos*-playing are forms all equally mimetic of life. In his
final chapter, in which he accords priority to tragedy over epic, he is not
basing his judgement on mimetic superiority. Plato, however, had already
initiated an insidious distinction, and it is this which seems to have
influenced subsequent cultural perceptions. At *Republic* 3.392c5, having
discussed the moral content of literature, Socrates turns to its formal
structure or *lexis*, and divides literature into two basic categories. (We are
not at all concerned here with the conclusions Plato himself wishes to draw
from the comparison – on the dangers of acting, for example – merely on
the possible deleterious effects on later thinking).

To exemplify his two categories, Plato makes Socrates take *Iliad* 1.17-42 and recast it without the direct speech of the heroes and without what he considers superfluous description. This new, second version is defined as 'pure narrative' or *haplê diêgesis* (393d5), narrative 'unmixed', *akêraton*, with direct speech. The poet is now speaking throughout in his own person (*legei te autos ho poiêtês*, 393) and does not attempt to persuade his audience that the speaker is anyone but himself.[18]

Opposed to this new 'pure' narrative is *mimêsis* or *to mimeisthai*, 'imitation' – Homer's original, in which he represents other characters by using direct speech in the manner of drama. This category is in fact mixed, as the direct speech of the other characters is interspersed with the poet's linking descriptions. However, the discussion of the two categories of 'pure' and 'mixed' forms of expression will serve well to exemplify considerations of apparent inherent virtues and defects to be found in 'narrative' and 'drama'.

Genette (1980, 162-5) has analysed the original *Iliad* passage and Plato's reworking at some length in his own brilliant and suggestive way. He makes the point that direct speech, when reported still as direct speech, as in Homer's narrative, appears to be directly mimetic, that is, exact quotation from a supposed real situation. Chryses' address to Apollo (*Iliad* 1.37), *kluthi meu, argurotox'*, 'Hear me, god of the silver bow', is certainly more striking than when it is recast as indirect speech, 'he offered many prayers to Apollo, invoking the god by his eponyms and reminding him and making demands ...' (*Republic* 3.394). How much more vivid to hear Chryses' own voice calling on the god by his eponyms, rather than being flatly told that he used them!

Plato's recasting of Homer into 'pure' narrative results in a changed length. Plato's version is only 136 words, Homer's around 200. A notable loss in the condensation are some of the stylistic formulas in the linking narrative sections , such as 'so he spoke' (33), or 'whom lovely-haired Leto bore' (36). These might be considered formulaic padding, but in fact one must conclude, with Genette, that these purely descriptive passages are important in creating Barthes' *effet du réel*. Of line 34, 'he walked silently by the shore of the loud-sounding sea' he writes, 'The loud-sounding sea serves no purpose other than to let us understand that the narrative mentions it only because *it is there*, and because the narrator, abdicating his function of choosing and directing the narrative, allows himself to be governed by "reality", by the presence of what is there and what demands to be "shown". A useless and contingent detail, it is the medium par excellence of the referential illusion, and therefore of the mimetic effect: it is a *connotator of mimesis*.'

In conclusion, the recast, 'pure' narrative shows us what a text might be like when a poet does not conceal his own *persona* behind another character (as in drama) and when he chooses to suppress all attempts at vivid *showing* and restrict himself instead to limited *telling*; there is no doubt that the result is lacking in vivid and lifelike detail, and that it is more distant from 'felt experience'. Nonetheless, it is clear from the narrated passages of the Homer extract that narrators do not necessarily abandon attempts at 'showing' or that narrative is in any way intrinsically less mimetic.

It is likely, however, that Plato's dreary rendition of Homer had a negative effect on the perception of narrative in general. Horace gives clear expression to the opinion that dialogue is intrinsically more effective:

> *Segnius irritant animos demissa per aurem*
> *quam quae sunt oculis subiecta fidelibus, et quae*
> *ipse sibi tradit spectator.* (*Ars Poetica* 140-2)

> What comes in via the ear stirs the feelings more slowly
> than what is put before the trustworthy eye, what the
> spectator himself takes in for himself.

This view was vigorously taken up again in the late nineteenth and early twentieth century, particularly by the Anglo-American school in relation to the aesthetics of the novel, cast this time in terms of the superiority of 'showing' over 'telling'.[19] It may be that this largely unchallenged ideology has caused critics to gloss over any real study of the intrinsic properties of message narrative in tragedy, and to fail to see that it might be a positive choice made by the poet, rather than one forced upon him by the alleged conventional restrictions of Attic drama.

Evolutionary or teleological views of tragedy have not helped here; especially the view that sees drama as an art form that originated in choral lyric, added solo narrative, and then became increasingly dramatic as it achieved its fifth-century form. There is sometimes a tendency to view message narrative as though it were an evolutionary weakness in what 'should' be a fully dramatic form, producing a narrow discussion in terms of functional necessity. While it is true that the continuous presence of the chorus implies a unity of place[20] which cannot lightly be negotiated away, with the result that events occurring within the stage building or 'abroad' must be conveyed by means of a messenger, the interesting exceptions to this 'rule'[21] point the way out towards a more generous understanding of narrative in drama.

Both dramatic 'showing' and narrative 'telling' are likely to have different characteristic strengths which ancient dramatists well knew how to exploit and contrast within an individual tragedy, just as lyric and non-lyric passages are exploited and contrasted, to make complex play with the audience's expectations and emotions. Given the persistent presence of messenger narrative in the latest surviving tragedies, it is insufficient to understand them merely as a survival of archaic practice, and to talk, as Bremer does, of the 'conservatism'[22] of playwrights when the evidence of the plays themselves points rather to continuous innovation throughout the fifth century.

Narrative has positive advantages unavailable to dialogue. First, in the case of dialogue, the audience must make continuous optical, aural and mental adjustments to take account of who is speaking, and work to assess the points at issue. By contrast the information transmitted in mediated narrative is 'pre-digested' and (arguably) at its easiest to assimilate. There is fairly good evidence that contemporary audiences liked messenger speeches.[23] Second, and this is particularly true of Sophocles, the culminating simplicity of mediated message narrative often comes immediately after the emotional and intellectual complexity of a lyric, providing perhaps the greatest contrast of mode possible within Attic drama. For example: the *Oedipus Tyrannus* messenger speech 1227-85 follows the choral ode, 'O generations of mortal men', *iô geneai brotôn* (1186ff.); the *Antigone* messenger speech 1192-243 follows the choral ode to Dionysus, 'God of many names, glory of the Cadmeian bride', *poluônume, Kadmeias numphas agalma* (1115); the messenger speech at *Oedipus at Colonus* 1586-1666 follows the choral ode to Persephone and chthonic gods, 'If it is lawful for me to reverence the unseen goddess', *ei themis esti moi tan aphanê theon ...* (1556). The pleasure we derive from the intellectual and aural contrast here could be compared to the way we respond to the different tempi and tonal colouring of the successive movements of a symphony.

The third, more central range of advantages offered by continuous narrative – its total control over its material – are best exemplified by using Bal's four basic categories of *actors*, *events*, *time* and *space*, these being the elements with which any form of literature may communicate. These examples are all taken from Sophocles' messenger speeches.

Actors: the number of participants in the event narrated can be unlimited. Hyllus' narrative about Heracles' downfall is strengthened by the description of the entire army as horrified witnesses frozen with fear (*hapas ... leôs*, *Trach.* 783), and Hyllus realistically describes himself standing among them until his father picks him out from the crowd. Similarly, the Paedagogus creates an internal audience for his story: everyone at Delphi finds Orestes glorious ('He made a brilliant entry, an object of awe to everyone there', *eisêlthe lampros, pasi tois ekei sebas*, *El.* 685). These internal mass audiences are a mirror and guide for the reactions of the theatre audience, and they help transform the narrative account into that of a reported drama. Such audiences can appear and disappear effortlessly, but they can have an effect on the onstage action too: the Greek soldiers who are described crowding around Teucer and calling for Ajax's stoning (*Aj.* 721ff.) raise onstage fears for Ajax's safety and hasten the chorus offstage to search for their leader.

Events: the supernatural and semi-supernatural can be effortlessly described; the miraculous death of Oedipus in *Oedipus at Colonus*; the whirl of dust which blinds the guard watching by the corpse of Polyneices in *Antigone*; Deianeira's account of the poisoned tuft of wool in *Trachiniae*. Acts of gruesome horror – murders, blindings, and so on – can be put across with the exactly salient or significant details. Events which could not be convincingly or clearly staged in dramatic form can in narrative be made completely intelligible to the audience.

Time and space: the playwright has an almost infinite freedom of opportunity to elide, magnify, pause, move anywhere instantaneously. Narrative has infinite powers: if it were possible to dramatise events on stage they would take much longer than the few minutes it takes the narrator to give his account. One of the virtues of mediated narration is that it can make temporal elisions at any point, cutting out the inessential and lingering at an important moment. Where the poet lingers, we are entitled to look for his particular concerns (for example, Seneca devotes twenty-four gruesome lines to an account of Hippolytus' mangling (Sen. *Hipp*. 1085-108) compared with Euripides' four (E. *Hipp*. 1236-9)).

The pace of the narration itself, accelerating inexorably from a slow, scene-setting start to climax and pause on the moment of horror, as is often the case, can heighten the tension. Space is similarly fluid, and the narrative, through the focalisation of the narrator can, like a camera, alter focus, pan, close up. Important other locations can be brought into play: the altar of Zeus at Cenaeum where Heracles is offering sacrifice in *Trachiniae*, the race track at Delphi in *Electra*, Antigone's 'hollow, rock-strewn bridal chamber of Hades' (*Ant*. 1204-5).

Given these infinitely flexible narrative possibilities, it is not surprising that messenger speeches have the power profoundly to engage the intellect and emotions of the audience. There is no doubt that the messenger speech frequently has supreme importance in the play overall. With its highly dramatic narrative content, often conveyed in the vivid present tense with bursts of direct speech, the whole delivered by an actor trained in the use of mime and impersonation, the narrative becomes a virtual drama in its own right. As Easterling remarks, 'The telling and the listening become the action for the duration of the story.'

Like Homer before them, all three playwrights seem to have had a highly developed understanding of the dramatic effects to be gained from the juxtaposition of sections of 'showing' and sections of 'telling' in the episodes of their dramas. We can see that however tense and thrilling the dialogues between stage figures may be, with their displays of aggression (*hubris*), persuasion (*peithô*), friendship (*philia*) or advice (*parainesis*), it is often rightly left to the extraordinary capacities of continuous narrative to convey the heart of the matter.

2

Narrative Time in Tragedy

> Narrative is a ... doubly temporal sequence ... : there is the time of the thing
> told and the time of the narrative .... This duality not only renders possible
> all the temporal distortions that are commonplace in narratives (three years
> of the hero's life summed up in two sentences of a novel or in a few shots of
> a 'frequentative' montage in film, etc.). More basically, it invites us to
> consider that one of the functions of narrative is to invent one time scheme
> in terms of another time scheme.
>
> Christian Metz, *Film language: a semiotics of the*
> *cinema,* quoted by Genette, 1980, 33

Genette's revealing work on narrative time in Proust indicates the importance of attempting to understand how time is used in any text. Narrative
is both delivered on an occasion in time, and creates its own temporal
existence; the meaning of a narrative is dependent on being able to order
its events in a chronological sequence.

Greek tragedy, speaking very generally, gives rise to two experiences of
time: the synchronic time of many of the stasima (lyric sections), capable
of vast shifts of temporal perspective, conspectuses and parallels, tangen-
tial reflections on age, the power of love, capacity of man and so forth, and
the more immediate, diachronic time of the iambic trimeter sections of
episodes (non-lyric sections) in which individual characters are seen moving through time towards fixed end points. The lack of exact alignment
between the two time schemes creates a dialectic unavailable to most
other modes of drama.[1] The disjunction or *parataxis* is more than a merely
formal distinction: in hermeneutic terms it tends to create a gap in our
understanding. To operate in this way – by the creation of gaps – is a
fundamental property of narrative, whether the gap is primarily temporal
or factual. 'It is the very lack of ascertainability and defined intention that
brings about the text-reader interaction. ... It is this very indeterminacy
that increases the variety of communication possible' (Iser, 1978, 166).

Tragedy frequently goes in for great temporal complexity. The work of
putting together information given at different times during the course of
the play to create a sequential narrative whole is a major part of the
interaction between the audience and the staged events. This is especially
true of the plays of Aeschylus and Sophocles. Tragedy is rich in different
kinds of anachronies: using Genettian terminology, achrony, analepsis,
prolepsis, metalepsis, paralipsis and so forth. These anachronies can be

left in various stages of disconnection with the main narrative, leaving junctures and conspicuous gaps, suggesting but denying the possibility of satisfactory interpretation: some choral odes of Sophocles work in this way – for example the epode of the first stasimon of *Electra* 504-15, set (in my view) at such an extraordinary tangent to the previous strophe and antistrophe.

After a brief look at narrative time and the chorus, this chapter focuses on the use of time in episodes, making a basic formal distinction between long-range and short-range narratives. Long-range narratives may point in either direction, looking either forward (proleptic) or back (analeptic). Short-range narratives may also be divided between those relating events in the very recent past and those describing events as they actually occur (simultaneous narrative). These contrasting narrative categories are helpful for analysing the creation of time and meaning in the overlapping and discontinuous form of tragedy, with its alternating sung and spoken sections. Tragic form is ideally suited for comment and reflection on the action as it takes place, together with suggestions about the play's ultimate outcome, involving the audience closely in the hermeneutic process.

2.1 Time and the chorus

Choral lyric has a natural reach into the past and future. This is due to the religious and civic ancestry of the chorus (which evolved long before tragedy itself), and its own highly developed mode of expression, its typical wishes, hopes, fears and long memory. For the past, choruses can be assigned real authority. The strongest expression of this comes at *Agamemnon* 104ff., *kurios eimi throein*, 'I have authority to tell ...'. Choruses can offer explanatory background, as in the opening lyrics (*parodoi*) of *Persians*, *Supplices*, *Agamemnon*; they can narrate myths of past events in the hero's family (e.g. *Trach.* 497ff., *Ant.* 582ff., *Phil.* 676ff.). The past they describe is rarely without significance for the future action of the play, and lyric narratives are not limited to the chorus' own experience, but can on occasion embrace the whole of human knowledge. All the same, the audience is rarely left unaware of the disjunction between their powers as narrators of the past and as predictors of the future.

Distinctions can be made between Aeschylus and the two younger dramatic poets in terms of the extent to which they evoke a *parallel* world existing outside the story that is being narrated. In the plays of Sophocles and Euripides, the stage figures and the temporal duration of their actions in the episodes tend to be firmly foregrounded and separated out from the more achronic choral odes and the secondary narratives and figures often evoked there (for example, the brief reference to the story of Amphiaraus, Sophocles *El.* 836f.). In the plays of Aeschylus, however, the mythical heroes are less modernised and the lyrics, in a much more unified, less problematic way, simply constitute the world of the play they inhabit. In

Supplices the fifty undifferentiated daughters of Danaus are both chorus and most important character; in *Eumenides* the non-human chorus of Furies are the major threat to the successful conclusion of the trilogy: the temporary evocation of parallel mythical figures is unnecessary. The section *Choephoroe* 585ff., when the chorus sing of Althaea, Scylla and the Lemnian Women, is the only surviving sustained reference to *external* myth in Aeschylus.

By contrast, the two later playwrights quite often use the different temporal tendencies of lyric to allude to other narratives. This can be for a whole variety of purposes (such as to align current problems to a pre-existing pattern, to provide comfort or offer advice), but sometimes and quite typically, the effect of the parallel choral narrative is to open up a gap between the 'now' of the stage figures – modern, pragmatic, questioning the past – and the 'timeless' voice of traditional community wisdom with its repository of tales.[2]

Since it is generally outside the brief of the chorus to leave the stage and gather its own news, its approach must be, in journalistic terms, essentially editorial: the immediate 'hard' news of the classic messenger speech comes at the opposite end of the narrative spectrum. This generalisation however, obscures interesting subtleties of practice. The chorus on occasion can be used to narrate recent offstage events. For example, in *Oedipus at Colonus* choral lyric serves as a virtual replacement of the messenger speech: Creon's men have made off with Oedipus' daughters and Theseus' men are in pursuit. Creon has been verbally worsted already when at 1044ff. the chorus wish themselves where the action is. By the time the brief ode is over, the encounter between Theseus' men and Creon's has been narrated through their imagination and expectation of what will happen to such an extent that the next scene can begin with the daughters' immediate return and reunion with Oedipus. This technique allows us to see the magnanimous authority of Theseus in full play and does not restrict Oedipus' display of paternal joy in the following scene. At the same time a full messenger speech has been avoided, enabling the action to sweep on and lead ultimately to the great speech (1579ff.). This ode makes an interesting comparison with *Oedipus Tyrannus* 463-82, in which the chorus similarly invoke an offstage situation as they imagine it; but here the description conforms to the more usual ironic pattern, since the chorus are mistaken when they describe Laius' murderer as a bull in the wild (476f.) – he is of course the king within their own city.

In *Hippolytus* Euripides too makes unusual use of the chorus as a narrator of immediate events in relation to Phaedra's suicide. In fact, Phaedra herself, the chorus and the offstage nurse all contribute to the news: Phaedra has already told the chorus she is set on death (723), then in the final strophe of their lyric (764-75) the chorus sing 'she will fasten the noose about her neck'; immediately afterwards through the wall of the stage building the offstage nurse confirms this to the chorus in a brief dialogue (776-89), and at 790 Theseus enters. The significant detail – the tablet on her body – we are later *shown* Theseus himself discovering (856ff.). Noteworthy also is *Hecuba* 98-152, where the choral entry-song is primarily a piece of news.

More typical, however, is the ironic Sophoclean pattern in which the chorus give themselves authority and style themselves prophets (e.g. *El.* 472, *OT* 1086). However, they are poor narrators of the future, and usually make wilder guesses than the stage figures; in fact they are well-known for offering false optimistic outcomes. The combination of authoritative, often paradeigmatic information about the past, coupled with emotive and sometimes misleading reaction concerning the present and immediate future sets up a typically complex dynamic; the chorus offer an intermittent stream of possible meanings with which the audience must at all points of the plot engage, and there is always the possibility that they will 'speak more truly than they know'.

More distinctions between sung and spoken sections can be made in terms of temporal elasticity: stage figures during scenes are constrained by the temporal rules that govern our own lives, that is, there is an apparent parallel between stage time and 'real' time (though naturally this effect is mimetic only: cf. Taplin, 1977, 291ff., also Genette, 1980, 86-8 on duration, isochrony and anisochrony). By contrast the time that elapses during a choral ode is far more elastic; in terms of stage time, there may be no time lapse while they sing, or perhaps, we discover from the next episode, hours have passed.

However, when the action of a play reaches its climax, the chorus are often left alone onstage to anticipate the coming horror (e.g. *Ag.* 1331, *Med.* 1251ff.). At this point their inability to intervene highlights the helplessness of humans in general, and reflects the sensations of the audience. Far from creating an elastic sense of the passage of time, the chorus at such moments make us experience the passage of every second with increasing tension.

2.2 Time in episodes

Within the episodes there is an apparently more restricted temporal scope. Here too, however, there is a specific category of stage figures who – outstripping the authority of the chorus – have definite authority to narrate both past and future: gods and prophets. When these figures speak, or when their words are reported, the temporal range within the episodes is greatly extended. Consequently within the episodes we can distinguish two temporally distinct types of narrative, those with a long temporal range and those relating to recent or immediate events.

2.2.1 Long-range proleptic narratives: portents, prophecies, dreams and curses

The use of dreams, prophecies and, less commonly, portents and curses is a striking characteristic of the narrative technique of Aeschylus and Sophocles – less so of Euripides.[3] Presented at a different narrative level running parallel to the major narrative, they exert a control on events and on the audience's perception of events. Although they generally point forward towards the climax of the play, they may also be used analeptically in the closing stages to create a sense of closure.

In tragedy's fictive world, dreams and prophecies provide a definite frame, since they always determine an outcome. It is in the nature of fiction that no element is irrelevant, however problematic. Dreams come true, prophecies and portents are infallible indicators, and curses are never uttered in vain. Roberts (1984, 24ff.) has a good discussion of the pattern of oracle stories both in tragedy and elsewhere. The narrative rules seem to be that predictions are fulfilled, oracular commands obeyed and oracular prohibitions disobeyed. This pattern is absolutely in accordance with the Proppian model that orders are fulfilled and interdictions violated.

The external audience of tragedy knows well that the events outlined will come to pass, but to the internal audience (the stage figures within the world of the drama), it is not so clear. Through the proleptic narrative, the audience is directed to view the unfolding action in a way that is both omniscient and teleological. The stage action manifests itself as a series of events seen with the heightened perception of foreknowledge as working towards an inevitable end. This perspective contrasts ironically with the stage figures' inability to understand what will happen (despite receiving the same advance notification) until too late.[4]

From one point of view, dreams and prophecies are a functional way of solving the problem of dramatising what are essentially small sections taken from a much bigger overall narrative. But apart from being a practical dramaturgical aid, if the earliest tragedies were, as Garvie suggests (1969, 105), 'little more than a messenger speech with lyric content', the development of pro- and analeptic narratives counters this tendency and contributes to the sense of profundity associated with tragedy.[5] Whoever the onstage narrator of dream or oracle may be, an ultimate narrator is indicated whose authority, however unspecified, must be more than human. In this way the brief and linear stage action can be opened out in space and time and made to appear in unity with the divine plan: in the plays of Aeschylus, it frequently links the action to the will of Zeus. In the other playwrights the relationship of the action to the gods is left comparatively unclarified, or becomes problematic.

As each scene and each lyric develops in an intricate pattern moving towards the end, the audience subjects the proleptic narrative to a series of interpretations. Proleptic narratives control not only the way the poet shapes his story but also the way the audience perceive shaping, and thus project possible outcome and movement towards closure. Any event in the play becomes heightened because it may be the moment at which the predicted fulfilment is beginning. As Herrnstein Smith writes (1968, 3) 'our pleasure derives largely from the tension created by local deferments of resolution and evasions of expectation'. These pleasures only become available when a frame has been created from which such effects can depend, and it is typical of Greek tragedy that portent, prophecy, dream and oracle are strikingly and repeatedly used to create this frame.[6] No study of tragedy using narrative theory could fail to pick out these features as a fundamental element of construction.

2.2.2 Narratives of recent or immediate past: the messenger speech and message narrative

Short-range narratives include one well-studied but ill-defined subset designated 'messenger speeches'. Such speeches are readily found in plays by Sophocles and Euripides.[7] They do not exist in the same form in Aeschylus. Typically, an anonymous stage figure relates offstage events occurring within the time-scale of the narrative itself, in the immediate or very recent past. We have only to think of the reappearance of the blinded Oedipus in *Oedipus Tyrannus*, or Creon in *Antigone* with Haemon in his arms minutes or moments after the narrated report, to find confirmation of the temporal immediacy at stake here. In many of these plays the poet's *sustasis tôn pragmatôn* (arrangement of events) seems to have been structured so as to make the information released in the messenger speech the climax of hopes and fears generated by the action. However, if the narrated offstage events often comprise the climax of the action, by an interesting paradox, during the messenger's narrative there is no onstage action at all, apart from any mimetic actions of the messenger and the (silent) reactions of the onstage narratees. On the diegetic level at which the culminating action of the play takes place, there is a marked *pause*.

That the familiar 'messenger speech' does in fact constitute an unquestioned, truly distinct and separate element of Attic drama is an issue that requires some rethinking when we look at it in the light of narrative theory. In the past, critics have selected only a fluctuating sub-group from the total number of informative speeches or *rhêseis* in iambic trimeters, applied the label 'messenger speeches' to them, and ignored the problem of relating them to similar *rhêseis*. For example, in *The Stagecraft of Aeschylus* (81-2) Taplin gives a tripartite definition of messenger speeches: '... anonymous eye-witness, set-piece narrative speech, and over-all dramatic function. When all three elements are combined we have an unmistakable *angelia* [message]; if one or two are absent then we have a scene with affinities or analogies to a messenger scene.' This definition ignores the extremely important question of how the time of the narrated event relates to stage time; furthermore, the three criteria do not adequately reflect the actual variety we find in the plays.[8] Taking Sophocles for example, the eye-witness may not be anonymous, as in the case of the speech describing Heracles' donning of the poisoned robe in *Trachiniae*, delivered not by an anonymous messenger but by Hyllus. Son narrates father's destruction to mother. Does the lack of anonymity debar it from being a 'true' messenger speech? If so, how should it otherwise be defined? Also, what of the Guard's two speeches in *Antigone*? He is certainly anonymous and unrelated to the ruling house, but he is still a highly characterised figure in his own right. Is anonymity still a criterion under these circumstances? And in what sense does the information from this part of *Antigone* fail to be a set-piece narrative speech, or to have an 'overall dramatic function' compared with other information given in the play? How should we define Deianeira's description of what happened to the tuft of wool at *Trachiniae* 663ff., or the kind of urgent sequence of messages between battle-field and general that occur in the shield scene *Septem* 375ff.?

By making a careful temporal assessment, widening the definition away from 'messenger speech' perhaps towards the less loaded phrase 'message narrative', and by looking hard at the poet's choice of narrator, whether anonymous or not, a more interesting investigation can begin.[9] A speech which does contain all of Taplin's criteria is better understood as operating at just one end of the spectrum of the large group of informative *rhêseis* spread throughout tragedy.

The two following translations from Sophocles are 'message narratives' but not 'messenger speeches' in Taplin's terms. Two areas of interest are (1) the many elements they contain which are paralleled elsewhere in traditional Sophoclean 'messenger speeches' and (2) the implications for the play of choosing a known, related speaker rather than an anonymous character.

Ajax 284-330: Tecmessa describes to the chorus Ajax's madness and subsequent return to sanity.

> You shall learn the entire action, since you have a stake in it.
> 285 At the dead of night, when the evening braziers
> were no longer burning, he took his sharp sword
> and made to go on a useless expedition.
> I reproached him, saying, 'What are you doing,
> 290 Ajax? Why are you starting this eager effort
> unsummoned, without call from messengers and
> having heard no trumpet? Well, at least
> the whole army is asleep now.'
> He replied in a brief, well-worn phrase:
> 'Woman, it's silence makes females attractive.'

Hearing this, I desisted and he sped off, alone.
295 I can't find the words to say what happened there,
but he came back in bringing with him bulls and
shepherd dogs bound together, and woolly prey.
He cut the throat of some of them; turning others
upside down he slaughtered them, splitting spines,
and others that were tied up he tortured, attacking
300 the herds as though they were human beings.
Finally he rushed out through the door, rapped out
words to some shadow, accusing now
the sons of Atreus, now Odysseus, laughing loudly
at the violence he'd repaid them with.
305 Then, rushing back into the house, eventually,
slowly, and with difficulty he came to his senses.
When he looked upon the room full of his mad folly,
striking his head, he cried out, then falling among
the wrecks of slaughtered sheep, he sat there,
310 grasping his hair with clenched nails.
He issued me with dreadful threats
if I wouldn't reveal the whole disaster to him.
[and he asked what sort of trouble he was in.]
315 In my fear, friends, I told him everything
that had happened, as far as I understood it.
He at once broke out into bitter lamentation
such as I've never heard before.
He always used to say such behaviour was
the mark of a coward, a low-hearted man -
320 but [though he made no shrill lament]
he kept groaning like a bellowing bull.
And now, prostrated by his great misfortune,
the man sits quietly where he fell, without
325 food or drink, among the herds.
It's obvious he will do something dreadful.
[for such are his words and his laments.]
My friends – this is why I have come -
Go in and help him, if you can at all,
for in such a condition, men are prevailed
330 upon by the words of their friends.

This speech relates the recent significant action of the play's central figure, presented complete in itself with scene-setting (285f.), some expansive detail (e.g. 295f.), and passages of direct speech (289f., 293f., dialogue reported in indirect speech 311f.). The speech describes the emotional aftermath (307f., 317f.) and returns us to the present circumstances ('and now', 322). All these features are also found in the major Sophoclean speeches (listed in n.7).[10]

We are soon prepared for the re-entry of the hero. In fact Ajax's offstage groans punctuate the ensuing dialogue between Tecmessa and the chorus at 333, 336, 339 and 341-2 until Ajax himself appears in a tableau to lament at 348. All this is absolutely the sequential pattern of 'messenger speeches' – after their delivery the hero is heard groaning until he too begins to speak: cf. Oedipus' groans (*OT* 1307), Heracles' groans (intermittently from *Trach*. 983), or Creon's groans (*Ant*. 1261ff.). A slight variant is to be found in *Oedipus at Colonus* and *Electra*: the hero is dead (or in the case of *Electra*, believed to be) so we have preparation for the entry of the hero's *remains* followed by the groans of Antigone (*OC* 1670) and Electra (*El*. 826ff.)

Some smaller typical features also occur: for example Tecmessa has been prompted into her message narrative by the question: 'Whatever was the origin of the evil that befell him? Tell us, who share in your sufferings' (282-3). For the question that triggers a statement of intent to give a full account, here 'You shall learn the entire action' (284), see also *Trach*. 898f., *OT* 1236f., *El*. 678f. and 681, *Ant*. 1191-3, *OC* 1585f. The request for full information and the declaration that the information is now underway no doubt serve as a preparatory signal to the audience as well.

In this example, the choice of Tecmessa as narrator gives the speech its distinctive edge. Far from being an anonymous bystander, she is an important, nobly-born figure in her own right, passionately participating in the action because of her relationship to Ajax and Eurysaces. In the embedded direct speech of 288-93 she addresses Ajax, and 'enters' the embedded scene as much as Ajax allows her to in an attempt to restrain him. Further, in the passage of indirect speech (312ff.) it is she who tells him what he did while mad (316).

At 328-30 Tecmessa concludes by turning to her addressees and asking for their help as friends. Persuasion, *peithô* is not a motive characteristic of the anonymous messenger but, as 328 shows, it has motivated her entire speech. The anonymous messenger's motivation is not normally particularly significant, though he may mention *charis* (his reward).[11] In societies more dependent on oral communication, it is probably an unquestioned assumption that anyone with news will spread it. Alternatively it may seem to satisfy the emotional need to tell, perhaps in an attempt to come to terms with the witnessed experience.[12]

The second example of message narrative is Hyllus' speech, *Trachiniae* 749-812. It is interesting for being the first half of a diptych of two message narratives, divided by a choral ode: the second speech 899-946 is delivered by the Nurse. Hyllus describes to Deianeira Heracles receiving the robe she herself had anointed:

> If you must learn, then all must be told.
> After sacking Eurytus' glorious city
> he advanced with the trophies and victory prizes.
> 750   There is a flooded shore in Euboia, Cape Cenaeum,
> where, in honour of the Zeus of his fathers
> he established altars and a leafy precinct.
> 755   Here, relieved from longing, I first saw him.
>   Just as he was about to offer many sacrifices

his own herald Lichas arrived from the house,
bringing your gift, the deadly robe.
He put it on, as you requested
760   and killed twelve unblemished bulls
– first fruits of the booty. In all,
he brought a hundred victims to the altar.
   At first, pleased with the lovely robe,
poor wretch, he offered prayers with happy heart,
765   but when the flame of holy rites burned
bloody from the oily wood,
sweat broke out on his skin, and his robe clung
close-glued to his side, as if by craftsman's hand,
at every joint. There came in his bones
770   a biting pain; then the poison, like venom of
a deadly snake, began to feast on him.
   Then he shouted for wretched Lichas –
entirely innocent of *your* ill-doing –
'What was the evil trick on the robe he'd brought?'
775   In his ignorance, the wretch said it was
the gift of you alone, exactly as despatched.
When Heracles heard this, piercing spasms
gripped his lungs; seizing Lichas' feet
where the ankle bends in its socket
780   he hurled him at a rock foaming from the sea.
His skull was split down the middle, and
brain-marrow and blood sprinkled his hair.
   The entire crowd wailed in horror at
the one man in agony, the other, destroyed.
785   No one dared go near Heracles.
Lying on the ground, or on his feet, he was
shouting, shrieking. The rocks resounded,
Locris' steep headlands, the cliffs of Euboia.
When he gave up flinging himself to the ground,
790   poor man, and crying out, cursing his
ill-fated marriage to you, wretch, declaring
getting you from Oeneus had destroyed his life,
he raised his eyes from the surrounding smoke
795   and saw me weeping among the great crowd. Staring
he calls, 'Child, advance. Do not flee my pain,
even if you should die with me as I die.
Lift me up, take me away, for preference
800   put me where none can see me. But if you pity me,
convey me quickly from this land.
Let me not die here.'
At this command we put him in a boat
and came to harbour here. It was difficult –
805   he was roaring in pain. Immediately now
you will see him – alive or newly dead.
This is what you planned for my father,
mother. And you've been caught. May avenging
Justice and the Fury make you pay. I pray for it.
810   It *is* lawful. You've given me the right

by killing the best of all men on the earth
whose like we shall never see again.

In its direct familial and emotional participation, Hyllus' speech is like Tecmessa's. Where she is motivated to conclude with *peithô*, his entire narrative is framed by angry condemnation. His earlier 'headlines' (734-7), which precede the full *rhêsis*, significantly had not even referred to Heracles, but had concentrated entirely on his denunciation of his mother, while the entire coda (807-12) repeats these opening expressions of hatred. The introductory line about 'learning' (749) found in many messenger speeches (see, e.g. *Ajax* 284) is grudging and, as Easterling's commentary notes, Hyllus 'reminds her of her guilt' throughout (at 758, 773, 775-6, 791-3). Like Tecmessa, Hyllus is not only witness but also participant, playing an active part in the scene he narrates. Hyllus is picked out of the crowd of stunned onlookers by his father, and his horrified passivity until forced to respond already defines the relationship between father and son we will see played out in the final scene.

These kin messengers – characters whose role is not restricted to the sole function of conveying a message – create intense pathos. They are deeply involved in the ruin of the husband or father they describe. Hyllus' speech also affects the subsequent action, specifically triggering Deianeira's suicide in an unexpectedly[13] premature way, creating a diversion away from the plot and causing, maybe, some traces of technical difficulty in rejoining it.[14] After her highly marked silent exit (813-20) and the following choral ode, comes the second messenger speech which reports her death; it is only after the chorus have reacted again to this second report that we hear Heracles' long-expected but delayed groans (983). Sophocles, having by a kind of domino effect produced not one but two speeches depicting the destruction of husband *and* wife, now has to bring the play back on course: the chorus seem to articulate the problem involved when they sing *potera proteron* (947), 'which of the two first ...?' (perhaps making use of the traditional expression of difficulty at the beginning of a lament and its common antithetical shaping (see e.g. *Antigone* 1343ff.).

The careful preparation made for the arrival of Heracles (803-6, 901-2) now has to be made to pay off: at 962ff. his imminent entry is indicated by the chorus. Presumably while they sing this last stanza or just after, Hyllus without motivation re-enters from the stage-building,[15] just as the cortège finish bringing on Heracles' body. *Ômoi egô sou*, 'How I grieve for you' he cries, words which could be understood to link back to the Nurse's picture of him distraught beside his mother's body: the bridge from Deianeira to Heracles is then economically made with the next word, *pater*, 'father'. Thus the two narratives are plaited together and the action continues. The visual focus helps here: the stage building which Hyllus leaves contains the dead Deianeira, the cortège he sees as he comes out carries the dying Heracles. Without the simultaneous arrival of the cortège the pattern of other plays would produce at least some momentary expectation that the Nurse's account will lead into a scene in which Hyllus laments his *mother*.

It seems that Sophocles has taken some dramatically risky steps to make Hyllus messenger and immediate cause of his mother's death. But his choice is consistent with the rest of the play, with its intense focus on the nuclear family of father, mother, son. Destructive actions done in ignorance of the consequences are performed by both wife and son, resulting in the tightly interwoven deaths of both parents. The parents are never shown together on stage; Hyllus the son provides the visible link between them. It is significant that the overt cause of it all, the silent Iole, is to be a future family member too; first, as concubine of Heracles, threatening Deianeira's role as wife; then as wife of Hyllus, thence mother of the glorious Heracleidae.

The implied reference to these mythical heroes with their positive Athenian significance[16] offers the audience a set of future perspectives unavailable to Hyllus in his anguish. It has an ambiguously mitigating effect on our view of the tragic action.[17] The choice of Hyllus rather than an anonymous messenger shows a highly effective dramatic economy: Hyllus the son takes the audience as close as possible to the tragic experience and then forward into a time when remote mythical past can form a link with the Athenian audience. The more Hyllus' role with his parents, including his role as narrator of his father's doom, can be understood, the better sense we can begin to make of the complex problems of the ending.

2.2.3 Simultaneous presentation of events

This category is a special development of the previous one in which the brief time-lapse between the offstage event taking place and its onstage narration is entirely collapsed. The offstage words or cries obviate the need for a messenger's report and create a vivid immediacy. We are virtually 'shown' rather than 'told'. The immediacy is both temporal and spatial: the implication of the audience being within earshot is that, were the door of the stage building open, the audience could see as well. Simultaneous presentation of events allows the action to flow on unhindered afterwards; both the event itself and the reaction to it are shown at the same time. The reaction inevitably dominates, to the extent that it is the part staged. Usually the chorus alone focalises the horror of the offstage action. Their intense involvement mirrors the situation of the audience, as does their conventional inability to intervene; this powerlessness is frequently treated ironically by the playwright: the chorus *talk* about intervening, but are helpless.

So at *Medea* 1271ff. we hear the offstage voices of Medea's two little boys to which the chorus then react: the boys use iambic trimeters, the chorus dochmiacs

Chorus	Do you hear, hear the childrens' cry?
	O wretched, ill-fated woman.
Child 1	Alas, what shall I do? Where escape
	my mother's hands?
Child 2	I don't know, dear brother. We're done for.
Chorus	Shall I enter the house? I should protect
	the children from slaughter.
Children	Yes, by the gods, protect us – we need it.
	We're facing the swords and nets.

In the Greek, the chorus' 'protect' (*arêxai*) is picked up by the children, 'Yes, protect us' (*arêxat'*): up to the moment of their death the children can hear the chorus who are clearly near enough to save them if they would. But the chorus now turn their thoughts to Medea's frame of mind, already treating the murders as a *fait accompli* (despite the future *kteneis*, 1281). Offstage events are not mediated by an extensive narrative: with great brevity the cries themselves substitute for the potential message narrative, 'Medea has killed her children'.

The recurring subject of such scenes of simultaneous presentation is what might be termed a 'lure-murder': the victim is tricked inside and killed. The plays containing such sequences are Aeschylus *Agamemnon*. 1331ff. (Agamemnon lured and murdered), *Choephoroe* 855ff. (Aegisthus lured and murdered); Sophocles *Electra*. 1384ff. (Clytemnestra lured and murdered); Euripides *Medea* 1271ff. (Medea's children simply murdered), *Hecuba* 1024ff. (Polymestor lured and – surprise – not murdered but blinded), *Heracles* 734ff. (Lycus lured and murdered), *Electra* 1147ff. (Clytemnestra lured and murdered), *Orestes* 1246ff. (Helen lured and intended to be murdered but – surprise – rescued). The presentation of information at *Hippolytus* 565ff. (dialogue between Nurse and Hippolytus 'overheard') is discussed below. Too dissimilar to be included here is the astonishing scene *Bacchae* 576ff., in which Dionysus' offstage voice 'creates' an *onstage* event, an earthquake realised by the chorus' reactions (and, perhaps, stage effects: see Dodds 1944 and Seaford 1996 ad loc.).

Apart from *Hippolytus* and *Bacchae*, the basic pattern each playwright develops is (1) the victim and the murderer(s) exeunt into the stage building, (2) leaving the chorus alone to chant or sing on the otherwise empty stage (anapaests, *Ag.* 1331-42, *Cho.* 855-869, lyric metres abounding in dochmiacs, Sophocles *El.*, Euripides *Med.*, *Hec.*, *Her.*, *El.*, *Or.*). (3) In all but *Agamemnon*, *Choephoroe* and *Hecuba*, the choral sections develop into an epirrhematic *kommos* (lament sung alternately by actor and chorus). The offstage voice(s) may initiate it, may form part of the iambic trimeter element of it, or be entirely *extra metrum* (probably *Heracles* – see Bond, 1981, at 734-62).

When both chorus and another stage figure are on stage while an offstage event is taking place, as Phaedra is in *Hippolytus* and Electra in both Sophocles *Electra* and Euripides *Orestes*, the different spatial positions of character and chorus can be exploited to set up a vivid chain of communication. Sophocles' Electra comes back on stage after the chorus' first strophe and antistrophe; in *Orestes* Electra remains onstage throughout. Nearer the stage building than the chorus, these Electras realistically pass on what they hear, giving a vivid blow-by-blow description, so that there is, after all, a narration of a kind. The Electras' onstage presence is explicitly motivated in both cases by the need to keep a look-out – premature enemy arrival may interrupt the deed. This possibility creates even more tension – there is danger from within *and* without and in *Orestes*, Hermione's untimely return does in fact interrupt. At the same time, Electra's passionate emotions, so important to both plays, can be shown not just by silent reaction (as they would be in response to a message narrative), but given an immediate voice (see especially *Orestes* 1302-10).

In Sophocles' *Electra* both Electra and the chorus have heard voices inside (1406-8), but at first the audience do not.[18] Then it is as if the volume from within increases and the offstage voice of Clytemnestra *is* heard. In her first cry she addresses Aegisthus, in her second her murdering son (1409, 1410-11). To this second offstage vocative (uniquely in extant tragedy) the onstage Electra replies in justification (1411-12). Clytemnestra's third and final cry announces her own death, and again the verse is an *antilabê* divided between mother and daughter (which reads like a deliberate recall of *Ag.* 1343 and 1345). The use of *antilabê* (a line of verse divided between two speakers) through the wall of the stage building creates tremendous immediacy. In this brief scene Electra both *narrates* to the chorus and holds a *dialogue* with her offstage mother; the effect is to make her virtually 'in at the death'. Interestingly, for the second half of this scene the chorus take over the role of the narrator (in their distinctively choric way) to offer the generalising comments of 1413-14 and 1417-21.

Hippolytus resembles *Electra* in as much as the scene begins well before the offstage event takes place. In both plays the tension builds as Phaedra and Electra get the chorus to be silent: there are excited questions and commands.[19]

What Phaedra overhears is the Nurse's failure to persuade Hippolytus to return Phaedra's love. In this case no lines have been given to either of the offstage voices, but Phaedra reports to the chorus 'verbatim' a couple of Hippolytus' expressions: 'evil matchmaker', and 'traitor to your master' (589-90). This offstage dialogue 'continues' onstage almost immediately afterwards when the Nurse and Hippolytus erupt onto the stage at 601, an extremely effective technique. Meanwhile, the scene of simultaneous narrative has already shown us Phaedra both reporting and reacting to the news and, significantly, deciding on death (599-600).

A little later (*Hipp.* 773-89) Euripides exhibits great craft and speed in the handling of Phaedra's offstage suicide. On this occasion we hear the Nurse's offstage cries. She calls for help and a knife to cut Phaedra down. The chorus' brief indecision recalls *Agamemnon* 1346-71. In the Nurse's following speech, she is already giving orders to lay the body out and, bang on cue at the mention of 'master' (787), Theseus begins to walk along the eisodos to begin speaking at 790. Phaedra's body is wheeled out on Theseus' order 808ff., and the play's second phase begins.

Considering the reasons why, in any tragedy, this very specific scene-type, with its striking brevity and immediacy, should have been preferred to a full message narrative should help to illuminate the narrative strategy of the play overall and its desired emphases.

2.2.4 Proleptic narrative in combination with message narrative

Proleptic narratives create a structure of expectation, mingled hopes and fears, towards a particular outcome. In a few plays, message narrative is positioned at the apex of a dramatic structure which has been largely built up by the use of prophecy or dream. A message narrative then specifically delivers that predicted outcome. The combination in this particular way of these two temporally-opposed sets of narrative is intuitively experienced by ordinary twentieth-century theatre-goers as constituting something centrally significant to the definition of 'Greek tragedy'. A list of such plays would include Sophocles' Theban plays and *Electra* (although a special case since the speech is deceitful), Euripides' *Hippolytus* and *Bacchae*. It is interesting that no surviving play of Aeschylus works in quite this way (Aeschylus' narrative strategy is discussed in Chapter 3). Listening to the lyric, dialogic and narrative sequences of these plays as they develop their familiar, inexorable pattern is a powerful aesthetic experience which it is difficult not also to describe as in some sense 'religious'.

In this kind of play the messenger tends to arrive and speak at the very hub of several different axes. First, his narrative describes a moment in which the divine design manifests itself in all the mundane contingency of human affairs; it is revelatory in the religious sense, in that it tells us about the implications of a curse or an oracle, or a ritual transgression or a religious dilemma. Second, this revelation is coincidental with a climax in the developing action of the play; it marks the moment at which *desis* becomes *lusis*. The conventional shaping of Attic drama will naturally give the report a strong sense of significance and inevitability: when a battle develops offstage or a crisis arises within the palace, the audience are conditioned to expect a messenger to tell them how it has been resolved. (The sequence *Trachiniae* 672-722 shows this: Deianeira tells the chorus her fears about the anointed robe; in 723-30 the chorus in distichomythia encourage her not to abandon all hope just yet, then announce the arrival of Hyllus. Hyllus necessarily recounts what the anointed robe has done. No other subject is at issue at this point in the play. See also *Oedipus at*

Colonus 1447-1555: this section immediately prepares the ground for Oedipus' exit to his end (the indications for which have been thoroughly established earlier). Left on their own, the chorus sing an ode to the chthonic gods (1556-78). The only question at issue for the audience now is how Oedipus has met his death: we must expect the messenger to tell the waiting chorus (and so us) what has happened.)

The third axis is the hero. The messenger's focus on the suffering and destruction of a paradeigmatic individual cannot fail to be profoundly moving.[20] The message narrative derives strength, not weakness, from being narrated rather than enacted. Given an effective production, the particular stillness and attention accorded to its delivery creates one of the most intense and concentrated focal points of the play.

2.2.5 Prophecies as analeptic narratives: closure

Sometimes prophecies are not used proleptically to create a climate of expectation leading up to the messenger speech. Instead, they are used to shape the material in the opposite direction, towards closure. They do this by absorbing present actions into the past. There is an interesting example of this at *Trachiniae* 1138ff. To exonerate his mother, Hyllus tells Heracles that she used a love charm given by Nessus. At the mention of Nessus, Heracles unexpectedly responds, 'Alas, wretch that I am, I'm done for. Now I really understand my situation' (1143-5). In his moment of recognition he forgets recriminations against Deianeira. It is time for him to abandon life, and the play moves towards dealing with this closing issue.

Heracles accounts for this new understanding of the inevitability of his death by recalling another oracle (1157-78) not previously mentioned in the play: long ago Zeus had told him that he would not perish by the hand of any living creature. Heracles brings this oracle into line (*sumbainont' isa*, 1164) with the one he subsequently received at Dodona, to double the confirmation that he has now reached the end of his mortal life. The references to the Dodona oracle earlier in the play (46ff., 76ff., 155ff.) had a clearly proleptic function, to help shape audience expectation towards the outcome of the action covered by the play. They offered a restricted either/or outcome. *Either* Heracles would die *or* he would come to the end of his labours (79-81, repeated with different phrasing 166-8), but the apparent antithesis was false:[21] the vague way the subject of this oracle was first raised as a 'writing', and the discrepancy of detail (see Easterling's note *ad Trach.* 824-5) help create a typically shadowy web of uncertain predication. All the same, there was insistence on immediate fulfilment one way or the other after a fifteen-month period, now past (173-4). That the function of the Dodona oracle was largely proleptic is confirmed by the fact that on hearing the news of Heracles' destruction from Hyllus, its fulfilment is the first thing the chorus sing about (first strophe of the third stasimon, 821ff.).

Now at this very late stage in the play the Dodona oracle is picked up again in association with the older oracle to put the entire action onto a larger frame: we are now concerned with the shaping of Heracles' entire life, not merely its last months. There is a tantalising inference from 1149-50 that under different circumstances[22] we would learn more of Zeus' prophecy to Heracles concerning the mysterious nature of his death. Instead, we have only Heracles' own brief account, together with his practical instructions to Hyllus. As Easterling remarks (1982, 9-11), the oracle and the commands point towards *some* significance without clearly indicating an apotheosis.[23] The resultant procession offstage to Mount Oeta which closes the play produces a typically open Sophoclean ending, in which new but indefinite lines of perspective have been sketched in.[24]

An oracle also produces closure in *Persians*, in a far less indefinite way than *Trachiniae*. Roberts (1984, 33f.) notes the reference Darius makes to old oracles (*Pers.* 739ff.), mentioned only after the news of the Persian defeat at Salamis has been announced. What is the point of introducing an out-of-date proleptic narrative at this late date, if not to create a sense of closure by the dawning of a new perspective? Xerxes' defeat is now to be seen not so much as a shattering defeat in the very recent past, a fit subject for the messenger's speech, but as the completion or fulfilment of an event long ago foretold by the gods.

3

Narrative Deceit: *Dolos*

dolos, prop. *bait* for fish, *Odyssey* 12.252: hence, *any cunning contrivance for deceiving or catching*, as the net in which Hephaestus catches Ares, *Od.* 8.276; the Trojan horse, ib. 494; Ixion's bride, Pi. *P*. 2.39; the robe of Penelope, *Od.* 19.137 (pl.) ... **b.** generally, *any trick or stratagem, pukinon dolon allon huphaine* ('he wove another cunning dolos') *Iliad*. 6.187,etc.: in pl., *wiles*, *doloi kai mêdea*, ('doloi and plans') 3.202; *doloisi kekasmene* ('surpassing in doloi') 4.339, etc. 2. in the abstract, *craft, cunning, treachery, dolôi êe biêphi*, ('with dolos and brute force') *Od.* 9.406; *epephne dolôi, ou ti kratei ge* ('he killed him with dolos, not with force') *Il*. 7.142; *ou kat'ischun ... dolôi ge* ('not with might, but with dolos'). A. *Pr*. 215, cf. *Ch*. 556, etc.; *dolois* ('with doloi') ib.888, S. *OT* 960, etc.; *ek dolou* ('as a result of dolos') Id. *El*. 279; *en dolôi* ('in dolos') Id. *Ph*. 102; *sun dolôi* ('with dolos') A. *Pers*. 775 ....

(Opening of the *dolos* entry in LSJ. Greek words have been transliterated and translated in brackets).

3.1 *Dolos*

The previous chapter analysed narratives of different temporal reach and considered how they could combine cumulatively to create particular effects and suggest meaning. Where the effect was essentially misleading – as in the case of the Dodona oracle in *Trachiniae* – it could be considered as a narrative deceit. The relationship between poet and audience is not an innocent one.

This chapter considers further the idea of an essentially deceitful, agonistic relationship betwen the narrator and narratees of ancient tragedy. In order to do so, it makes use of Detienne and Vernant's suggestive researches into *mêtis*, a mental category defined as 'wiley intelligence, effective adaptable cunning' (1991, 3), and *dolos*, any of the complex devices employed by *mêtis* to prevail over its adversary. The authors' study of *mêtis* uncovered a significant semantic field consisting of the key nouns and adjectives *dolos*, trick; *mêchanê*, device; *technê*, craft; *apatê*, cheat; *aiolos*, shifting; *poikilos*, variegated; *haimulos*, wily (p. 43). *Mêtis* (and associated *dolos*) encompasses 'the whole extent of the cultural world of the Greeks from its most ancient technical traditions to the structure of its pantheon' (p. 2). It is applied to all situations which are 'transient, shifting, disconcerting and ambiguous' (p. 3) and it operates between two opposite poles with objects 'that are not yet stable' (p. 5).

I take *mêtis* as a model for the poet's mind-set and use the term *dolos* to describe any of the poet's devices which act as bait to keep the audience's attention and to deceive them as to the ultimate outcome of the narrative.

Dolos in the sense of 'trick' plays an overt part in many pre-tragic narratives. The *Odyssey*, for example, is a cunning and self-reflexive poem whose *polytropos* ('versatile', 'ingenious') hero famously defines himself in terms of *dolos*: 'I am Laertes' son Odysseus, involved with all human tricks, and my reputation reaches Heaven' (*Od.* 9.19-20.) His trick-filled escapes, disguises, artful narratives and elaborately-delayed ultimate recognition form the very substance of the poem,[1] especially the second half with its four cumulative lying narrative sequences (*Od.* 14.192-359; 17.415-44; 19.165-202 and 269-307; 24.259-79). *Dolos*, however, can have wider implications than a hero's stratagems. In Hesiod's *Theogony*, *dolos* is no less than a cosmogonic principle of the universe by means of which the gods themselves and the world are created. Later, through the stories of Prometheus and Pandora (see *Works and Days* 47-105), *dolos* develops into a defining principle of all subsequent relationships – those between gods and humans, men and men, and men and women.

As a general principle, Detienne and Vernant's description of the operation of *mêtis* could provide no better model for the way any creative poet, then or now, operates with his flexible narrative material, giving and witholding information and continuously engaging his audience by means of a stream of suspense-sustaining narrative *doloi*. The audience can be 'in' on one character's deception of another, wondering at every moment if the disguise will be penetrated or the lie detected. Alternatively, they too can be misled – to an unquantifiable extent – as the audience of *Agamemnon* are by Clytemnestra's extraordinary mixture of truth and lies and by the chorus' contradictory, unresolved remarks about her. They can be played upon by delays, diversions, counter-expectations, false dawns and so forth.

Once *doloi* have started to take effect, it seems that previous familiarity with the outline story of the myth makes surprisingly little difference to audience engagement. The fact that we know how the story ends does not make us any less focused on the course of Oedipus' inquiry, as we watch it unfolding minute by minute in performance. The sheer power of unfolding narrative seems to suppress our awareness of our own *ex eventu* knowledge.

Deceits are essential features of all tragic narratives, whether simple or complex in plot terms. Analysis of *doloi* in the plays enables us to see not only repeated patterns across all three playwrights, but also the characteristic experimental handprints of each individual in his relentless pursuit of new devices to entrap his audience. *Mêtis* has 'suppleness and malleability' to give it victory in domains 'where there are no ready-made rules for success, no established methods, but where each new trial demands the invention of new ploys, the discovery of a way out that is hidden ... *Mêtis* is in itself a power of cunning and deceit. It operates through disguise. In order to dupe its victim it assumes a form which masks, instead of revealing, its true being' (p. 21). Its essential features are 'pliability and polymorphism, duplicity and equivocality, inversion and reversal ...' (Detienne and Vernant, 1991, 40); in short, the very essence of drama.

One ancient narrative *dolos* much employed by Aeschylus and Sophocles is the presentation of ambiguous proleptic information, often in the form of a dream or oracle (see 2.2.1). Homer had already richly developed the tricky and ironic implications of dreams, making use of discrepant awareness between internal characters as well as between internal and external audience on receipt of the message. Zeus sends a 'deadly dream', *oulos oneiros*, explicitly to deceive Agamemnon, with resultant chaos as Agamemnon in turn attempts to deal craftily with it. There is great irony in the dissembling of Zeus the narrator and Agamemnon the narratee, and in the different function of 'Nestor' the dream-figure (*Il.* 2.23-34) and Nestor the wise councillor (79-83).

The source of Penelope's dream (*Od.* 19.535ff.) and her decision to hold the contest of the bow is more mysterious: the dream's provenance remains firmly unknown, as do the exact import of the horn and ivory gates from which they issue (19.560-7).[2] Whatever its source, the dream resembles the *oulos oneiros* in being intricately surrounded by deceit. As she narrates it to her disguised husband, Penelope's dream is all too simple in its meaning, and has in fact been clearly interpreted by the eagle figure within the dream itself, when Penelope (still dreaming) weeps because her geese have been slaughtered. The dream thus includes its own interpretation, and Odysseus has merely to confirm that, disguised as an eagle, 'Odysseus himself' (556) has spoken to her. But Penelope does not accept this. She makes the mysterious remarks about the origin of dreams from the gates of horn or the gates of ivory: dreams are *amêchanoi akritomuthoi*, 'inexplicable, impossible to interpret' (*Od.* 19.560) and the ones from the ivory gates bring no fulfilment. Her conversation takes a different turn.

Penelope's dream gates are interesting. Narrative theory disproves her statement that some dreams have no fulfilment: fictive dreams are infallible pointers to the future, even if the dreamer does not understand how until the moment of fulfilment. Her sad remarks delicately highlight the level of deceit which her husband must continue to operate against her. We enjoy the fact that she is ignorant of the procedural rules of the narrative in which she is a character. Athena gives Odysseus and Telemachus outright proleptic information, and with this additional help they are better able to shape their own narrative ends.

From Odysseus' and the listeners' point of view, the dream narrative is readily understood as an image of Odysseus' forthcoming defeat of the suitors. It finds an immediate context for fulfilment in the next subject Penelope takes up, the contest of the bow. *She* mentions it with gloom, since for her it represents the unwelcome selection of a new husband. But the dream has already suggested that the outcome will be everything she could desire. Odysseus can take at second hand the dream dreamt by his wife as a good omen applicable to his own situation. (It is at second hand too that Orestes interprets his mother's dream in *Choephoroe* – with less fortunate results.)

In tragedy a dream or oracle may set up a pair of polarised outcomes (see Chapter 2 n. 21). This device seems in fact a thematisation of an inherent property of narrative, which progresses by a series of bifurcations, since any potential objective can be realised or fail to be realised (see Bal, 1985, 19-23 and Rimmon-Kenan, 1983, 22-7 on Bremond's theory of narrative bifurcation). In some plays a *dolos* is made from this bifurcation: ultimately we realise that the alternatives presented were false and the outcome incorporates *both*. Thus in *Choephoroe* Apollo's oracle threatens him with affliction if he does *not* carry out the command to kill his mother: he commits the act *and* he is afflicted. The same device is at work in Sophocles: at *Trachiniae* 79-81 Deianeira tells Hyllus of a prophecy coming to fulfilment that either Heracles will reach the end of his life or he will go on to live in happiness (repeated with different wording at 166-8); at the end, both outcomes have been fulfilled: he is dying, but the suggestion of some afterlife is there.[3]

Discussing Aeschylean narrative technique in terms of 'surprise', 'variation' or 'deviation', Garvie associates these *doloi* with the fact that Aeschylus' surviving plots are simple ones in Aristotelian terms[4] which necessarily require deviation from what would otherwise be a straight line from the beginning of the play to its climax at or near the end. Like proleptic narratives, *doloi* provide shaping and suspense for a form which might well have lacked it originally (see Aristotle's comment, *Poetics* ch. 4, 1449a17, on early tragedy's 'short plots and ludicrous diction'), acting to prevent premature, over-predictable and consequently insignificant closure. Then too it is clear that a *nostos* play (*Persians*, *Agamemnon*, *Choephoroe*) requires material to intervene between the news of return and the return itself, and the second half of the *Odyssey* is a pattern book of narrative deceits and delays for just this purpose.

In the later years of the fifth century, pressure to reflect the changing contemporary world, and a need to create new twists for audiences saturated with familiar material, as well as the desire to convey his own particular vision, may account in part for the striking Sophoclean deviations or 'loops' discussed in Part III and also for some of Euripides' novel plot lines, as in e.g. *Orestes*. To repeat Herrnstein Smith, 1968, 3, 'our pleasure derives largely from the tension created by local deferments of resolution and evasions of expectation'. The whole area of narrative strategy and the phenomenology of the reading/audience process is at issue here. *Dolos* functions as the bait, that which plays on the perception of the prey, constructing and sustaining a fictional reality in order to keep it 'on the hook'.

3.2 *Dolos* and narrative theories

In fictional communication some measure of deceit or at least ambiguity will always be present. Different theorists have different ways of expressing this idea; from a structuralist point of view there is an inherent trickiness in the narrative process itself: 'the mainspring of the narrative activity is to be traced to that very confusion between consecutiveness and consequence, what-comes-*after* being read in a narrative as what-is-*caused by*. Narrative would then be a systematic application of the logical fallacy denounced by scholasticism under the formula, *post hoc ergo propter hoc*' (Barthes, 1975, 237; see also Culler, 1975, 183ff. on Nietzsche's mosquito bite and the problem of causation).

As regards the narrator-narratee axis, deceit must be present to maintain the relationship between narrator and narratee throughout the course of the narrative. At any moment the narratee can put an end to the narrative transaction, withdrawing his attention out of sheer lack of interest or because he has prematurely gained all the information inherent in the communication. The flow of information must be manipulated continuously so as to maintain the audience' interest, directing them towards full recognition without including all the data to complete the process until the end, if at all. Enough information must be given to provoke speculation, but not too much. Withholding and hiding information, setting up false expectations, controlling the reader's response not only by the creation of frames but also by leaving gaps, ambiguities or unresolved contradictions, is absolutely the way of all narratives (see Perry, 1979).

There are different models here. To Barthes (1974, 89), narratives are 'legal tender, subject to contract, economic stakes, in short, *merchandise* ... narrative is both product and production, merchandise and commerce, a stake and the bearer of that stake ....' This model finds some measure of thematic confirmation in ancient drama where the messenger might expect *charis* (monetary reward) in return for his story, as suggested at *Trachiniae* 190ff.; *Oedipus Tyrannos* 1005ff.; *Electra* 772; *Philoctetes* 551ff. (and see Longo, 1978, 83ff.). In *Trachiniae* and *Philoctetes*, Sophocles draws attention to the messenger's information as a narrative transaction contained within a much larger piece of 'trading' or 'transaction' that is taking place.

Chambers' model is slightly different, emphasising a power structure: 'To tell a story is to exercise power (it is even called the power of narration), and "authorship" is cognate with "authority". But the authority is not absolute but relational, the result of an act of authorisation on the part of those subject to the power, and hence something to be *earned*' (Chambers,

1984, 51, with my emphases). Etymologically, as we have seen, the narrator is *the one who knows* (Latin *narrare*, **gnarare*, related to *gnarus* = knowing, skilled); in Chambers' view, 'where the narratee offers attention in exchange for information, the narrator sacrifices the information for some form of attention'. From another point of view, narration can be viewed as a seductive act, a kind of strip-tease in which an unrestricted view is deliberately and tantalisingly denied. (This view was explored in Barthes' *S/Z* (1974), essentially a meditation on the erotic functioning of narrative in Balzac's *Sarrasine*.) All these different narrative models, which of course derive from the real world, perhaps unsurprisingly are often thematised within the narrative as well.

I find useful the model of narrative as a kind of game (see the entry on game theory in *The Oxford Companion to Philosophy*, ed. T. Honderich, Oxford, 1995). Fiction is essentially *ludic*, and works by continuous interplay of illusion, allusion, elusion, collusion, delusion, and so forth. Tragedies are of course *plays*, and plays, with their concrete, three-dimensional falsehoods, disguise and dressing-up, most superficially and most profoundly exemplify the ludic. When disguise is thematised by plots involving overt deceit, a whole complex of effects can be created in which discrepant awareness is always significant. Rich effects can be created, dependent on an interplay of engrossment and detachment, and the play may draw attention to its own theatrical status, reminding us that it is second-by-second constructing a reality rather than constituting one. We are both drawn in and kept out; the design of the play is exposed – and so is our response to it.

In Aristotle's discussion of tragedy in *Poetics*, ludic elements of deceit, disguise and dissimulation are hardly considered; they are merely those preliminary conditions which give way to the elements of reversal and recognition, items which Aristotle considered to be 'tragedy's greatest means of emotional power' (Halliwell's translation of *Poetics* 1450a17). But reversal and recognition could not be produced without initial *doloi*. In the plots of tragedy, we see a rich and continuous interplay between the need for knowledge, and *doloi* which frustrate the need. In this way, plots often thematise the basic narrator-narratee situation by highlighting the struggle to get certain information and achieve an understanding of what is going on. The movement from ignorance to knowledge, from deceit to recognition of the truth, is the major movement of many tragedies. *Doloi* deserve consideration.

3.3 *Dolos* and Greimas' actantial theory

Actantial theory is an essentially dramatic model, introduced here to highlight the opportunities for *doloi* in the relationships between actants in tragedy. Actantial theory isolates fundamental roles at the deep structure level of narrative. Its actants represent not actors but narrative

functions. Stage figures may share the same actantial function and conversely, one stage figure may assume two actantial roles. Greimas' model
(a development of the earlier work of Propp and Souriau[5]) assumes that
each narrative inhabits its own *micro-universe*[6] in which fixed actants
perform fixed actantial functions.

In using this model one assigns all figures to one of six actantial classes
at the deep structure level. I say 'figures' because not only the *dramatis
personae* who appear on the stage may be included but more abstract
entities as well such as gods, Necessity, Fate, and so on, if justified by their
functional role in the text. The actants are divided into three pairs, and
since actantial theory (like most narrative theory) has a linguistic under-
pinning, the relationship between each pair should have the capacity of
being verbally expressed as subject – predicate – object, to constitute a
sentence of the *fabula*.

1. First pair: Subject / Object
Subject is often but not always the main character of the narrative surface
structure, typified by his teleological wish or fear directed towards Object.
A modulation of power is envisaged. The actantial structure at the start of
Philoctetes might be expressed as: Odysseus (Subject) wishes to get control
over Philoctetes (Object).

2. Second pair: Destinateur / Destinataire: Sender / Receiver or Power / Receiver[7]
Forces of various kinds, human and non-human, whatever may be legiti-
mised by an analysis of the text, bring about or thwart Subject's hopes and
fears. These are designated 'Power'. At the deep level, Power communicates Object to Receiver, and the relationship between this pair is aetiolog-
ical, showing a modulation of knowledge: at the end of *Philoctetes* Heracles
(Power) commands Philoctetes (Object) to go to Troy and help the Greek
army (Receiver).

3. Third pair: Helper / Opponent
These less central actants are modifiers and may be regarded by analogy
with sentence structure as having an adverbial function in relation to the
other four ('notwithstanding', 'owing to'). They represent the circumstances under which the enterprise may or may not be fulfilled. In the
micro-universe of *Philoctetes*, Neoptolemus spends the play oscillating
between the functions of Helper and Opponent.

The very process of attempting to find a satisfactory actantial structure
for individual tragedies is a worthwhile activity: in confronting the various
possibilities and ambiguities which emerge and then disappear during
reading, we are no doubt experiencing the tricky interplay between
narrator and narratee typical of all texts. In fact, however, the actantial

structure at the end of tragedy seems to be, in part at least, invariable. Unsurprisingly, Power is a god or gods, and the final Receiver of Object is society itself, or its representative group of individuals within the micro-universe of the play (e.g. the chorus).[8] Object may well be a corpse or corpses requiring community ritual: see Aeschylus *Persians, Septem, Agamemnon, Choephoroe*; Sophocles *Ajax, Trachiniae, Antigone, Oedipus at Colonus* (although the body itself is absent) and *Electra* (though Aegisthus is not yet a corpse when the play ends). Corpses are significant at the end of most Euripidean plays too, creating the *aition* in *Medea, Heraclidae, Hippolytus, Andromache, Hecuba, Supplices* and probably *Bacchae*. The corpses of Jocasta, Eteocles and Polyneices are on stage at the end of *Phoenissae*.

Dolos is inherent in any micro-universe, and underlies much of tragedy's irony, pathos and suspense. From the point of view of Subject in a tragedy, the extent of the micro-universe of the play cannot fully be known. Subject is subject to misprisions, ambiguities and deceits. In the opening scenes of many plays we see his/her initial aim towards Object modified by scenes of help or opposition. Meanwhile, in an oblique and usually disguised relationship to Subject, Power also makes a movement towards Object: given the unfinished teleological relationship between Subject and Object at the outset and the separate, disguised movement of Power, an outcome will occur not envisaged by Subject at the outset (even though in tragedy, with its heavily marked ironies, it may well have been overtly predicted). By the end, two distinct but connected events have occurred: the Subject/Object relationship has reached a *telos*, and Object has been communicated to Receiver.

Actantial theory brings into focus some typical *doloi* in ancient tragic narratives. For example, Aeschylus and Sophocles can create an initial surface structure which heavily disguises the actantial structure at the deep level: in *Septem* the opening structure appears to be Eteocles (Subject) confronting Polyneices (Object). The two brothers, one attacking and the other defending Thebes, appear to be at opposite poles. In fact, however, after the moment of *anagnôrisis*, the actantial role of Subject disappears and the two brothers become one actant, joint Object of a stronger Power than either of them had perceived. Similarly in *Oedipus Tyrannos* it initially appears that Oedipus is Subject, searching for the murderer of his father (Object). But again, the moment of recognition reveals these two apparently separate individuals to be one identical figure, Object not Subject. In both these plays, the figure who initially appears to be Subject is the victim of ignorance.

Bacchae, however, employs a quite different *dolos*. Dionysus, we understand by the end, has consistently been both Subject *and* Power throughout (Euripides had used something like the same strategy in *Medea*). Dionysus is in control of everything that happens in the drama and indeed he foretells it (in disguised form: see 10.3) to the audience in the prologue. In this case Object (Pentheus) is the ignorant party, and raw divine actantial Power overtly disguises itself into the actantial Subject, the figure of a youth whose gentle effeminacy seems to be the reverse of divine power, just as it is also the reverse of Pentheus' military strength. Dionysus disguises himself (and later his victim) in order to destroy him. Building on two of Dionysus' traditional aspects, Euripides' stage figure is in fact *two separate actants*. Pentheus is crushed between the two.[9] The *dolos* operating in *Septem*, *Oedipus Tyrannus* and *Bacchae* has the capacity to make identities shift disconcertingly from one pole to its opposite, revealing a dangerous instability in items of knowledge that seemed previously certain.

3.4 Aeschylus

It is possible that there was a fixed actantial structure at the end of all Aeschylus' trilogies of which we have at least one play, and for the single play *Persians* too. *Doloi* have dropped away and the gods, particularly Zeus, are manifest as Power, while the community has two actantial roles – it is both Subject and Receiver (cf. *Septem*, *Agamemnon*, *Eumenides*, *Persians*). The double actantial role of the community is at its simplest in *Persians*: the chorus hope and fear for Xerxes' success at the outset (Xerxes is Object), and lament his losses at the end.[10] The *Oresteia* both opens and closes with plays in which the community functions like this.

The adaptation made by Aeschylus in *Agamemnon* to make the community Subject and Receiver rather than Aegisthus (cf. *Od.* 4.514-25) is particularly striking. Aegisthus is the traditional protagonist of the revenge plot, but Aeschylus makes him so insignificant that his appearance can wait until the closing minutes of the play. (No equivalent displacement has taken place in *Choephoroe*, where Orestes is both protagonist and actantial Subject.) In *Agamemnon* a double displacement has occurred: it might at the outset seem that Clytemnestra has taken over Aegisthus' actantial role (Homer's account had already been modified by variants composed by Hesiod, Hagias, Xanthus and Stesichorus and no doubt other lyric poets, which gave a bigger role in the murder to Clytemnestra), but in fact it is clear that it is not she but the chorus who function as Subject: in their enormous singing role they express the hopes and fears which fulfil the basic teleological conditions required of Subject, while all the information delivered in the episodes 'breaks onto' them. Like Oedipus in *Oedipus Tyrannus*, it is the very limits of their cognitive competence which involve the audience most intensely and which provide much of the tremendous irony in the play.

At the same time, the use of the chorus as an agent of *dolos* in *Agamemnon* is fundamental, pervasive and extremely striking (see, particularly, Goldhill, 1984). Essentially, Aeschylus gives the chorus a complex double game to play. They have self-professed narrative authority (*kurios eimi throein*, 'I have authority to utter', 104). With it they provide the audience with background information, *framing* the play, but at the same time they leave *gaps*. They act as an emotional transmitter throughout: they feel fear; they long for their king; they suspect Clytemnestra but cannot clarify their suspicions. In the lyric sections they encourage the audience's hermeneutic inquiry by using the language of interpretation themselves – for example with reference to *mantikê* (prophecy) or Helen's name. At the same time, in their search for religious and philosophical understanding, they put the action of the play on the highest possible plane. But the very loftiness of their vision and the very depth of their experience, together with their age, make it difficult for them to see anything unequivocally: like even the most experienced of human beings, they are fallible. This noble short-sightedness somewhat resembles the brilliant but defective intellect of Oedipus in *Oedipus Tyrannus*.

The audience, dependent on the chorus for its information, are (as often) able to interpret the information better than the chorus themselves. The narrative deceits which open a gap and invite the audience's own interpretation are highly marked.

Deceits as narrators: at a certain point in the parodos Aeschylus makes the chorus, like the guard before them, *refuse* to narrate (the guard refuses at *Ag.* 36-9, the chorus at 248); the word *enthen*, 'subsequently', in the line *ta d'enthen out'eidon out'ennepô*, 'what happened subsequently I neither saw nor speak of', encourages us to puzzle out the consequences at the very moment that the chorus abandons its account. The chorus presents much predictive material such as the portent, Calchas' prophecy and, in the so-called hymn to Zeus, a notion that Zeus permits human understanding when it derives from suffering. They stress the authority of such elements (249, 'Calchas' art is not without fulfilment'). They seem to have the information necessary to map out the future; however, they are only human, and cannot do so. Long-range narrative is intersected with the hymn-like refrain *ailinon ailinon eipe, to d'eu nikatô*, 'Cry woe, woe, but let the good win out' (121, 139, 159), the effect of which is to maintain a binary opposition between hope and fear, leaving no space for analysis.[11] Fatalistic expressions (such as 251-4) avoid interpretation, and their following wish (255-7), 'May it all turn out as this nearest bulwark, sole guardian of the land of Apia wishes' – whether by 'sole guardian' they mean (by inadvertent *dusphêmia*) Clytemnestra, or merely themselves – is woefully inadequate to the situation. Thus as narrators, despite their breadth of knowledge, the chorus in their fear are characterised by (a) refusal and (b) unwarranted openness about the future. This second feature reflects Bremond's model of narrative progression in which each potential action gives rise to two possibilities – fulfilment, or lack of fulfilment. Here their fear for the future motivates them to keep both alternatives open.

Deceits as narratees: the chorus show the same characteristics. During the episodes they are unable to interpret the information they are given. This is demonstrated most clearly in the Cassandra scene where they fluctuate between (a) expressions of incomprehension as far as prophecy is concerned: 'I know nothing of prophecy' (1105); 'I haven't got it yet. I'm at a loss with prophecies obscured by riddling talk' (1112-13); (b) ready acceptance of past events: '*That* I know – the whole city's talking about it' (1106; see also 1162-3 and 1242-5), and (c) gloomy verdicts on the efficacy of prophecy in general, e.g. 1132-5. The stichomythia of 1246-7, like that in the earlier Herald scene, is a miracle of compressed non-communication, marked by the final comment of the chorus, *dysmathê*, 'hard to understand' (1255).

Part of the richness of the *Oresteia* lies in its strategic manipulation of the audience's perception of Power across the three plays of the trilogy: initially Zeus is described as the sole exception to the rule of flux. He is beyond comparison (*Ag.* 163-5); *panaitiou*, 'the reason for everything'; *panergeta*, 'contriving everything'. The idea is floated that he has initiated a plan for mortals to learn through (generational) suffering (cf. also 1563-4); but the oxymoron *charis biaios*, 'violent favour' (182) highlights the paradoxical nature of this idea, and Zeus himself is only part of a generally puzzling kaleidoscope of confusing and inconsistently-linked deities operating in the universe ('Some Apollo or Pan or Zeus perceiving high above', 55-6). By the end of *Choephoroe* this confusion has become critical. Sub-elements of Power conflict and no sense can be made of Zeus' role in relation to the other forces in the universe. At last in *Eumenides* the divine structure is clarified by the creation of a strict hierarchy and a defined separation of function between the divinities constituting actantial Power.[12] Without minimising the importance of the trial, Orestes' matricide, an agonising dilemma in *Choephoroe*, has small significance from the perspective of this conclusion. By this time, none of the actants are individualised humans (or indeed human at all), apart from the participants in the final procession.[13]

3.5 Sophocles

Part III will discuss one example of Sophoclean *dolos* in detail; here there is a brief discussion of *doloi* remaining on closure.

We saw that in Aeschylus' completed narratives, a turbulent, tricky past may have given way to some better civic present in which gods are no longer a threat to the community. The *telos* of the final plays from the surviving trilogies and of *Persians* is manifested by group ritual, in the case of the *Oresteia* a procession, in the case of *Persians* and *Septem* a lament.[14] The concluding tone is comparatively positive, even if the community laments, since what has been demonstrated is the working out of some 'process' which is also 'progress'. The tragic fate of individual char-

acters in the play is absorbed into the demonstration of group continuity
in the form of ritual performance. With this the audience no doubt identified, feeling themselves strengthened and made secure by what they
witnessed. No *dolos* remains at the end to reduce the strong finality of
closure. (I would not wish to over-generalise: at the end of *Eumenides* of
course the Erinyes retain their power and the future can only be expressed
in terms of prayers and hopes.)

In Sophocles' plays, the same closing actantial framework where Power
= gods, and Subject and Receiver = the community is still nominally in
place, but the whole structure comes under pressure in all kinds of ways,
subjected to Sophocles' incessant irony and his fascination with the portrayal of single individuals reacting and relating to their social
environment. Actantial categories and the relationships between them
undergo a different, more subtle kind of shift in comparison with that
required for their original conversion from myth to tragedy in the first
place[15] and *doloi* tend to persist unresolved beyond the end of the play.

Sophoclean gods still deliver a traditional, mythical Object to the community – in *Ajax, Trachiniae, Antigone, Electra* and *Oedipus at Colonus* a
corpse or corpses requiring ritual – but there is often little sense that this
is part of a positive process. There is little evidence of an ultimately
consistent divine interest in earthly affairs (an interesting contrast with
Zeus' offstage attention to onstage events in *Prometheus Bound*, although
that is perhaps a special case). In comparison with Aeschylean endings, it
is striking that the satisfactory burial at the end of *Ajax* seems to be
achieved without the aid of Athena, who opened the prologue, and that
while Heracles' appearance at the end of *Philoctetes* wrenches the action
back onto its destined track, his intervention – even if we call it persuasion
– mirrors Athena's in *Ajax* for its lack of concern for human suffering.

Sophocles tends to focus on the suffering individual, rather than the
community which benefits from their suffering, and his plays tend to break
off abruptly, usually adumbrating but not including the closing community
ritual which seems to be Aeschylus' normal practice. (The exceptions here
are *Philoctetes*, where no immediate ritual is indicated – though there will
be a healing ritual in Troy – and *Oedipus at Colonus* which uniquely *does*
end in a lament.)[16] The sense of communal benefit (Object communicated
to Receiver) is implicitly present, certainly in the plays which take cult-
heroes such as Ajax, Heracles and the Colonean Oedipus as their central
figures, but the treatment is subtle and various.

Sophoclean endings are of extraordinary interest. In the first three
surviving plays (*Ajax Trachiniae* and *Antigone*), all of which close, traditionally enough, with a corpse requiring burial, there seems to be a
tendency to end earlier and earlier. The culminating example of this is the
later *Electra*, which concludes with Aegisthus, one of the two traditional
corpses, still arguing with his murderer in perfect mental and physical
health.

To take the first two surviving plays, *Ajax* and *Trachiniae*. At the end of *Ajax* realistic, immediate details of preparations for the first stage of Ajax's interment (digging the nearby grave, heating water, fetching the arms that will be buried with the body) fill the last speech, and the play closes as brother and son, with assistance, raise the still-bleeding corpse and the cast process offstage with it. The second stage, burial itself, is also felt to be imminent – the body, after all, has been lying visible on the ground since its discovery at 891 – but is not shown. All the same, we understand that Ajax will have a family burial with wife, brother, son, Salaminians and possibly others in attendance. Significantly, Odysseus and other Greeks may attend. While this is a very different, low-key kind of treatment from anything we could expect from Aeschylus, there is all the same a modest sense of rightness and completion here.

In *Trachiniae*, Heracles, carried in unconscious on a stretcher, gives an initially strong visual impression of a corpse laid out on a bier. But this image is not fulfilled within the course of the play itself. He is still alive at the end, and this final scene, we eventually understand, is only a preliminary one which makes arrangements for the subsequent death on Oeta. Trachis itself, setting for the play, turns into a merely transitional place, a mere halt on a longer death journey Heracles is making from Zeus' altar at Cape Cenaeum to Zeus' sacred mountain. This ending, while it fills in gaps in our previous understanding (cf. 1145), creates many more which remain partially or completely unresolved (if not so much to the original audience).

Oddly, it is Heracles himself who, with no explicit reference to divine command, designates his own pyre on Zeus' mountain, and demands to be burned alive by his son. In verses 1145-50 Sophocles delicately tempts us to think that Heracles might have told us more detail of Zeus' commands, including orders for death, if Alcmena and his remaining children could have been formally assembled to listen.[17] Since this is not possible (1151-6) Heracles gives Hyllus an abbreviated account of the Dodona oracle before issuing direct orders about the manner of his death, orders which we, if not Hyllus, might suppose to be equally enjoined by Zeus.

It is interesting to consider other ways the information about Heracles' death could have been given. As at the end of *Philoctetes*, a *deus* (some appropriate emissary from Zeus) could have been used, making every detail clear and incontrovertible and commanding instant obedience from Hyllus. What we have instead is a dialogue in which a series of horrifying orders from a brutal man dying in agony are issued to his traumatised, confused son, from whom he has forced an oath of obedience. The depiction of paternal bullying is almost unbearable.[18] This tone of intense mental and physical pain is maintained right through Hyllus' final speech, and includes the closing lines 1275-8, whoever is the speaker.[19] The final expression, 'and none of these things is not Zeus' is Aeschylean in its concluding emphasis on the power of Zeus in human affairs, but the speaker has turned the thought on its head and is referring to human suffering, not achievement. Any idea that this might not be a final view is only hinted at.

Emotion and dramatic irony counterpoint one another: the orders at which Hyllus shows most distress are those where the audience have the greatest extent of superior information. Hyllus manages to negotiate with Heracles over the pyre: he will see to the building of it but not touch it. There is a narrative gap in which Philoctetes, the man who will light it and receive Heracles' bow in reward, is not mentioned: the audience know there is a solution for this dilemma. But the most painful order of all is that Hyllus must marry Iole, and this we know cannot be denied. That the noble Heraclidae were generated with such initial repugnance creates a whole spectrum of possible responses in the audience.

Trachiniae is not alone in 'gratuitously' reminding us of future events near the end. *Oedipus Tyrannus*, *Electra*, *Philoctetes* and *Oedipus at Colonus* do the same. The proleptic references disturb any sense of closing harmony that might otherwise be created; but at the same time, paradoxically, they might indicate closure to those members of the audience who are reminded that they have been watching *this* particular story, one among many possible renditions (see Easterling, 1981, 69, Roberts, 1988, Segal, 1996). Sophocles' innovative skill is to allow *doloi* to persist past the closing lines of these plays.

Part II

Aeschylus

He used to say his tragedies were slices from Homer's great banquets.

Athenodorus, *Deipnosophistae* viii.347e

[Early tragedy consisted of] little more than a messenger speech with lyric content.

Garvie, 1969, 105

... there is strikingly *little* [emphasis added] in the way of messenger scenes in Aeschylus. They are characteristic of Sophocles and above all of Euripides, but not, it seems of earlier tragedy. Aeschylus expends his skill on diversifying his narrative elements, and there is no clear sign of any prototype for the familiar scenes of later tragedy.

Taplin, 1977, 84-5

4

Narrative Shaping

4.1 General outlines

The surviving plays of Aeschylus, which all derive from a fourteen-year period at the end of his life, indicate that, at the time he was composing, the possibilities of dramatic form were comparatively unhardened into conventional practices – inasmuch as this was ever the case for a form which, for as long as we have evidence, seems to display continuing experimentation. The antecedents of Aeschylus' diversity are unknown, yet at the same time critics usually stress that Aeschylus himself was a great innovator (e.g. Else, 1967, 83ff., who plots a nine-point development from *Persians* through the remaining plays).

It is certainly useful to consider that his basic task was to convey the narratives of epic in an increasingly dramatic *poiêsis* (see, e.g. Herington, 1985, particularly 125-44), but with so few plays surviving it is hard to trace this progress. Each play, whether or not we include *Prometheus Bound*,[1] is very different. Aeschylus' use of the formal elements of tragedy is fluid, and the separation between lyric and trimeter, actor and chorus, is less clearly distinguished: while there are many examples of *rhêseis* which have a narrative function (for a typology of these see Peretti, 1939), choral lyric is also used to convey important information. Only in *Persians* are proleptic narratives used in combination with a sustained message narrative to promote anything like the sense of outcome described at 2.2.4 above. Even with the Herald (*Ag.* 503ff.), the entire *Oresteia* lacks any kind of straightforward messenger speech; in the first two plays in particular, information is notoriously deceitful, defective and ambiguous. *Supplices* and *Septem* both contain a brief messenger speech (*Supp.* 600-24 and *Sept.* 792-820), but these almost pale into insignificance between the powerful lyrics which surround them on either side.

Portent, prophecy, dream or curse occur in all the seven surviving plays, and with great significance in five. Of the other two, *Eumenides* deals with the consequences of Clytemnestra's curse in *Choephoroe*. This final play in the trilogy does not need to end with a further long-range narrative, since it achieves closure by giving authority to Athena and 'fixing' the Erinyes into the aetiology of the Areopagus. This in itself creates strong lines of perspective away from the past, returning the audience to their present circumstances; the reference to the Argive alliance (see especially *Eum.*

767-71) which Orestes as a dead hero will safeguard, also returns the
audience to its own time. The other play with no major proleptic narrative
is *Supplices*, first play of the Danaid trilogy, and here indeed the lack of
any proleptic narrative is striking and makes an understanding of the
trilogy very difficult.

We need to distinguish, on the one hand, between dreams and oracles
as significant structural components of any given drama, and on the other,
mere reference to them or, to put it another way, between their narrative
and non-narrative function. Thus while *Choephoroe* and *Persians* include
a major dream narrative, *Agamemnon* lacks one – despite abundant
references to dreams and dream language.

But in fact the mere language of dreams and of prophecy, interpretation
and 'reaching the goal' shapes and informs much Aeschylean tragedy
(perhaps even more than the language of sacrificial ritual does). In particular, the very structure of the *Oresteia* could be said to mimic the
delivery of an oracle and its fulfilment. From many separate voices heard
directly and indirectly – the chorus, Calchas, Clytemnestra, *prophêtai* of
the house of Troy, the Herald, the anonymous person who named Helen,
Cassandra – the audience hear authoritative pronouncements of various
kinds such as 'learning through suffering' (*pathei mathos*) and they struggle to interpret and understand so as to reach the goal (*terma* or *telos*).

At a structural level, Aeschylus' proleptic narratives are often alter-
nated with analeptic narratives of equal extent. These are often delivered
by the chorus and usually do far more than point forward or back in a
simple way to one definite action and its consequences. They work in a
complex and continuing way to manipulate audience expectation and
emotions. The eagles-hare portent[2] is an example of this technique. It
serves ambiguously both as a prediction of success at Troy and also as a
symbol of dark causality stretching far into the future, since Artemis'
anger brings about the sacrifice of Iphigeneia with all its implications. The
snake dream in *Choephoroe*, besides prefiguring Clytemnestra's murder at
the hands of her son, also operates throughout the play as a complex
symbol of ambiguity and deceit.

Aeschylus' iambic trimeter *rhêseis* are equally hard to grapple with.
They are diverse, idiosyncratic and often in catalogue form. Narrative
strategies may be heavily-marked and self-referential, but are used fluidly
to serve the individual design of each play rather than fitted regularly to
an extant template.

There is an important overall narrative shaping in many of Aeschylus'
plays: huge central scenes based on the elaborate communication of significant information. The Cassandra scene of *Agamemnon*, the Io scene
from *Prometheus Bound*, the shield scene of *Septem*, (less so the Darius
scene of *Persians*) exemplify this tendency. Each scene is unique and
serves its context in its own play, but nonetheless shares significant
similarities with the others. All are positioned at least half way into the

play at a point when many of the themes are already well-developed and a certain amount of tension has been created; the scenes build extensively on what has gone before and deliver much new and crucial information.[3] The Io and Cassandra scenes, which both occur in late stages of the opening play of trilogies (but see Griffith, 1983, 281ff. for the view that *Prometheus Bound* is the middle play), convey important advance information which will carry through to the second play. The element of *communication* between internal narrators and narratees is emphasised; each scene has a strong phatic frame,[4] emphasising the narrative as a performance.

The rest of Part II picks out some of the distinctive ways in which the earliest surviving playwright exploited different elements of the rich formal mix comprising *tragôidia*. The discussion is deliberately not cast in chronological, developmental form. Given the complexity and late dates of the small proportion of his surviving work, it is clear that any kind of model that sets out to show diverse narrative techniques developing morphologically from initial simplicity is doomed to failure – even more so than attempts to show development in *dramatic* technique. If drama was a reasonably new form when Aeschylus was composing, Homer's *narrative* mastery was always available, if it could somehow be adapted to the medium of drama.[5]

4.2 Scale, openings, focalisation, suspense and emotion

Aeschylus' plays typically have vast narrative *reach* and *extent*,[6] presumably due to their origin in the expansive epic tradition; the plot-line of the *Oresteia* moves from the mythical sack of Troy to the historical foundation of the Court of the Areopagus in Athens, an institution familiar to the contemporary audience; the Theban trilogy, represented by *Septem*, moves down three generations. Even the single play *Persians* takes in the whole of Persian history from Zeus' grant to Medus (759ff.) to the battle of Plataea (817f.) The Danaid trilogy, inasmuch as it can be reconstructed, would appear to have dealt only with the single generation of Danaids in Argos over a brief, if eventful, period of time (the Danaids are of bridal age, *numphai*, throughout), but here too the frequent references to Io and Zeus create a significant extension to the trilogy's timespan.

Yet paradoxically, Aeschylus opens up his mighty narratives in a very small way, and this seems an important strategy typical of every play. The scale is never flagged at the outset by using proleptic material in prologues and opening scenes to give a synoptic, unifying view across the separate action of each play. Instead, Aeschylus prefers to involve us in a complex hermeneutic process, lifting only a corner of the veil, as it were. He begins by showing us a tense situation focalised through a stage figure or figures characterised by expectation and fear and perhaps faced with a crucial dilemma. He emphasises their ignorance, and both we and his stage figures are variously brought to a position of knowledge only after a lengthy and involving process which takes up much of the play. Great *ekplêxis* is created in the shocking moment when the climax of this process is reached and knowledge attained (although we have noted already that message narrative does not play such a crucial role in the central revelation as it does for the other playwrights). Aeschylus' shaping of the narrative material in this way brings us to a consideration of 'suspense'.

Suspense has been defined as 'an emotion or state of mind arising from a partial and anxious uncertainty about the progression or outcome of an action, especially one involving a positive character' (Prince, 1987, 94-5; see also Bal, 1985, 114-15 and Pfister, 1988, 98-102). Suspense may be Aeschylus' greatest contribution to the development of drama. Herington writes (1985, 141-2): 'At creating suspense in a plot, Aeschylus is by common consent one of the greatest masters of them all ... The heroic episode must be so treated that it will not flow at the same even pace but with mounting speed and excitement, towards a climax which will fall near or at its end' (see also Else, 1967, 78-102).

The effects Aeschylus creates are almost synonymous with drama itself and the general view of what is meant by 'dramatic'. Suspense is arguably created on all possible fronts at every level, as if this was the main effect at which he was aiming. To achieve it he uses a galaxy of complex and overlapping effects of predication, created by riddles and word play; the archaic language of *hubris*, *kotos*, *atê* etc., with their loaded implications; prayers and foreshadowing expressions of hope and fear.

Of the suspense created by his narrative strategy, it seems absolutely typical that while Phrynichus' play on the collapse of Persia, *Phoenissae*, probably performed in 476,[7] began by acknowledging the obvious fact of the defeat at Salamis, Aeschylus in *Persians* begins by making it the crucial question to be answered. The Queen's dream is created specifically as a vehicle for highlighting and prolonging the ignorance of the stage figures. The main thrust of the play indeed, in all but the last scene, is to build up and sustain suspense so as to make critically important the effect of the news of defeat as it 'breaks' on the living and dead members of the royal house of Persia. Making an uncertainty out of a known fact and resurrecting a dead man onto the stage to hear about it, are both examples of extraordinary, almost perverse, ways of handling the given material.

In the rest of his plays too, which deal with mythical subjects, Aeschylus sets about re-inventing the relationship between the audience and a familiar story. Our own familiarity with the plays should not make us underestimate the extreme boldness at times of the framing techniques which get the audience to 'forget' (at some level) story material which it in fact knows very well (and could indeed narrate in its own right).

Audiences have specific knowledge to draw on (e.g. Jason always goes off in the *Argo* and finds the Golden Fleece), as well as a general understanding of story-patterns (heroes must overcome mighty opposition and jealous women are extremely dangerous).[8] How can an audience be made to *forget* what it knows? There is the point that in epic the bard's activity is frequently described as one in which events of the past are remembered or recalled, with the aid of the Muses who represent recollection. Given the 'forest' of myths with their overlapping boundaries and local sub-species, it is likely that the average audience member would not have immediate, clear recall of all the stories to do with all the heroes; the poet is the expert in this respect. In submitting their attention to the poet's narrative, the audience of epic seem to be thought of as in some way subjecting the content of their own memories to the temporary control of a higher authority: we can apply this also to tragedy.

Theoretical distinctions of various kinds can help show how this response is possible: first, the simple but fundamental distinction between story (*histoire*) and discourse (*discours*). Structuralist theory has usefully argued that each narrative consists of two parts: a story, which is the content or chain of events together with existents (e.g. characters or items of setting), plus a discourse; that is, the expression or means by which the content is communicated. 'In simple terms, the story is the *what* in a narrative that is depicted, discourse the *how*' (Chatman, 1978, 19). Thus an audience familiar with the story can nonetheless still be played upon by all manner of techniques employed in its discourse.

Secondly, there is a useful distinction between *the world of the theatre* and *the world of the drama* (Elam, 1980, esp. 87-97 and 98-114), and this distinction associates very closely with Rabinowitz's quite separate suggestion (1977, 121-42 and 1980) that audiences or narratees have their own 'morphology'. To simplify his ideas, any audience obviously consists of flesh and blood individuals, reacting in their own individual and group ways. The theoretical narrator of any drama may, however, address himself to either of two theoretical narratees, both co-existent within the same spectator. First, the *authorial* audience, a group of people with a similar cultural and historical background to the author himself, people well equipped to appreciate his metatheatrical references to other plays, allusions to recent political events, etc. Second, the *narrative* audience. This audience temporarily assents to believe that the fictive world is real (people long dead appear and speak, for example). They react in a simple way to the story as it unfolds, forgetting what they may know already about its outcome. Drama would not have the power to move without the narrative audience's 'willing suspension of disbelief', its ability at some level to forget known facts and assent to the validity of others.

All ancient dramatists in the course of a *tragôidia* appeal to both authorial and narrative audience in order to create a range of effects, now directly evoking the sympathy of the narrative audience for the stage figure in his predicament, now, with self-reference, reminding the authorial audience that the play they are watching is admirably constructed, and that they know other versions of it.[9] The audience may be consciously aware of the sheer beauty of an ode at the same time as they 'helplessly' respond to it. The combination of, and gap between, these different appeals (often strong enough to produce physical symptoms – extreme stillness, tears to the eyes, involuntary gasps, altered heartbeat, bristling of hairs[10]) is part of the extraordinary experience of watching tragedy. A watching audience is in a liminal condition in which it is susceptible to all sorts of suggestion.[11]

It is a particular *dolos* of Aeschylus to create opening suspense by starting in a small way with a narrow focus and a high emotional charge, a technique calculated to give immediate stimulus to the narrative audience. He gives little sense of what the structure of the play will be like overall, but the question of an end point is raised early on and is identified as the subject of much hope and fear. Sometimes he creates an elaborate linguistic texture in which proleptic elements, *angelia* and physical symptoms of fear are densely interwoven (see n. 10).

This way of beginning could not be more different from the opening strategy of Euripides, whose plays characteristically begin with an expository monologue addressed directly to the audience (discussed in Chapter 9). Contrast instead the anxiety of the chorus in *Persians*, the crisis Eteocles must deal with in *Septem*, the emotional watchman who has waited so long for news in *Agamemnon*, Orestes with his prayers and uncertainties in *Choephoroe*. Ironically, the Pythia in *Eumenides* begins in expository fashion – but this soon gives way to terror. *Supplices* 1-39 in some ways comes closest to a Euripidean prologue for its comparatively direct exposition. However, the sheer bulk of lyric and dialogue that then intervenes before the arrival of Pelasgus at 234 is most un-Euripidean, as are the formalities of recognition that ensue before the issue of asylum is discussed. It is typical of Aeschylus to delay definitive action.

4.3 Typical progression: use of time

Aeschylus' stage figures hope, fear and wait. They are enmeshed in the passage of time, which is somehow to determine their fate. Time has critical importance to the structure of Aeschylus' dramas, and interference with its natural sequence is a crucial tactic to arouse suspense. The plays typically develop by an alternation of truncated analeptic as well as proleptic narratives, setting up a narrative pendulum which swings repeatedly and tantalisingly to and fro over the 'now' of the present without developing it; instead we receive glimpses of selected events from past or future.[12] Aeschylus' narratives of the past are experienced as crucial to gaining an understanding of the present. Aeschylean choruses, repositories of traditional wisdom, regularly refer present problems to the mythic past of their own communities (see, for example, the repeated invocations of Zeus and Io by the Danaids in *Supplices*; the panoramic knowledge of the house of Labdacus shown in *Septem* 720-91).

Narratives from the past may be paradeigmatic, illuminating present and future. Aeschylus exploits this implicit narrative function by parataxis, juxtaposing known past with uncertain present and creating a highly idiosyncratic hermeneutic structure. This structure associates superbly with his deceits (3.4) and delays (4.4).

The chronological pendulum can be demonstrated well in any play, but is particularly marked in *Agamemnon*. Early on the goal or *telos* of the action is presented as Agamemnon's return, and the temporal extent of the action is thus set up as reaching from news of return to return itself. We know the beacon has been seen (22ff.) but we go back repeatedly to the setting out of the expedition ten years earlier. Further embedded into Calchas' interpretation of the portent is the so-called 'hymn to Zeus' which takes us back to the earliest time of all, when the universe was created by Ouranos and Cronos. Now we swing forward again to the previous night when Troy fell (264ff.) In the following ode (355-487) we move back to a period before the ten years' war when Paris broke the laws of hospitality by seducing Helen, and forward to a virtual present where young Greeks lie dead around the city walls. Again, we look forward to the moment of Agamemnon's return. The Herald tells us more about the recent victory and about the fragmentation of Menelaus' ships. This prompts the chorus to return into the past again with an allusive narrative beginning with the shadowy figure who named Helen (681ff.), presumably at her birth. Agamemnon enters, but before he is persuaded over the carpet, Clytemnestra insists on describing her ten years waiting for him (855ff.).

Cassandra's scene is one of those particular central scenes in which narratives of future *and* past are brought together and a wider, more panoramic vision allowed: in a disjointed sequence which leaps to and fro through time, and across the space between Troy and Argos, the prophetess touches on a wide range of past and future events many of which have not yet been brought into the consciousness of the play. I cite them in chronological order – but this is not the order in which they appear: first in the sequence is the 'primal and original disaster', *prôtarchos atê*, when Thyestes committed adultery with Atreus' wife; the feast of his own children prepared in revenge; Cassandra's childhood in Troy and her association with Apollo; the Furies presently in the house; the two murders that are about to take place; Orestes' return.

It is only at this stage in the play that any material is given us with which we could construct a future for the trilogy; even so, information leading to an idea of closure is still largely withheld. (Similarly at the end of *Prometheus Bound* we have some idea of the leverage over Zeus that will enable Prometheus to be released, but inconsistencies are left unresolved.) All the same, *Agamemnon* 1279-85 does constitute a virtual synopsis of the action of *Choephoroe*:

> I shall die – but not without honour from the gods; for there
> will come another as avenger, born to kill his mother and
> avenge his father, a wandering fugitive, exiled from this
> land. He will put the coping stone on these woes for those
> he loves; gods have sworn a great oath that his father
> lying supine will draw him home.

After this scene Agamemnon is murdered and the *here and now* for the
first time takes over. But Clytemnestra ranges over the past in justification of her deed, and the typical see-saw effect continues right to the end:
only in the final scene does Aegisthus supply a full narrative of the
significant rivalry in the previous generation between Atreus and
Thyestes.

4.4 Delay

This is another temporal *dolos* highly typical of Aeschylus and productive
of suspense. Delay might be defined as a prolongation of expected narrative duration. Delay experienced by an internal audience gives rise to
scenes of anxious waiting, as at the beginning of *Agamemnon* and other
nostos dramas. Or, lulled into accepting a false prolongation, chorus or
characters may be surprised by an unexpected entry like that of the
Danaids at *Supplices* 825ff. The external audience may or may not be
subject to the same treatment. When they know that an event is imminent
but something delays or obfuscates it, tension is created, as when Orestes
hesitates to kill his mother in *Choephoroe*. Or they may share the *ekplêxis*,
astonishment, of the internal audience at a sooner-than-expected entry.
Three examples follow:

Supplices: entry-speeches

Supplices gives us some lengthy entry-speech narratives, after which the
person or persons announced do *not* arrive for a considerable time. At 180
Danaus tells his daughters that he sees dust,[13] but Pelasgus himself does
not arrive and speak until 234. In the interim we are shown Danaus giving
his daughters directions, like a stage manager, for the scene that is to
follow. Under his eye they take up their suppliant positions at the altars
of the city gods, invoking them in turn. This interim delay generates extra
tension and gives the following scene with Pelasgus an excellent and
sophisticated frame for the audience: we can watch the Danaids' behaviour
in terms of its success as acting, seeing how it conforms to their father's
directions (186-203) and the effect it has on Pelasgus, who for his part has
certainly not had the opportunity to prepare for the confrontation in
advance.

A more complex example occurs later in the play at 710ff. Danaus
announces that the Egyptian ships are approaching, news that is unex-

pected (712). He can not only see them (713, 714, 716, 720, 722) but hear them too (718). The heightened sense of their imminent arrival is explored in the *kommos* (lyric dialogue) between Danaus and his daughters (736-63); there is fairly frequent convention of a (lyric) delay at a critical moment, so this delay is in itself not surprising. However, we certainly expect the entry of the Aegyptii to follow on immediately afterwards. But in a surprising overthrow of expectation, Aeschylus now has Danaus deliver a speech of at least twelve lines (more than twelve lines if Hartung's proposal of a lacuna after 773 is correct), delaying the Aegyptii's entry yet again. He begins 'It's not a quick business moving a fleet ...'. There will be a lengthy mooring procedure to be completed; the fact that night is approaching makes this particularly tricky. His narrative overtly slows the pace, slackening the sense of tension and immediacy created by the earlier announcement. Danaus departs to plead the Danaids' case to the Argives, and the fact that he risks leaving them alone at this juncture feeds into our supposition that the Aegyptii will not now land until the following morning. The maidens sing a beautiful flight song from which all sense of contextual urgency has been removed; the result, in fact, is similar to the first example in the sense that we are encouraged to appreciate their choral skills in general and enjoy the lyric as a piece of composition. Our surprise at their shrieks when the Aegyptii actually do appear at 825 (sixty-two lines after they were first announced but still much sooner than the Danaids and we have been led to expect) is a theatrical *coup* (see Easterling, *Nott. Class. Lit. Studies*, 1, 1992, 21).

In each case a linear narrative is avoided; a delay between announcement and entry initiates scenes of heightened emotional tension and expectation.[14]

Septem: the pairing of Polyneices with Eteocles

Garvie makes the point that once the symmetrical narrative pattern of the speeches in the arming scene 375ff. has been established, the rules of dramatic logic come into play and we know that Polyneices will be matched with Eteocles, whether or not we also know this separately through familiarity with the myth. Aeschylus increases tension by the very symmetry and appropriateness of each of Eteocles' choices and by delicate deviations from straight-line development which are richly suggestive (Garvie, 1978, 71ff.), while the continuing ignorance of Eteocles, who has shown himself so full of leadership qualities, creates a terrible irony. His reversal from ignorance to knowledge is deliberately delayed; the longer it continues the deeper and more painful the sense of inevitability.

Prometheus Bound: deferred story-telling

This play has a structure which particularly needs narrative variety since there can be little significant action: after the first scene the main character is immobile and Zeus, his antagonist, never appears (perhaps he cannot be shown). Twice in the play an expected narrative is deferred: at 271f. Prometheus tells the chorus to dismount and learn everything from start to finish. The chorus sing their readiness (277-83) but Oceanus unexpectedly appears and the promised revelation is not forthcoming. Then in the Io scene the chorus intervene just at the point where Io has persuaded Prometheus to reveal her future (with their cry 'Not yet', 631), and that account is delayed until 703ff.

4.5 Prophecies and dreams

Aeschylus makes great use of dreams and oracles to shape his dramas and provide suspense, and in this he is undoubtedly indebted to Homer, who in the *Iliad* makes cumulative prophetic statements about Troy's fall and Achilles' death, which control our response and contribute to the poem its shape and tragic colouring. Oracles tell of 'things that are, will be, and were before', *ta t'eonta ta t'essomena pro t'eonta* (*Il.* 1.70). They are 'a statement of plot' (Lattimore, 1964, 72), but also a frequent agent of ambiguity, despite the fact that the commission of their commands and the unavoidable fulfilment of their prohibitions are in accordance with clear narrative rules. They are an important hermeneutic device, inspiring intense mental activity in the audience.

Aeschylus too allows proleptic narratives to accumulate and converge on a fixed point (see particularly *Septem* and *Choephoroe*).[15] The tragic medium, with its inherent lack of omniscient focalisation, can readily be used to create even greater internal ambiguities. The foreboding atmosphere of a given play has usually been established before the oracle or dream appears. The subsequent predictive material is presented through the focalisation of a stage figure during an episode rather than, as in Euripides, by an initial prologue speaker who may be giving the audience a guide to the whole action. In Aeschylus initially the oracle or dream seems merely to feed into the fear or expectations of the stage figures. For example the chorus of *Persians* are full of foreboding even before the Queen has told them of her dream (and, paradoxically, once they have heard the dream narrative with its fairly clear presentiment of disaster, their belief in a 50-50 chance of success is restored). The female chorus of *Septem* is initially depicted fearing the future directly (78-180, 287-368), not because of any oracle they have heard – despite the enormous amount of proleptic material at issue in the play of which they later show deep understanding. In *Choephoroe*, Clytemnestra's dream and Apollo's oracle are initially merely added to the situation of watchful tension already created by Orestes' return.

Despite the initially tentative effects on the internal narrator and narratee however, the message itself is certainly understood by both authorial and narrative audience as a guide to the action, providing a sense of structure and direction which the course of the play then fulfils: in *Persians* the Queen's dream is followed by the Messenger's news which explains it, then Darius' recalled prophecies give perspective to Xerxes' final lament. Cassandra's predictions in the second half of *Agamemnon* are an important preview of *Choephoroe*; Apollo's oracle in this play is only to be resolved at the end of the entire trilogy. Any reading of *Septem* must stand or fall by the great irruption of oracle and curse into the central scene.

> O race of Oedipus that gods drive mad,
> that gods so hate, race of endless tears!
> Alas, his curse now bears fruit. (*Sept.* 653-5)

Persians

Aeschylus gives the actual substance of the dream a shifting, symbolic importance stretching unexpectedly over the entire length of the play. (This technique contrasts, for example, with the simpler functional use Euripides makes of the pillar with hair and voice representing Orestes in Iphigeneia's dream *IT* 50f. See 9.1). The dream in *Persians* initiates motifs the audience will understand only later. After violent action described 194-6 there is a curiously static, frieze-like quality about the figures at 197-9. The Queen describes Darius pitying his son and Xerxes tearing his garments when he sees his father. These are not mere decorative details to border the main image of the dream: in fact, the brief appearance of Darius here prepares for the scene 681ff., in which he rises from the dead, pitying his son, ('Poor wretch!', 733); while the motif of Xerxes' rags will be re-introduced again and again in the subsequent movement of the play (see 469, 832-6, 845-51, 1017, 1030), culminating in the final appearance of the ruined king, his ragged finery symbolising the grief of Persia.[16]

The Queen's dream of Xerxes' attempt to yoke Europe and Asia cannot fail to be understood as a prediction of Persian failure, and the chorus' open verdict on it must be perceived ironically. Apart from the audience's historical knowledge, the chorus' own earlier presaging words strongly invite a negative interpretation. The stage figures' treatment of the dream as an entirely ambiguous, even neutral communication is in fact part of an established dramatic convention: it is exactly how the Clytemnestras of both *Choephoroe* and Sophocles' *Electra* react.[17]

Choephoroe

Here dream and oracle intertwine and build cumulatively towards the main action of matricide, and beyond to its aftermath and final resolution at the end of *Eumenides*. Dream is female and internal to the house, oracle male and external, but both are agents of ambiguity as much as truth.

The dream snake makes a rich, unexpected movement from dream to eventual onstage presence – or at least hallucinatory presence. At first Orestes straightforwardly interprets his mother's dream and identifies himself as the snake in it: 'I turn into a snake and kill her' (549-50). This interpretation of the snake as a symbol of Orestes is confirmed by Clytemnestra: 'Alas for the snake I bore and nursed – how truly prophetic was the fear in my dream!' (928-9). At the time this appears to be the moment of insight on Clytemnestra's part which completes the relevance of the dream and the snake to the play. But the dream here, more than the dream in *Persians*, is a slippery motif of multiple relevance and still has an important part to play. At 1047 the chorus praise Orestes for having freed Argos by 'easily cutting off the heads of two snakes' (1046-7). This phrase reverses the attribute of *snakiness*, taking it away from Orestes himself and applying it to his enemies. But this is not the final movement: at the very end, when Orestes sees the Furies he describes them as 'thickly wreathed with snakes' (1049-50), and 'multiplying' as he watches (1057). So snakes symbolise first the righteous avenger, then his enemies, and finally become a symbol for the Furies and the revenge *they* inspire. The snake's multiple valency is a *dolos* operating thematically to underline the ambiguity of retributive action (like the web/robe imagery of both the first two plays of this trilogy).

The oracle is equally deceitful. Its first mention is carefully positioned between the lyric presentation of the dream (32ff.) and its apparently lucid interpretation (526-52). The oracle provides direct motivation for action, and Orestes asserts that the god who ordered the act guarantees its fulfilment (269-70). But what of the oracular description (273ff.) of the fate of those who *fail* to avenge their kin (for attempted rationalisations, see Garvie ad loc.)? The lengthy details are puzzling at this point because they appear redundant. The point, only to be understood later, is that, like the snake dream, the oracle is setting up a double bind: in carrying out the oracle's command Orestes will suffer these symptoms both despite and because of his matricidal action: the situation (discussed in 3.1) is not 'either/or' but 'both/and'. The symptoms are therefore proleptic in function and admonitory in a way that only becomes clear through time.

The second mention of the oracle (556-9) comes immediately after the interpretation of the dream, in language which, with apparent innocence, juxtaposes trickery and truth: again it is stressed that Apollo is never a deceiver – despite advising deceit.

> Since they killed a worthy man by deceit, let them be
> caught also by deceit, dying in the same noose which
> in fact Loxias has prophesied – Lord Apollo, a prophet
> who has never lied in the past.

There is a slight but ominous difference between 'Apollo who never lies' and 'Apollo who has never lied in the past'. The qualifiying phrase suggests a dangerous gap between secure past and insecure future.[18]

The oracle is mentioned for a third time at the critical moment when Orestes is on the point of killing his mother. Unexpectedly he turns to the non-speaking figure of Pylades, asking the question (899):

Pylades, what shall I do? Should I shrink from killing my mother?

The question creates an extraordinary moment of suspense. Temporarily, the urgent action halts and the fleeting possibility arises of the narrative taking a completely unexpected turn (Orestes decides not to kill his mother). Aeschylus now resolves this impossible situation with another piece of *ekplêxis*, by having Pylades make an answer which involves the oracle, and which is itself 'oracular'. That Pylades, up till now a non-speaking role, is given a voice at all is a shock to the audience. Under any circumstances, when a figure speaks after long silence, their words must have a particular intensity. Here, when Pylades recalls the binding power of the oracle the effect is almost as if Apollo himself spoke.[19] Pylades' reference to the oracle provides the important final impetus to prosecute the matricide, marked by Orestes' brutal command at 904 (particularly peremptory without the usual transitional *su de*, 'but you', as Garvie notes).

In conclusion, each time the oracle is mentioned in the play, two opposing effects are created: on the one hand, the stage figures press the plan of murder further towards its conclusion, while on the other, the language used and the precise contextual situation cumulatively increase the level of ambiguity about the validity of the deed itself.

Aeschylus also uses dreams and oracles quite differently as small, locally significant items for persuasion or confirmation: confirmation may include the moment of recognition or *anagnôrisis*.[20]

Persuasion. The narrative of Io's separation from her family which makes reference to dreams and oracles (*PB* 640-86) is not central to the overall story of Prometheus, and their effect on Io has been completed by the time we hear about them – she is already a goaded wanderer. They do not arouse the audience's interpretative skills. The most interesting feature of both is the unusual way they are presented as yet more examples of Zeus' strong-arm tactics: at 667-8 the oracle delivers an outright threat to Inachus if he is disobedient and fails to cast his daughter out. The dream and the oracle together constitute threatening messages from Zeus which persuade Inachus to expel his daughter (671-2).

Unexpanded proleptic elements can also be presented singly or in a group to provide confirmation. Prometheus declares in *prophecy* (908) that, without his help, Zeus' rule will fail through a marriage, and if this happens it will be the fulfilment of the *curse* Cronos uttered when Zeus deposed him (910ff.). Confirmation of an ineluctable divine will also seems to be the reason for Eteocles' glancing reference to his *dreams* (*Sept.* 710f.). There is no reference to Cronos' curse or to Eteocles' dream elsewhere in the plays in which they occur, nor anywhere else in ancient literature: again, both must owe their existence entirely to the rhetorical needs of the moment.

Dreams and prophecies also play a strong part in *anagnôrisis*. Several plays of Aeschylus display a learning curve which arches up towards the fateful moment when the hero or heroine reaches full understanding. Almost invariably a dream or prophecy is then referred to which may or may not have been mentioned already, as confirmation that the moment of outcome has arrived. The irony of such expressions of recognition – frequently using *karta* or *agan* 'too (much)' – is striking.

Thus at *Pers.* 518-19 the Queen cries to the chorus, 'O vivid vision of my night's dream, how all too clearly (*karta*) you showed my disaster – and you interpreted it far too trivially (*agan*).' Darius echoes her (739ff.), 'How quickly came the outcome of the oracles! Zeus inflicted their fulfilment on my son, and I somehow thought the gods would bring it about much later.' Clytemnestra cries (*Cho.* 928-9): 'Woe is me for this snake I bore and nursed. How true a prophet (*karta*) the fear in my dreams!' Eteocles declares (*Sept.* 710-11), 'How all too true (*agan*) the visions in my dreams, dividing up our ancestral wealth!' Cassandra even *prefigures* just such a moment (*Ag.* 1240-1), 'Face to face, you'll soon be saying with pity how true a prophetess I was! (*agan*)'.[21]

5

Three Major Narrative Scenes

5.1 Framing, structure, verbal functions and time

Septem's Shield scene, *Agamemnon*'s Cassandra scene and *Prometheus Bound*'s Io scene have striking underlying similarities. All three occur at or after the mid-point in their respective plays, and in importance each must be considered *the* central scene. Thalmann (1978, 28) gives a diagram showing *Septem* as a ring structure with the Shield scene (369-719) at its centre. The Cassandra scene (*Ag.* 1072-1330) holds the key position between the scene of Agamemnon's return and his murder. The Io scene (*PB* 561-886) is at the heart of the drama, functioning as a kind of play within a play.[1] Positioned as they are, these scenes substantially advance themes and issues already set up by the poet.

Each scene is a bravura performance with words, but given that the scenes' essential function is informative, it is striking that the straightforward referential function, so prominent in the messenger speeches of the other two playwrights, is in these scenes almost overwhelmed by other competing codes, notably the phatic.[2]

An example of marked phatic emphasis occurs at *Supp.* 234f. where the chorus and Pelasgus call for mutually identifying narratives in an elaborate recognition/greeting scene. The repeated references to speaking, saying, naming, declaring, remain largely unsubordinated to what is being said, creating a highly formalised situation onstage in which attention is focused on each successive act of narrating, and the reciprocal listening and responding (see *Supp.* 243, 245, 246-7, 249, 271-3, 274-6, 277, 291, 293, 295, 301, 304, 310, 318, 320, 322). The structure is not so much, 'What is your name?' but 'Make a declaration of your name to me.' When attention is so focused on the act of speaking, the internal and external systems, usually kept apart, begin to coincide and the audience (to whom, of course, all speech in drama is ultimately directed) is alerted to take note of distinctive *telling*, with emphasis on the *process of communication itself* as much as on the *content*.

The sustained use of the phatic function thus frames and makes conscious its own discourse. In *Agamemnon* the marked difficulties of communication between the chorus and Cassandra contribute to one of the major themes of the play; in *Septem*, the phatic emphasis heightens the audience's receptivity to the symbolic language games at work in Eteocles' verbal counters. The phatic function in *Prometheus Bound* draws attention to the continous re-arrangement of narrative material in that scene.

Each scene capitalises on the time-scheme already established to create powerful effects. In terms of Aeschylus' 'narrative pendulum' discussed earlier (4.3), the rhythm quickens. Areas previously swept straight over (creating a narrative *gap*) are now explored. Put in terms of narrative theory, partial analepses are completed: thus at *Septem* 70 Eteocles refers to his father's curse and the Erinys without placing them in chronological sequence. This partial analepsis is completed at 653-5 when we finally gain an understanding of how they fit into the sequence of the play's events. Increased revelation is made possible by the exceptional qualities of the major narrator, in each case an exceptional figure at the opposite pole from conventional anonymous messengers. Eteocles can find repeated omens (*clêdones*) in the information the scout gives him; Cassandra is a prophetess inspired by Apollo; Prometheus is the son of Themis who has told him all the future (*PB* 101-5; 209-21; 873-4; 913-5).

The range, function and general effect of these panoramic message scenes is far wider than those of the so-called 'classic' group. Information given is certainly not restricted to the recent or immediate past. Motivated by a crisis, Aeschylus' narrators widen out the temporal perspectives of the drama enormously; their elaborately-structured narrative sequences tie together past, present and future to create an essentially predictive effect. The delivery of proleptic narrative is particularly important in those scenes which come from first plays of trilogies (*Agamemnon* and *Prometheus Bound*;)[3] but in *Septem*, a final play, the past too is suddenly revealed and leads to closure.

These scenes, however, do not deliver the moment of outcome, like the message scenes of, for example, Sophocles' Theban plays. All the same, outcome follows closely in both *Septem* and *Agamemnon*. In *Septem* it erupts from the same scene, in *Agamemnon* it follows after a choral interlude of only twelve verses. (*Prometheus Bound* is different, offering cataclysm without resolution.) It is interesting to see that *Septem* and *Agamemnon* contain, in their own idiosyncratic ways, much of the narrative detail one would expect to find included later in a conventional message narrative. It is the Shield scene that gives us the disposition and elaborate detail of the champions, whereas no detail is admitted into the messenger's later brief report. Cassandra's far-reaching visions include, in brief snatches, most of the details of Agamemenon's death that we are going to get (though we hear the victim's offstage cries and Clytemnestra's exultant, self-justifying description at 1382-92).

All three scenes greatly increase the knowledge of the external audience, if not of the internal one. In *Septem* there is Eteocles' famous outburst of understanding at 652; in *Agamemnon*, while the audience learn much, and Cassandra comes to an understanding of her imminent death, Aeschylus is at pains to point up that the chorus cannot take in what

Cassandra tells them; in *Prometheus Bound* the three-way discussion about what may and may not be known receives almost as much attention as the information itself.

5.2 The shield scene from *Septem* (369-719)[4]

Strong frame and strong verbal function

There are seven messenger speeches to which Eteocles responds seven times,[5] after each of which the chorus sing a brief song. This pattern is made clear from the start, e.g. 42f., 56-8, the vexatious 282-6.[6] At the opening of the scene itself, the unusual double entry of Eteocles and the Scout (369-74) and the repeated *spoudêi/spoudê*, 'with haste/haste' (371, 374) create, on the visual level, an immediate image of a pair of critically opposed men, challenger and counter-challenger. Taplin, 1977, 149, writes: 'The visual handling of the entries sets the pattern for the seven pairs of speeches, each reply of Eteocles meeting perfectly each challenge set up by the Scout.' The exchanges begin with the Scout saying that he knows the disposition of the enemy at *each* of the seven gates (*hekastos*, 376) before going on to describe the first enemy, Tydeus, and asking Eteocles to make a counter-disposition. After Eteocles has responded the first time and the chorus have responded to *his* response, the audience know this pattern will be repeated another six times. The phatic emphasis (verbs of speaking at 373, 375, 400, 451, 457, 489, 490, 526, 553, 568, 631-2) continuously reinforces this structure.

Because the scene is so heavily stylized and uses language in so many ways other than the merely referential, attempts such as Wiles's (1993)[7] to read in stage action which will naturalistically accommodate the fluctuating tenses (see below) may consequently be futile. 'Eteocles' words ... are as good as action, and ... for the audience they are supposed to be translated into action *off-stage*' (Taplin, 1977, 155-6). 'The important thing that he (Eteocles) is doing in these speeches is *verbal*' (Cameron, 1970, 101, my emphasis). The scene portrays an unreal, symbolic encounter; the disparity of tenses give it the overall feel of a complex 'still': seven Theban champions stood, stand and will stand forever urgently at the Seven Gates to face their Argive opponents.

Each of the Scout's ornate descriptions of champion and shield device is countered by a parallel description from Eteocles. Hybristic boasts are 'turned' by a more modest approach. Within the simple frame 'challenge/counter-challenge' a complex pattern is set up and repeated through the first few speeches so that later variations will be perceived as such (de Hoz, 1979, 228, ' ... a sort of movement, a differentiating tension can be discerned'). Any deviation is a source of immediate and close attention, provoking from the audience efforts of interpretation – mimicking the activity in which Eteocles himself is engaged.

The 'turning' depends largely on the metareferential and metalingual functions of communication. The Scout's *rhêseis* function as riddles, *clêdones*.[8] Like the material of a dream or portent, every detail is capable of yielding an interpretation, and Eteocles has the ability to produce readings which mean a victory for Thebes; he can indeed, in the words of the first line, *legein ta kairia*, 'say what the hour requires'.[9] The exact way in which each threat is 'turned' varies each time, and the complexity of detail defies easy generalisation and invites a plurality of critical interpretations.

Through the descriptive power of the two contrapuntal sets of narratives, the seven pairs of contestants and their contests (*agônes*) achieve virtual reality. Furthermore, although the outcome of each single combat is treated as yet to be known, the visible control over the entire situation exercised by Eteocles up to 652 can leave little doubt that the result will be in Thebes' favour.[10] The effect is similar to that of the carpet scene of *Agamemnon*, where Clytemnestra's superior verbal agility successfully brings Agamemnon over the tapestries and into the house.

It is striking that the controlling structure is not abandoned when Polyneices is described at the seventh gate; despite the emotional outburst of 652, Eteocles' response to this champion comes in the same form as his response to the others. The continuance of this formal pattern past the powerful moment of recognition helps mark out all seven confrontations as part of the inevitable design of the gods. Six of these Eteocles could counter, while the seventh is his doom; here the emphatic contrapuntal structure contributes strongly to the meaning: form is fate. The shaping up to the revelation of Polyneices reinforces the idea of the two brothers as an opposite pair; after this point the language stresses them as identical: 'I shall stand leader with leader, brother with brother, enemy with enemy' (674-5).

In the ensuing scene of *peithô* between the chorus and Eteocles, we do not expect Eteocles to be convinced that this encounter, any more than any of the others, can be avoided. Eteocles is revealed as no longer an authoritative narrator of the future but a puppet in another narrative fixed earlier. This does not make the *clêdones* null and void, but it puts them into another perspective and indicates that the quasi-mantic activity Eteocles has been engaged in is of lesser authority: he must give way before the oracle and the curse, whose language has higher power.

Time

The use of time in this scene is extraordinary. The play began with a sense of extreme urgency (cf. entry-speeches 371 and 374). The Argive champions had much earlier been selected and sworn a mighty oath (42ff.), and in the parodos the Theban women described their acute fear at the sights and sounds of the host already approaching over the plain against them

(78-180). Yet Eteocles has spent his time so far dealing with the emotions of the chorus rather than making dispositions against the Argive champions.

But the sense of acute crisis is soon suspended within the scene itself. There are several reasons for this: first, onstage narrative inevitably constitutes a pause in the action (unless one holds Wiles's view that the Theban warriors are on stage and sent off as each selection is made), in the sense that no new character will enter and no topic other than the information to be communicated will be raised until the narrative is over. Time becomes elastic and Eteocles has as much of it as he wants to counter each of the Scout's narratives. The process of description and counter-description with all its elaborate detail and interpretation holds our attention in its own right. Its present time becomes almost timeless, a feeling assisted by the present tenses used by the Scout, and also by the offstage dictates of Amphiaraus.

The mantic Amphiaraus, apart from his other functions in this scene, is explicitly in control of offstage, Argive action. He both locks and unlocks their movement. Almost the first piece of information learnt from the Scout is that Amphiaraus has forbidden the Argives to cross the Ismenus and attack (377f.). The enemy, fully armed, are thus 'frozen' in full armour until we hear of Amphiaraus' counter-order in the direct speech of *machômeth'*, 'let us fight' (589). From this point on, the pendulum starts to swing again. Meanwhile, in this artificial, timeless present Eteocles finds his *clêdones*. His words predict the outcome of the contests and so point to future fulfilment.

This brings us to the problem of the tenses used for the verbs in which the postings are made. Eteocles replies to the Scout with three futures, two perfects, an aorist and a present tense. Winnington-Ingram is surely correct in saying that they are not arranged at random: we begin logically with a future (408) and return to the future when the sense of urgent time begins to bite again (the posting of Amphiaraus' opponent Lasthenes is in the future (621). In between, the present, aorist and perfect tenses connect up this surreal onstage present, together pointing to the eternal antagonism of the Seven Against Thebes.

The tenses also have an effect on the resolution of the entire trilogy. Aeschylus must bring events to a satisfying conclusion. We know that the oracle to Laius, its fulfilment by Oedipus, and Oedipus' curse directed at his sons have, however presented, already played their part in the workings of the earlier plays, and would consequently be present somewhere in the audience's mind. They would already have seen or heard of *outcome* in the murder of Laius by his son, and the dramatic presentation of Oedipus' understanding of his parricide and incest. They would have heard the curse against the sons, and be waiting for *its* fulfilment. But by a bold stroke, all reference to this inevitable fulfilment has so far been temporarily obliterated in this third play so as to focus on the success of Eteocles' planning. The past tenses delicately adumbrate the pre-determined pat-

tern events must take, and the slight logical incongruity seems a tiny price
to pay for the resulting effect. The pay-off will come at the tremendous
moment of Eteocles' outburst at 653, an *anagnôrisis* (moment of recognition) and *peripeteia* (moment of reversal) which, like other great scenes in
Aeschylus, marks a great shift of direction and temporal perspective.

After the mention of Polyneices, what had been seen as developing
freshly moment by moment before our eyes, something new and in Eteocles' control, is equally to be understood as part of something old and
inevitable, the fulfilment of Oedipus' curse. The shaping of the whole play
is made so as to show, through the figure of Eteocles, the ability of the past
to fix the apparently fluid present. The variation of tense, probably unno-
ticeable in performance, is a deliberate manipulation which keeps in play
all three time frames – past, present and future – to be reactivated or
dropped when required. This technique is unparalleled but not impossible,
given Aeschylus' narrative boldness elsewhere.

The effect is particularly rich because this scene, with its cledonic
structure, was already showing one kind of verbal battle, in which Eteocles' narrative superiority made him clear victor. Now, however, at the
name of Polyneices, an ancient narrative of greater predictive authority
emerges from within the same structure of control and containment.
Eteocles' control crumples, and his cry of recognition 653-5, 'O great hatred
of the gods, maddened by gods, O desperately wretched house of Oedipus,
alas, now is my father's curse brought to fulfilment' brings back all the
previous proleptic elements of the trilogy in a rush; the historic perspective
engulfs the carefuly controlled present and future.

5.3 The Cassandra scene from *Agamemnon* (1072-1330)[11]

Speech / silence

Cassandra's scene of prophecy is significantly preceded by her onstage
silence throughout the carpet scene and by her silent presence throughout
the ensuing lyric, 975-1034. Still silent, she becomes the centre of attention in the pre-scene in which Clytemnestra, attempting to induce her to
make the same fatal journey into the house as Agamemnon, is seen to
fail.[12] Clytemnestra and the chorus (who politely suggest compliance 1049
and 1054-5) discuss Cassandra over her head. Is the reason for her silence
ignorance of Greek (1051, 1060) – perhaps an interpreter is required (1062)
– or psychological damage (1064ff.)? There is even a suggestion that she
uses gesture to communicate (1061).

All this emphasises her resolute refusal to speak, for which we are never
given a motive.[13] But the effect is significant in several ways. We see that
communication requires the participation of two parties; Cassandra's
refusal to share communication with Clytemnestra is a form of success
which contrasts with Agamemnon's fatal compliance.

The Cassandra scene takes place at one minute to midnight, as it were: Agamemnon has gone inside, and all the preparation to date leads us to expect his imminent death. Instead, the powers of a special narrator create a temporal extension. We experience an unnatural timelessness as before; the scene is long and highly wrought with its own rhythms and pacing, and as long as it lasts, it delays the critical moment when the axe falls.

Cassandra's ability to describe the future to some extent balances the chorus' earlier authority to describe the past; if the Argive chorus provided the opening background information, much of which concerned Troy, Trojan Cassandra supplies us with the knowledge we need about Argos to carry us past the stark ending of this first play into the rest of the trilogy. The barbarian slave knows more than any other character in *Agamemnon*, even Clytemnestra, and her knowledge springs infallibly from direct contact with a god. By showing this infallibility operating through a narrator doomed to be incomprehensible, Aeschylus gives us perhaps the richest development of one of the major themes of the play; what Goldhill (1984, 81), calls 'the problem of exchange of language'. The scene acts out the polarities of speech/silence, ignorance/knowledge already in operation. While it gives so much information externally to the audience it is also a pathetic display of the failure of communication between prophetess and chorus. Such inadequacy on the chorus' part helps prepare for their *aporia* (lack of resources, perplexity) when Agamemnon's cries are heard.

Cassandra gives voice to a pitiful and unusual lament for herself as she moves inexorably offstage to her death (cf. *Ant.* 806-928: Sophocles may well be influenced by this scene). Her fate, a side-issue in terms of the trilogy, becomes the uppermost concern of the scene. Without ever detaching Cassandra's fate entirely from Agamemnon's, Aeschylus, with subtle *dolos*, makes use of the chorus' focus on Cassandra's plight to draw our attention away from Agamemnon's coming murder.

Structure

Aeschylus has not here created a formal structure as fundamental to the movement of the play as the paired speeches of *Septem*. All the same, the intricacies of the 'lyric plus *rhêsis*' structure are illuminating. By using both, the same narrative material receives different treatments, and the poet can tease out themes, motifs, developments and relationships which play to the strengths of either form.[14] The murder of Agamemnon and the plan of the trilogy are conveyed both in immediate, allusive lyric and in the more rational *logos* of iambic trimeter.

In other Aeschylean epirrhematic scenes (e.g. *Supp.* 347ff., *Sept.* 203ff.) the metrical pattern is more regular and the distinction between speaker(s) and singer(s) constant. In this scene, the two are slightly interwoven to heighten the tension delicately, and underline the themes of the scene. Cassandra fails to get her information across to the chorus in either genre; she fails both as the mad prophetess in frenzied lyrics and as a calmer, more statesman-like Teiresias-type of soothsayer in iambic trimeters. Aeschylus uses the difference between the two genres to create a gap. In the first half, Cassandra thrillingly describes her hallucinations in lyric – a bath, a hand, a net – while the chorus, who do not see what she sees, respond in iambic trimeters. Their flat comments undercut Cassandra's passion ('very dull', comment Denniston and Page, 1957, on 1088-9). Then from 1121 the chorus break into lyrics too – dochmiacs expressive of their fear. Fear does not sharpen their powers of understanding however, and it is Cassandra who now begins to 'climb down' from her frenzy, show an increased awareness of her surroundings, and adopt some iambic trimeters. The narrative flow is maintained at a complex level quite different from that of the previous scene. At the same time, the chorus as internal audience – like us, sympathetic but not directly affected – guide our responses.

Narrator-narratee

At the outset, Cassandra's silence designated her as an 'outsider' in relation to the established, Clytemnestra-dominated communication system of the play. Her 'outsiderness' continues to be applicable in the following scene: despite their sympathy the chorus fail fully to 'accept' or 'hear' her. The phatic, appellative and metalingual codes repeatedly point chorus and Cassandra *away* from each other, a situation thematised by Cassandra's revelation (1212) that Apollo has doomed her to prophesy without being believed.

Cassandra is also externally manipulated and does not control the time when each separate vision occurs and demands expression. To create such onstage immediacy and disjuncture is a tremendous *coup de théâtre*, all the more impressive if Aeschylus is largely innovating in making Cassandra a frenzied prophetess.[15] Her 'involuntary' cries, questions, and general absorption in her own experience, indicate pain: 'My terrible pain ... makes me giddy' (1215-16); 'How like fire – it's coming for me' (1256).[16] A sympathetic production might emphasise the uncontrolled timing of these bursts of vision, with irregular silences between the strophes.

When she begins to sing, a totally new kind of voice comes into the play, highly disturbing and initially incomprehensible: her voice does not utter language, only cries and the name of Apollo. It is to Apollo that she addresses herself (e.g. 1087f., 1138). She does not directly address her audience, rather they overhear her involuntary utterances. These phatic codes and their different metres point narrator and narratee away from each other, opening a hermeneutic gap. Failing to get an answer to their question (1074), the chorus revert to talking about her in the third person as they did earlier (1078-9, 1083-4, 1093-4), commenting on her prophetic ability and their own powers of interpretation: but the way the chorus doggedly emphasise the validity of the very simple fact they utter 1088-9 (note the phatic emphasis of 1089) as though they, not Cassandra, were the significant narrators at this point, highlights the difficulties of their communication.

Cassandra's visions from 1090 make her an eye-witness of crucially important action about to occur off stage. The referential function, however, is small. More like simultaneous narrative than anything else (see 2.2.3), each strophe is as much an expression of her *reaction* to what she sees as descriptive of it. She produces incoherent cries (at the outset of each strophe), tears (1096), many apostrophes, and questions in the third person (1100-1, 1107-9, 1114, 1115), second person (1107), or first person (1109). She also gives something of a running commentary on her own ability to interpret what she sees (1095ff., 1101, 1161), just as the chorus do. In terms of verbal functions, a profusion of emotive, conative, phatic, poetic and metalingual codes overwhelms the simply referential.

All the same, Cassandra is not totally oblivious to the chorus' responses (*men oun* at 1090 and *gar* at 1095 show something of a reply (see Denniston and Page ad loc.), and *soi legô*, 'It's you I'm talking to', indicates direct communication). What begins further 'enmeshing' between the two parties, after the chorus have abandoned their staid trimeters for dochmiacs, is their sympathetic comparison of Cassandra's fate with Procne's (1140ff.): in the sequence that follows, the chorus use second-person markers at 1150, 1153, 1154, 1162, 1173, 1174, (Cassandra only at 1158 – and she is addressing the Scamander): they are clearly in stronger communication, demonstrably acting and singing as joint participants in lament. Throughout the scene, the chorus express sensitivity and understanding when it is a question of Cassandra's own fate: but the central issue eludes them.

In the first *rhêsis* of the second half Cassandra tries to involve the chorus directly as witnesses to prove her powers (*martureite ... ekmarturêson*, 'bear witness ... bear me out', 1184, 1196). But the chorus are more interested in her relationship with Apollo (stichomythia 1203-13), and by the end of her second speech it is clear to her that she has not got across to them, as the despairing conclusion 1239-41 indicates. At the beginning of the second section of stichomythia, a particularly clear statement from Cassandra ('I say you will look upon the doom of Agamemnon', 1246) is still unaccepted. Although she goes on to say more that is vital to the trilogy, the chorus express no more concern for the future of Argos and restrict themselves entirely to Cassandra's own fate.

Three times Cassandra delays her final entry into the house and three times finds more to say before she goes, reinforcing the unnaturally vivid present time of the play, since it is set against the chorus' remark at 1300 'the last part of one's time has greatest value' and Cassandra's beautifully resigned response *hêkei tod' hêmar*, 'my time has come' (1301). This, and her remarks 1327-30 which close the scene, focus our attention almost exclusively on her plight. There is a powerful sense of finality here, which is at the same time a clever manipulation of our responses: we have (I think) lost contact with what we were expecting at any moment from 1035 so that, despite the chorus' brief lyric attempt to grapple with the thought of imminent disaster for Agamemnon (1331-42), his death cries come as a redoubled shock.

5.4 The Io scene from *Prometheus Bound* (561-886)

The essentially narrative form of the Io scene is turned into a kind of game with rules set up and broken, diversions, delays and surprises – *doloi* found in other scenes of *PB* as well.[17] The concentration of such techniques here seems sometimes overtly playful, bearing not a little resemblance to Plato's *Symposium*, where the drinkers' speeches on love are similarly intercut with comments which track away from the agreed order and where, in a frame of seeming arbitrariness imposed on the entire proceedings, the audience/reader is in fact offered a continuous and sophisticated 'reading' of the subject under discussion. The Io scene, perhaps not to be compared aesthetically with the scenes from *Septem* and *Agamemnon*, is all the same particularly interesting from a narratological point of view, since attitudes to narrative and narrative itself sometimes become the overt subject of discussion among the three parties.

Narrators and narratees

Io superficially resembles Cassandra. Both girls, desired and maddened by a god, are given a scene of onstage frenzy. Cassandra's cries are produced by bursts of prophetic inspiration, Io's by the gadfly's sting. Their raw pain and vivid emotion provide the backdrop to the information which is released. In each play, the girl's suffering and ultimate fate becomes an object of strong narrative interest, temporarily rivalling and somewhat masking the central themes of the trilogy.

Hyperactive Io contrasts with Prometheus, immobilised in a remote spot. He can *do* nothing at all and, except in the opening and closing scenes, nothing happens to him either. His role is restricted to that of narration and (apart from the bullies at either end) his visitors have little narrative to contribute themselves. Prometheus is the immortal, omniscient son of Themis, and it is stressed that he has infinite narrative powers, implicit in his very name, emphasised throughout (and reconfirmed 824ff. and 873-4). His narrative flow is potentially inexhaustible and he has indefinite leisure to exercise it (818, 875). Portrayed in the previous scene as benefactor of mankind (*dotêr, ôphelêma*), now he can be seen in action, like a teacher warning, advising, sympathising, predicting reactions, dividing his attention between two parties, recapping on the structure, at all times asserting his benevolent authority. His earlier general predictions are now focused on a specific individual.

The chorus are essential to sustaining the excitement and complexity of the scene. Although the communication is essentially binary (between Io, narratee and Prometheus, narrator), the chorus play an unusually active role as a vociferous internal audience. There is much question, refusal, promise, demand, denial over narrative between Io and Prometheus on their own, but it is the added voice of the chorus which constitutes the scene's essential shape. Without their intervention we should have no narrative delivered by Io herself. The effect of the chorus' contributions is to embed the narratives themselves into a three-way discussion of what often amounts to *narrative procedure*.

At 631 the chorus insisted on splitting the role of narrator between Io and Prometheus; at 782 they insist on splitting the role of narratee: let Io hear about her future, let them hear about Prometheus' (they remind him of this two-fold agreement at 822). Their insistent presence is reflected in the stringency with which Prometheus summarises the course of the narratives so far (700ff.) and in his clear demarcation of which of his two potential addressees he is addressing (700ff., 788, 842-5). The narrative flow is thus maintained at a complex level quite different from that of the previous scene. At the same time, the chorus as internal audience – like us, sympathetic but not directly affected – affect our own responses. Their interest and curiosity[18] work on our own: the time spent listening is an *axia tribê*, time well-spent (639). A significant and hostile off-stage nar- ratee is Zeus: the knowledge that he is listening to every word when so many of them concern him also heightens the tension.

Opening

The entry of Io at 561 is a surprise to the audience, and surprise seems to be deliberately maintained throughout the scene. The disjointed, urgent questions of Io's anapaests and lyric monody set up a complex requirement for information falling into two groups: questions about Io herself (present and future – a new area of interest in the play) and questions about Prometheus (past and present). These questions initiate the elaborately programmed process of combining the future stories of Io and Prometheus which constitutes this scene (cf. 773-4, 871-3).

Io wants to know where she is, who Prometheus is, and why he suffers (561-5). Then she wants to know where she has to go and why Zeus makes her suffer (576-8). On Prometheus' recognition of her *phthegma*, utterance (588-9), she breaks into even more disjointed questions. How does Prometheus know her? When will her sufferings end? (593-608). She demands that Prometheus *speak*, and, as with the other scenes, the many synonyms for this activity (588, 593, 594, 595, 596, 604-5, 607, 608) highlight the phatic content. The audience expect *a narrative performance*, and Prometheus' response (609-10) indicates it is forthcoming:

> I shall tell you plainly everything you desire to know, not
> weaving riddles, but in simple speech.

However, neither here nor later does the playwright allow the narrative progression to become predictable. At this point stichomythia rather than *rhêsis* unexpectedly develops as Io, once Prometheus has identified himself, asks the reason for his sufferings again, and between 615-630 Prometheus modifies and delimits his opening declaration in several ways: he has just stopped (615), he has said enough (621), it is better for Io not to know (624) as the information will shatter her heart (624, 628). Many of these forms of narrative refusal have already been directed at the chorus in earlier scenes and will come into play again later in this scene: e.g. he may not speak (766), his audience would not benefit (876). A little later Prometheus signals for the second time that he is about to begin a continuous narrative (*akoue dê*, 'listen then', 630), when this time it is the chorus, silent so far, who make a strong and unexpected intervention; *mêpô ge*, 'not yet', 631. They want to change the narrative rules and request both a change of subject and a change of narrator: let Io herself first describe her past, and then let Prometheus describe her future. This design is formally agreed (635-6, 640), then at least partially carried out until it falters (735) and a replacement plan is made (778ff.). At this point Prometheus offers Io a choice between two narratives: the rest of her travels (breaking his previous promise that she would hear this) or his future.[19] The chorus demand both and ultimately get them, though not without further excursions *en route*, nor with sufficient fullness at the end.

Narrative sections

The five major iambic trimeter narratives are set into a fluid and lively context of female emotion – a contrast to the masculinity of Prometheus. The first is narrated by Io at the request of the chorus, the rest by Prometheus. Thus (1) 645-82 a narrative of Io's past is followed by (2) 707-35 Io's future wanderings, (3) 790-815 Io's future wanderings continued, (4) 829-41 Io's recent past, (5) 846-73 the story of Io's descendants including Prometheus' liberator. Something like the chronological pendulum discussed before is at work here. The element of surprise is also sustained in the progression: nothing in the dialogue sections helps us expect (2) and (3) to be separate *rhêseis*, and (4), introduced unexpectedly by Prometheus as proof of his prophetic abilities, runs into (5) without an intervention by another speaker.

In terms of the trilogy, only (5), describing the birth of Heracles, is of relevance. Io's past and her future exotic peregrinations are redundant, just as the details in the Cassandra scene relating only to the prophetess' fate were. In that play and this, the 'vital' information is introduced tangentially and elusively – in the 'intermission' between narratives (2) and (3) and at the end of (5).

The first narrative contains many features of 'classic' messenger speeches, giving it, however redundant, great performance potential in its own right: declaration of intent to narrate (641-2), emotional state of speaker (*aischunomai*, I am ashamed, 642[20]), brief but vivid scene-setting (note imperfects 645-6 and 659), direct speech (647-54), indirect speech (665-8), and suffering of protagonist, which in this case consists of exile and metamorphosis (673f.). Io ends by neatly pointing forward to the next item of narrative on the programme (*sêmaine*, 'indicate', 684) before closing the ring (683-5).

Prometheus' following speech takes the form of an exotic list rather than a narrative proper.[21] The break-off at 735 is striking and introduces the 'intermission' between narratives (742-85): a *dolos* manifest throughout the play figures here: the prominent *rhêseis* reveal little vital knowledge, this being reserved for the gaps between, in the stichomythic or dialogue sections. With apparent randomness, Io's talk of suicide, 'Why have I not already flung myself from this cruel rock ... to the ground?' produces an important shift. Prometheus puns on Io's remark that she will hurl herself down from a rock, declaring that she would certainly bear *his* misfortunes with difficulty, *duspetôs* (derived from *dus* + root **peto* from *pipto*, I fall), since he is immortal and must endure until Zeus is expelled from power, *ekpesêi turannidos* (pun on *pipto* again). The word-play delicately binds together Io, Prometheus and Zeus.[22]

By this masterly casualness, Prometheus re-introduces one of the most important themes of the entire trilogy – the threat to Zeus' power. It is only to be touched on, and is left in a paradoxical and contradictory state. Two new potential narratives are begun but left unconnected. Io is baulked when she asks the name of the mother of the son who will be stronger than Zeus (first narrative line), but is then told that she will bear a son who will liberate Prometheus (second narrative line). The audience understand that the Titan and the daughter of Inachus are now linked into the future, but presumably share her view, 'This prophecy is not yet easy to interpret' (775).

The characters return to discussing narrative procedure. Prometheus attempts to alter the rules by making Io choose between two possible narratives, either the previously agreed account of her future sufferings, only half described so far or, developing the new thread, a story about the liberator. As at 631, the chorus now interrupt the dialogue again, demanding both stories.

Prometheus consents and begins 'to you first, Io' (788) as if the second story was indeed to follow. However, there is another diversion until Prometheus, addressing himself to *both* narratees and using the language of 'tracks' for 'narrative paths', talks of the two stories 'coming together' (*es tauton*, 845). The idea of a final, unified story uniting Io, Zeus and Prometheus is the more exciting because so long awaited and so readily delayed by all the disparate narrative requirements, conditions and resulting prophecies.

All the same, fresh ambiguities surround the account of the birth of Epaphos and the return to Argos of the Danaids. Zeus appears to have softened: Io will be impregnated without normal intercourse and Zeus will allow the Danaids' cousins to be murdered for attempting sex with them against their will. Hypermestra seems already a figure of compromise and reconciliation. But how can all this be reconciled with an antipathy between Prometheus and Zeus which is meant to last well beyond this point? Then too, mention of the liberator is restricted to the very end and framed between almost identical phrases indicating that more time would be needed to explain properly (see 870, 875). In effect we learn only one vital item of information – that the figure to free Prometheus is 'one who will free you with his bow' (872-3).

Proleptic narratives

Of the play in general, Griffith writes (1983, 16), 'Every scene, except for the Prologue and the Ocean scene, is built around a prophecy of some kind from Prometheus.' Up to the Io scene, however, Prometheus has only spoken with any clarity about the past.[23] The arrival of Io with her questions prompts fresh information first about her own future and then, because the two are connected, his own. The developing sense of Prometheus' potential control over Zeus' future is greatly increased by the Io scene, and gives rise, after her departure, to his powerful assertion (908ff.): 'I swear that Zeus, despite his stubbornness, shall yet be humbled, such a marriage he is preparing, which will hurl him in destruction from his throne.'

All the same, an audience still worshipping Zeus as father of all the gods could not feel this prophecy to be unequivocal. Furthermore, by the end of the play we still cannot see how Io's descendant will free Prometheus. Zeus' omnipotence is manifested by the fact that he has overheard everything that is said on stage – he can immediately send Hermes to carry out his commands: yet his extremely prompt reaction reinforces the idea that Prometheus' prophecies contain a dangerous truth. The cumulative but confusing proleptic references create a strong interest in the action of the following play(s).

Other long-term narratives have no such proleptic importance. Io's account of her past mentions dreams (645f.) and repeated visits to oracles (658f.). The messages contained in both of these precisely carry out the desire of Zeus: the wooing dream voice (direct speech 647-54), and the eventual command of the oracle with its threat of the destruction to

Inachos' family if the order is not obeyed, make this more than usually clear. Dream and oracles form part of the propaganda battle between Zeus and Prometheus and concern Io's past, not Prometheus' future.[24]

This self-reflexive scene demonstrates that narrative performance gives pleasure (*hêdonê*, 'pleasure', 631; *gluku*, 'sweet', 698). The language of *charis*, 'gratitude' (635, 782, 821) and 'gifts' (616, 626, 778, 821-2) reinforces this. The unstressed kin relationship between the three participants – the chorus are Io's aunts and their father is Prometheus' father-in-law (while Io's line, we learn, will one day produce Prometheus' liberator) – also links them almost cosily together into the entire narrating situation.

As well as pleasure, however, the scene discourses on the pain that narrative may arouse: Io suffers, and Prometheus suggests that to relate her suffering to a sympathetic audience is worthwhile (637-9): the chorus react with extreme horror (687-95) but suggest all the same that Io's 'sickness' will be alleviated by improved knowledge of her situation (698-9), a view she holds herself (625, 629) against Prometheus' attempts at protection. Prometheus turns out to be right: his narrative reduces her to incoherence (742) and thoughts of suicide (747ff.). The gadfly sting drives her offstage without acknowledging receipt, so to speak, of Prometheus' final narrative.

The Io scene magnificently opens the trilogy out into time and space. The descriptions of Io's wanderings over the world turn Prometheus' remote Scythian rock into a central cross-roads in world space, while his powerful narratives reach out inexhaustibly into past and future time. The final narrative about Io's offspring, which describes the generations in Egypt and the generations in Argos before Heracles will be born, opens up a huge temporal perspective to the audience in which they realise that what they are seeing onstage belongs to a period of the very remote past. This sort of technique, which we have seen produced a sense of closure in *Persians*, here also prepares us for the closing scenes of this first play, while at the same time the sheer magnitude of the vision offered will affect the audience's expectations for the subsequent plays.

Part III

Sophocles

The ultimate expression of *mêtis* is the circle, the bond that is perfect because it completely turns back on itself, is closed in on itself with neither beginning nor end, front not rear ... through its continuous curve which closes on itself, the circle unites within it several opposites each one giving birth to its own opposite. ...

Detienne and Vernant, 1991, 46

6

Sophocles and Narrative 'Loops'

6.1 Introduction

Aspects of Sophocles' narrative strategy have already come under scrutiny in earlier chapters. Sophocles was used to exemplify the advantages of narrative over dramatic presentation in Chapter 1, he provided the major model for the discussion of narrative time throughout Chapter 2, and the *dolioi* endings of several of his plays were discussed in Chapter 3. It might at first sight appear that of the three dramatists, Sophocles is the least interested in narrative *doloi*. Rather, he is perhaps the most crafty strategist of them all, so subtly and imperceptibly are his devices woven into the texture of the plays.

This chapter will focus on one particular strategy, a *dolos* of major importance apparent in many plays which, for want of a better term, I call a narrative 'loop'. The idea of a circular narrative device relates powerfully to the central idea of *dolos* as 'bait' or 'trap' explored by Detienne and Vernant.[1] Baits, nets, weels, nooses and snares are all circular traps formed of flexible materials which have the property of being imperceptible to their prey, but which at the right moment can reveal themselves in a moment of reversal in which the opponent becomes entangled and hunter becomes prey: an excellent model for the strategy in question.

Narrative loops occur when Sophocles makes a temporary deviation from a plot line, rejoining it again later at the point of exit. All these deviations contain deceitful or at least ambiguous narratives, and this is the case not only when the plays dramatise established myths (in which case the false nature of the narrative and the return to the traditional story line at the point where it broke off is inevitable), but also when the plot is apparently original and thus unbounded by traditional constraints. In the second case the 'loop' is all the more to be understood as a deliberately chosen, free creation of the poet.

The function of these deceitful narrative loops is complex, debatable, and necessarily dependent on the concerns of each individual play. All the same, one can observe some general characteristics: the stage figures can be tested out against a wider range of experience than would otherwise be possible. They can experience powerful emotions in quick succession – joy, sorrow, anxiety, grief, resignation. Different outcomes can be explored on a temporary basis, perhaps ultimately reinforcing the authority and inevitability of the one that is ordained. Themes of time and mutability can be explicitly or implicitly explored. Irony is inevitably created, often made all the more telling because the movement towards disaster is made to spring spontaneously out of quite innocent and 'natural' human reactions. At the same time a highly sophisticated appeal is often made to the authorial as opposed to the narrative audience (see 4.2 for this distinction), who are forced to question the normally unchallenged truth-value of dramatic narrative. The play may draw attention to its own theatricality by showing the fictive stage figures taking on further fictive roles. Finally, the content of the false narrative often imitates the main story, so that different elements of it are shown is if refracted through a prism.

6.2 *Ajax* (646-865)

The so-called *Trugrede*, 646ff., is the only deceitful Sophoclean *rhêsis* (in surviving plays, at any rate) not delivered as a message narrative to other stage figures. It is a one-speech episode which it is difficult not to call a soliloquy, except that Tecmessa and the chorus are still on stage (Ajax sends Tecmessa inside and gives the chorus an order, 684ff.). Given the gravity of Ajax's reflections, I take the now widespread view that it is only the other stage figures who are to be deceived into supposing he intends anything but suicide (see Stevens' article: it is clear that critics are never likely to agree on the exact reference of each separate sentence).

The significant new perspectives adopted by Ajax accord with those he makes in the suicide speech 815ff. which *is* a soliloquy. Why then does Sophocles not run the two speeches into one and have Ajax kill himself then and there? This would be infinitely simpler and not beyond the possible conventions of Attic theatre. After the end of the single speech Tecmessa and the chorus, still on stage, could merely be depicted as too slow or physically incapable of preventing him, as Iphis and the chorus cannot prevent Evadne leaping onto her husband's pyre, or as Oedipus and the chorus cannot prevent the capture of his daughters (Euripides *Supp.* 1034-71; Sophocles *OC* 816ff.) The *phthanein* 'anticipation of another' and *lanthanein* 'escaping the notice of another' necessarily involved in this could add to the sense of *dolos* and tragic irony. Why take the risk of making this tremendously significant speech ambiguous, thereby possibly weakening its impact and confusing the audience? Why follow it with the misleading *ephrix'erôti* ode ('I trembled with desire') and then the possibly inessential messenger scene which tells us nothing of crucial importance for the future of the play, but brings about the great disruption of emptying the stage of the chorus and bringing them on again?

We can answer some of this by saying that the loop begins and ends with two speeches in which Ajax develops a series of important insights into his situation, finding perspectives about time and change originally indicated by Athena 131-2. His mood of aggressive, angry rejection gives way to a superb philosophical resignation (646-9, 669-84). He feels pity for his wife (652). He makes some provision for his family (687-9, the prayer of 848ff.) His hatred for the Atridae and Odysseus is unabated (835ff.), but he speaks of reconciliation with enemies and with the gods (666-8). In particular, the series of prayers to different gods in his suicide speech indicates a change of heart from the man who at 589ff. thought his relationship with the gods was over. Although his thoughts arise from critical circumstances, the beauty and elevation of their expression remove him, while still alive, from the immediate to a more timeless realm. Contrast helps achieve this: the two *rhêseis*, uttered in actual or virtual solitude, contrast violently with the 'busy' group activities that come between them, characterised by misunderstanding, urgency, futility, even muddle.

Throughout this part of the loop Sophocles makes continuous play with our expectations and emotions by a series of subterfuges. First, as authorial audience, privileged to see the prologue, we know better than to share the chorus' delight at Ajax's supposed decision to stay alive. All the same, as narrative audience it is hard to be unaffected by their exuberant joy especially at 710-14, ending with the thematically significant *panth'ho megas chronos marainei*, 'There is nothing great time does not extinguish'. In fact, looking back on the antistrophe of this ode from the perspective of closure, the chorus will later seem to be not so much wrong as merely premature.

Sophocles' next subterfuge plays on the conventional shaping of tragedy: the entry of the messenger immediately after the lyric seems, as so often, to be about to give the lie to the chorus' hopes[2] – but no, the audience is as much surprised as the chorus when instead an entirely unexpected narrative of recent/immediate past now begins (note vivid present tenses at 720, 722). An angry offstage army is economically evoked, baying for Ajax's and his brother's blood.

The long perspectives established in the *Trugrede* have vanished and for the first time the anger of the army and of the Atridae becomes a very real threat – one which will later develop from its offstage position here to take centre stage. But despite its proleptic importance, this introductory narrative is soon abandoned. The exchanges 733-9 refocus our attention into a second, equally unexpected area. Psychological naturalism motivates the movement from one topic to the next. At the same time, tremendous ironies are generated. When the chorus say Ajax is absent the long-expected idea of 'too late' is at last expressed and the messenger cries *iou iou*. The audience, by convention, would naturally have associated the messenger's cries with news of the hero's death – but as it is, we are ignorant of their reference. The chorus' optimism is rightly dismissed as 'words full of great folly' (745), and audience and chorus share total ignorance and apprehension.

There seems to be no tradition for 748-83, the narrative of Calchas'
prophecy. The prophecy increases our understanding of both past and
future. The frame of the speech (751-6, 778-83) has immediate proleptic
relevance: it is the risk to Ajax of divine punishment from Athena *today
only*, stressed 753, 756, 778 (see also 801-2). The warning has the obvious
important function in stage terms of removing the chorus and allowing for
Ajax's solo suicide speech. The emphasis on *today* makes a polar contrast
with Ajax's panchronic sense of time:[3] now we are back in the minute-by-
minute, blow-by-blow world of panic and confusion.

The prophecy gives the audience much to grapple with. The familiar
possibility of open outcome is raised at 778-9, but as so often with Sophocles it is unclear whose interpretation this is in the first instance – Calchas'
or Teucer's. It resembles the Aeschylean technique of sustaining unrealis-
tic optimism encountered in the choruses of *Persians* and *Agamemnon*.
Probably, discrepant awareness between the stage figures and the audience is recreated: the stage figures go to look for a living man – the
audience think the search will be for his body. Given the audience's
fore-knowledge, the chorus' eager anxiety is all the more pitiful, especially
after the previous scene in which they have displayed their helpless
dependency. The time at which the prophecy enters the world of the play
is another feature which possibly puzzles the audience. Has not Athena's
punishment already, perhaps, been carried out in the form of Ajax's
madness during the hours of darkness? Is his suicide part of her punishment too? Again, the anomaly and general vagueness are never explored
and are not to be logically understood. What the audience see displayed is
the pain and confusion of the human condition.

The speech is also important analeptically. We learn (1) that at the
ritually significant moment of setting out for Troy, Ajax contradicted his
father and insulted all the gods, and (2) that at Troy itself he specifically
insulted Athena. These two linked items of information help redefine Ajax
as a typical *theomachos* hero, a 'fighter against god', and give us a wider
background from which to understand Athena's cold cruelty towards him
in the prologue. Perhaps too, his heroic restitution is paradoxically assisted by this alignment to the '*theomachos*' hero-type.

Like Deianeira in *Trachiniae* and Eurydice in *Antigone*, Tecmessa has
missed the messenger's initial information. The exchanges 784-814 are
busy with fresh informing, reacting, clarifying the issues, and making a
plan of action which involves ordering the chorus offstage. The bustle and
urgency here could not provide a greater foil to the reflective dignity of the
following suicide speech, itself followed by the almost comic dochmiacs of
the returning chorus, concerned for their own unheroic toil.

This loop achieves a great deal – a separation between Ajax and his
dependents which is not only spatial but also *qualitative*. Sophocles focuses this separation round the two parties' very different reactions to
what can happen in *one day*, juxtaposing *one day* and 'all long unnumbered

time'.[4] The chorus' all-too human fallibility is distinguished from the hero's profound heroic insight and controlled suicide. Information about Ajax's past acts of *hubris* mitigates the divine harshness of the prologue, giving him paradeigmatic status. The longer perspective of this information, reaching back over ten years, and the infinitely longer time-frame of Ajax' first soliloquy have pulled the audience back from the immediate, urgent action to give a new view *sub specie aeternitatis*.

6.3 *Trachiniae* (180-496)

Through the interplay of Deianeira with the Old Man and Lichas – a false and a true messenger duo – Sophocles creates an extraordinary scene of *dolos*.[5] The investment in it is large; it is long and intricately shaped. Like the other deceitful/ambiguous narratives in the loops under investigation, it is also, in a sense, quite unnecessary. Why have the Old Man and Lichas' lies at all instead of proceeding straight to the true account?

Within a brief space the scene provides for two miniature reversals rather than one, exemplifying the theme of mutability which is so prominent in this play: first, anxiety to joy (*chara*, 'joy' vocabulary at 179, 201, 227-8, 293; *terpsis*, 'pleasure', 291 – this passage provides the only relief from the otherwise unrelievedly sombre tones of the play) then, joy to apparent resignation. Like other scenes from *nostos* dramas, it exploits the 'waiting for news' context to underline the ironies of getting true information, of acquiring knowlege. This is manifested most clearly in the extraordinary, almost comic dead-end *agôn* (verbal contest) between the two messengers (402-35). The loop also touches on two other possible endings – Deianeira does not find out about Heracles' relationship with Iole (329-34); alternatively (this option is explored more thoroughly) she finds out, but out of pity and noble generosity decides to take no action (436-96).

Above all, the loop seems created as an ironic test of Deianeira's love and loyalty – beyond the trials of any Penelope – and as a demonstration of how that most natural and tender of emotions, a good wife's love, can produce the most terrible Medea-like consequences.[6] Sophocles' version suppresses Megara and represents Deianeira as the only true, long-term wife: she knows about the many other women Heracles has loved, but Iole is the first threat to her wifely status. She learns that, despite outward appearance, Heracles has not sent her as a slave (367); this scene shows her *moving in*, 'a pain under the roof' (376-7).

Given the slight disjunction between the noble, sympathetic and resigned Deianeira of 1-496 and the actively scheming, deceitful figure of 531-632, it is tempting to look back to possible earlier versions of the story which might have represented Deianeira as a woman who deliberately destroyed her husband out of jealousy.[7] However, I do not follow Reinhardt (1979, 46f.) in believing that Deianeira's speech to Lichas (*Trach.* 436f.) is intended to deceive. Reinhardt is right to compare it with the so-called *Trugrede*, but not for shared deceptive qualities. Rather the opposite: in both cases the dignity and elevation of the rhetoric – in the case of *Trachiniae* contrasting sharply with the 'near-colloquial brawling'(Davies, 1991, 129) of Lichas and the Old Man – surely preclude the possibility of deceit. Out of surviving Sophocles, only in the Paedagogus' false speech in *Electra* is rhetoric used to assist deceit, and the audience have been well-prepared for it. Deianeira's fatal action, by its very *lack* of consistency with the noble character (see Winnington-Ingram, 1980, 78ff.) developed particularly within the loop (and most of all in the speech calling for honesty 436-69), reveals not her guile but rather, 'the beast-like strength and violence of *erôs* at work in human beings' (Easterling, 1982, 5).

The opening scenes are of anxious waiting, rather like the openings of *Persians* and *Agamemnon* except that the focus is exclusively on Deianeira's personal life of dread.[8] When the Old Man enters, Deianeira has just released the information Heracles gave her when he departed: now three months and a year are up: 'Then at this time he would either have to die, or, live happily for the rest of his life ... and now this is infallibly coming to pass' (166-8, 173-4).[9] The chorus hush Deianeira by referring to the need for *euphêmia*, propitious language, and by pointing out the garland worn by the approaching Old Man, indicative of good news.

Deianeira is deceived (180-334)

With his headline *oknou se lusô*, 'I shall set you free from doubt' (181), the Old Man provides an immediate contradiction to Deianeira's forebodings. The danger from the oracle appears to be already over, but the movement of this loop away from the oracle is another *dolos*. The plot slides from one point of narrative bifurcation – life or death for Heracles – to develop another, 'Which of the two women will be Heracles' wife?'

After cautiously questioning the messenger's credentials (187, 192) Deianeira allows herself to cry out exultantly 'O Zeus' (200) and orders the chorus into their brief lyric (its jubilance only faintly stained by the sinister epithet *mellonumphos*, 'about to be married' (if correct, and if correctly taken with *domos*, house: see Easterling *ad loc*.)).

Lichas enters with a train of slave-women (229). No advance reference prepares us for the deceptive content of his speech and (ignoring various ironies) until 335 everything that is said seems to confirm that all is well (cf. his opening line *eu ... eu*). Despite judicious questions 236, 239, 242-3, 246-7, Deianeira's address 'O dearest of men' indicates the overflow of excitement and generous love triggered by the good news, which will also produce her pity for the slaves (243-4) and later, Iole.

Lichas' long *rhêsis* (248-90) is initiated by a question which tries to make sense of *time*, another theme in the play: the unusual contradiction of the opening line of his speech, 'Not so, the greater part of the time he was detained in Lydia', might suggest some fudge about how Heracles has in fact been spending his time. However, the complex abundance of Heracles stories and our ignorance of pre-Sophoclean versions of this one in particular, make it hard to guess at the level of discrepant awareness likely to be evoked in the audience by the details here and in the following speech.[10] At the least, though, Lichas' *rhêsis* contains some oddities. It has an unbalanced time sequence (b-c-a-b-c), lacking the usual symmetry of ring composition. Eurytus' insults and Heracles' act of revenge become the central focus (260-73), thus appropriately highlighting the major falsehood of the speech, i.e. that the motive for the sack of Oechalia was revenge alone.[11] The oddly interrupted pattern of Heracles' revenge, coming in two instalments with first the murder of Iphitus and, after the sojourn with Omphale, the destruction of the city, may already have been traditional; that might not entirely dispel the sense of its strange circularity.

Lichas' anxiety is revealed by frequent phrases which attribute his own statements to Heracles himself (249, 253, 261). These expressions possibly trigger audience suspicion about the entire speech. Lichas' central anxiety seems to be having to say that Heracles has been forced into servitude: on the face of it, surely misplaced anxiety, since servitude was the well-known and entirely acceptable condition for the most glorious sequence of events in Heracles' life – the mighty labours performed for Eurystheus. The anxiety is better understood to be over the idea of serving a woman. Since he is addressing Heracles' wife, Lichas refrains from alluding to his well-known *sexual* servitude to Omphale,[12] one among the many women subject to Heracles' desire (cf. 459-60). It could be that alert audience members would find concealed in Lichas' speech reference not to one but *two* episodes of Heracles' sexual enslavement.

Sophocles' deceptive speeches, unable to contribute directly to the forward action, contribute richly to the developing themes of the play. For example, Lichas will suffer the same violent fate at the hands of Heracles as Iphitus, a *rhiptos moros*, 'death by being hurled' (357, cf. 775-82). More significantly, the references to Heracles' slavery to Omphale (250, 252, 276) and to Eurytus (267), later joined by references to the slavery of Oechalia and its women (257, 283, 302), combined with the concrete onstage presence of Iole, silent among other slave-women, all together accumulate into a dense motif in which over and again we experience the power of *Erôs* or *Cypris* as a force which subdues, destroys and particularly, enslaves. At the end of the loop, Lichas' closing couplet focuses this motif of subjection onto *Heracles* (488-9): 'For he, pre-eminent in everything else, has been utterly defeated by his love for this girl'; in the lyric that follows (497ff.), this same motif is focused on *Deianeira*.

Deianeira responds guardedly to the chorus' joyful reaction to Lichas' account. Their suggestion of 'open delight' (*terpsis emphanês*, 291) is manifestly ironic when Iole is silently present on the stage. Deianeira's speech (293-313) and the dialogue up to 334 also point up many painful

ironies: the glancing inset prayer (303-6) prefigures the sufferings of the
Heraclidae and the little genitive absolute 'while she yet lives' (305) with
reference to herself, hints at her own, unsuspectedly close death.

Deianeira's understanding of the mutability of good fortune (296-8) – a
wisdom about the human condition – is the personal characteristic that
arouses her *oiktos deinos*, 'terrible pity'. It is a quality strikingly similar to
that displayed by Odysseus in the earlier *Ajax*, where it produced reconciliation. The movement here is in the opposite direction (as it is in *OT*: see
n. 6). Such feelings, far from preventing disaster, are ironically stressed as
directly causal in bringing about the slow change from deceit to fatal
knowledge. It seems important to Sophocles to emphasise the causal
connection: Deianeira's noble understanding of the human condition (expressed again, 436-69), will be overtly acknowledged by Lichas' opening
words 472-3 as he confirms the Old Man's report: 'Since I see that you are
a mortal thinking as a mortal should, and are not unfeeling ....'

As Deianeira turns to address Iole directly (307), the audience experiences the horrible unease of those watching a deceit about to collapse. The
flow of narrative information disintegrates and ceases. The audience
presumably understand that with three speaking actors already on stage,
the silent figure of Iole is indeed a *kôphon prosôpon* (non-speaking character) and cannot tell her own story, but Lichas' unconvincing ignorance
(314-15, 317, 319) adds to the strong sense of discomfort and the uncertainty of not knowing what will happen next. Into this discomfort, the
conjunction of the two women is ironic too. Overtly, wife and slave are at
opposite poles of fortune, but in fact we know they have identical fates as
ill-starred objects of Heracles' love. One narrative of destructive male
violence describes both their lives, and Deianeira's sympathy has infinitely
more self-identification in it than she realises.[13]

In this section of the loop Sophocles has created a brief pause, ironically
offering the audience the opportunity to contemplate a happy outcome of
simple reunion between husband and wife, while all the time the source of
future tragedy, Iole, stands on stage.

Deianeira understands the truth (329-496)

At 329ff. Deianeira gives marching orders to all the onstage figures except
the Old Man. There could hardly be a clearer indication that the scene is
to end.[14] Then the Old Man's sudden intervention initiates some moments
of confused questioning about who is to remain. Another occurrence of brief
uncertainty about what will happen next and who is to be on the stage to
make it happen comes again at 387-92 when Deianeira is about to leave in
search of Lichas.

How should these deliberate confusions over exits and entries best be
understood? In both cases, Sophocles arouses and then defeats audience
expectation. By imitating life's contingent nature, he highlights how ran-

dom and exiguous the threads are which, bound together, create a fateful action – and the parts of it that, by the dramatist's fictive powers, we are going to see on the stage.

The first part of the loop created a *dolos* in which Deianeira was initially deceived into joy. The strategy pays off in the second half: joy makes pain doubly painful. The scene of painful discovery is extended by the requirement that Lichas confirm the Old Man's report (mirroring his confirmation of the good news earlier). As official herald he, not the Old Man, is authorised narrator. The scratchy *agôn* (402-35) juxtaposes, on the one hand, a random messenger without offical authority, speaking up initially for reward (190-1) and now, perhaps, out of a disinterested concern to establish the truth (373-4) and, on the other, a man overtly authorised to speak the truth producing (unprompted by his master, 480-3) a stream of half-truths and persistent evasions. Whether Lichas' lies were motivated out of pity for Deianeira's feelings (as he says), fear of her anger or overriding loyalty to his master cannot be completely clear, and different performances are likely to produce different emphases.

The Old Man cannot get Lichas to acknowledge the truth. The stalemate prolongs the uncertainty. Both have appealed to Deianeira (400, 409, 429, 434), and this helps provoke the striking *rhêsis* (436-69) in which she demands the truth. The difficulty of obtaining an acknowledged truth has temporarily become the critical issue, and it is possible to read Deianeira's *rhêsis* as an ironical extension of this theme of deception/truth: that way, Deianeira's appeal for truth succeeds only by her conscious creation of lies about herself. But this view would run counter to Sophocles' purpose for his heroine in this loop which, I believe, is simply to cause us to admire her. Along with a repetition of the gentler virtue of *sophrosunê* Deianeira has already displayed, she now shows herself a fit wife for a hero, arguing cogently and showing an intellect and an ability to marshal appropriate arguments with admirable rhetoric. Only when she acknowledges the power of *Erôs* over herself (444) we might find a hint of irony. The scene ends on a note of uncomfortable harmony, possibly disturbed by the phrase 'gifts should be appropriately matched' (494): Deianeira confirms her inactive position (490-2) and exits in a calm and queenly fashion, giving orders and promising rewards.

The end of the loop is not the end of the irony, however. Immediately after the choral ode, Deianeira comes onstage *lathrâi*, secretly, to speak to the chorus. She now describes Iole without pity as 'freight' (*phortos*, 537) and 'merchandise' (*empolêma*, 538). The prospect of sharing Heracles' bed with a younger woman is, not surprisingly, intolerable, and she will take action to restore Heracles' affections to herself. In an elegant transformation of narrative situations, the ignorant Lichas is now duplicitously entrusted to deliver to the husband a fatal object in return for his own fatal domestic gift: Deianeira achieves this by deceitfully capitalising on her successful narrative (436-69). At the same time, the horizon of trickery has widened: her words are indeed consciously deceitful, but she is also the innocent agent of another's deceit and bringing Nessus' fatal *dolos* to fulfilment at last.

The use of words relating to Iole here recalls Heracles' slavery (he was 'purchased' 250, 'bought' 252). In both cases we are in the world of trade, where, at some level, people and objects are items bought and sold for profit. *Narrative transaction* is thematised here, as it is even more clearly *Philoctetes* 578ff. Earlier Deianeira successfully bargained for Lichas' true narrative about Iole by offering a valuable narrative of her own (436ff.). Now she 'trades' on it again: to send 'merchandise' to her husband in return for the 'merchandise' he sent home. In all this, Lichas serves as the go-between. For all three parties the transactions are fatal.

6.4 *Philoctetes* (541-627)

The narrative gaps, lies and ambiguities in this play are manifold, and yet the twists and turns of the story evolve out of one another with great psychological naturalism in a seemingly inevitable flow.[15] More than most, this play is a particularly delicate web, to be unpicked at any one point with extreme peril.

The narrative loop with the False Merchant, which is set into the long first episode (270-675) between Neoptolemos and Philoctetes, marks perhaps the peak of false narrative in the play – although an unfathomable number of lies have already been told and will remain unresolved. The False Merchant's lies act as a kind of foil to the lies Neoptolemus has been telling earlier, forcing a moral revaluation of what is entailed in *dolos*. In the loop, dialogue gives way to *dreigesprach* and the False Merchant, carrying out Odysseus' orders, is almost a disguised version of Odysseus himself (and indeed the same actor, differently masked, would have played both parts). Fresh possible lies and fresh possible truths are superimposed over existent half-truths, and compounded by yet more metatheatrical references, teasing and taxing to the limit the understanding of both narrative and theatrical audience in a heightened play of ludic elements.

Thanks to the survival of Dio's *Orationes* 52 and 59 we have some knowledge of Aeschylus' and Euripides' preceding *Philoctetes* plays.[16] This gives us an insight into the high level of *allusion* and audience *collusion* in the scene, which must be set alongside the *delusion* of Philoctetes. The effect of all this is that the dramatic situation cannot be relieved of its ambiguity by close inspection of the words in the text or even by an analysis of the interplay of narratives.

Significantly, the loop also makes little sense in terms of furthering the plot to get Philoctetes off the island (this problem is the starting point of Osterud's analysis). And yet, like the arrival of the disguised Paedagogus in *Electra*, the False Merchant's arrival is fully prepared for in the prologue (125-31), and the level of detail and the emphasis given to it mark it as an important part of the play's design: Odysseus tells Neoptolemus exactly how to respond once the False Merchant appears: 'When he goes in for artful talking, pick up what is expedient from what he keeps saying' (130-1). Yet unlike the situation of *Electra* there is no need for this intervention – Philoctetes is already only too eager to come with Neoptolemus. Nor is there a direct consequence afterwards. The narration of Helenus' prophecy creates no obvious major impact and does not contribute to the sense of urgency in the way that the report of Calchas' prophecy does within the *Ajax* loop. Certainly, the False Merchant's entry reminds us of the external urgency of the mission and of Odysseus, who had said he would send the scout in disguise if he thought they were loitering (127). Later on, at 974 and 1293, the audience discover that Odysseus has been snooping, but there is no evidence that this is the case here: 24 suggests Odysseus will be too far away to overhear. (It is just possible that the audience can infer that Odysseus, counting the minutes, presciently intuits that a dangerous friendship has developed between Philoctetes and Neoptolemus to the detriment of his own influence.) But none of this justifies the scene's inclusion and other grounds must be found.

A major underlying purpose of this loop seems to be nothing less than to force the audience to focus on *acting*, and bear witness to the effect both of participating in it, and of observing it. The onstage situation, which has been created so naturally, is in fact highly complex and artificial. Neoptolemus is acting. He is also acting with, and observing the acting of, the False Merchant. He is observing the effect of the joint acting on Philoctetes. Meanwhile the audience is observing all of this. At this point, how can they assess Neoptolemus' real frame of mind? As Neoptolemus' and the False Merchant's words have no simple truth-value, only the audience's emotional responses can guide them to Neoptolemus' concealed feelings and help them assess whether any speech of his is 'true' or not. There is no escape from subjectivity here. Proof of Neoptolemus' change of heart comes only at 895ff., finally triggered by Philoctetes' outburst of pain and dependence. Sophocles' decision to focus on the role of the actor must remain implicit. There can be no overt reference to the world of the theatre since the epic world dramatised by the Athenian poets did not know drama.[17]

The False Merchant joins an already complex 'double act' going on between Neoptolemus and the chorus to deceive Philoctetes. In this earlier *dolos*, Neoptolemus is the major narrator and falsely informs Philoctetes, the narratee. Despite some superior knowledge, the audience too is caught by the playwright's *dolos*, since Sophocles has provided little guidance to discern true items of information from false.[18] The boundaries between true and false discourse have broken down.[19] This confusing breakdown happens in conjunction with what is emotionally very positive – the growing friendship between Neoptolemus and Philoctetes. Neoptolemus, we perceive, is good at lying, but part of his success, like that of any good confidence trickster, stems from his ability to empathise with his victim. We empathise with both these characters and in a very simple way are pleased to see the developing sympathy between them. The entry of a fresh liar gives us a sharp reminder of the deceitful grounds on which the relationship has been established.

In narrative terms, the Merchant is a new false narrator superimposed on the previous one. This time the False Merchant is the major narrator while Neoptolemus takes over the (now silent) chorus' supportive but subordinate narrative role. But because Neoptolemus does not know exactly what the Merchant is going to say next, the young man, 'scriptless' at this point, is also forced to some extent into the helpless position of narratee – one subjected to the authority of another's (lying) discourse, even though he is also colluding with it. His partial ignorance of the narrative situation thus overlaps with that of the utterly duped Philoctetes. Part of the function of this subtle 'loop' is to get the audience to infer changes in the young man's moral perspective through seeing him forced to improvise this difficult double role which puts him in close emotional touch both with the False Merchant and with Philoctetes.[20] His convergence with each merits discussion.

Neoptolemus and the False Merchant

The False Merchant – played by the same actor who played Odysseus in the prologue – is a base stooge of Odysseus. The scene points up the fact that Neoptolemus too is a stooge (*problêma*, screen, 1008). Coming within the same scene, the Merchant's patently false opening speech forces the audience to re-evaluate the integrity of Neoptolemus' earlier words. Like Neoptolemus', the Merchant's introductory speech 542-56 is resonant with circumstantial detail. Talk of journeying home to the island of Peparethos (modern Skopelos), is resonant: the island, famous for grapes, lies off the Malian Gulf near Philoctetes' home and its mention is not only convincing but might also be calculated to reinforce his homesickness: so much for the narrative audience. At the same time the Merchant is subtly colluding with the authorial audience by playing on Homer's reference to the wine trade from Lemnos which supplied the Greek army while it was camped at Troy (*Il.* 7.467). (In this play Lemnos is wild and deserted.) All this brings home the similarity of what went on before – Neoptolemus' *variatio* on his own story, and the story of the fates of Greek heroes, with its selective chronology and suppression of variant epic versions in favour of the presentation most likely to move Philoctetes.[21]

I take the difficult phrase at 553, *prostuchonti tôn isôn*, to mean 'When I've got my just reward':[22] the False Merchant is colluding with the audience here in showing a typical messenger's desire for reward, but the phrase also reinforces the parallels between the Merchant and Neoptolemus, pointing up that both are lying for *kerdos*, profit. In the stichomythia of the prologue, Odysseus had convincingly used the idea of *kerdos* to motivate Neoptolemus (111-12). (Later in this scene the False Merchant, true to his *persona*, expresses unheroic anxiety for the profits of his regular business (582-4).) Then, after some deceitful stage business between the merchant and Neoptolemus, Philoctetes cries (578-9):

What is he saying, boy? Why is the sailor furtively trading in words with you?

The phrase 'trades in words' again recalls *kerdos*. The model of narrative as a commercial transaction is strongly thematised here.

Neoptolemus is forced to 'chime in' with the False Merchant, just as earlier he had made his story 'chime in' with Philoctetes (*prosaidein*, 405). But 'chiming in' with a tradesman is a lowlier, more degraded form of deceit than telling your own lies. Reduced to this level, Neoptolemus is manifest as an unheroic agent of Odysseus' plotting. Odysseus suggested lies and Neoptolemus has spread them. Philoctetes' indictment of Odysseus 407-9 had already suggested a reformulation of the moral perspectives adopted in the prologue. The loop subtly reinforces this revised judgement.

Neoptolemus and Philoctetes

Neoptolemus has already established false or at least ambiguous parallels between Philoctetes and himself. Both are victims of Achaean *doloi*. With subtle irony Sophocles makes both concur in the division of heroes at Troy into two basic groups: the deaths of noble heroes characterised as incapable of falsehood, such as Ajax, Antilochus,[23] Patroclus and of course Achilles himself are lamented, while the survival of braggarts and liars such as Diomedes, Thersites[24] and of course Odysseus is a matter of scorn. No doubt the authorial audience enjoyed the judicious selection of heroic fates employed here. However, both Neoptolemus and Philoctetes are explicitly linked in other ways unconnected with deceit: their mutual respect for Achilles, for example. Both express filial concerns. Both too start off in a position of emotional isolation. This is more than obvious in the case of Philoctetes, but it is clear that Neoptolemus is solitary too. Sophocles has not chosen to give him a companion or mentor. The relationship between Odysseus and Neoptolemus in the prologue lacked any warmth. Odysseus used formal patronymic address to Neoptolemus (4, 50, 96) and Neoptolemus responded in kind (26, 87). Their pragmatic, military relationship is defined entirely by the job in hand. Now Neoptolemus has just had the experience of being the one to fulfil Philoctetes' intense longing for friendship, *philia*. (*phil-* compounds are used by Philoctetes at 224, 229, 234, 237, 242, 242.) Philoctetes repeatedly calls Neoptolemus *teknon*, 'child'. We cannot tell how far Neoptolemus is responding, but by such sympathetic remarks as 339-40 ('Poor fellow, I would think your own troubles are enough for you, without mourning for others'), Sophocles leaves it open for us to think that, while arousing and exploiting affection, the fatherless young man is beginning to return it.

The effect of the loop must be to sharpen the ambiguity of this relationship. We seem to see Neoptolemus experience the confusion of siding with the False Merchant, mouthpiece of Odysseus, to deceive his friend, when his sense of *philia* towards him has developed at cross-purposes to the needs of the plot. The experience of *acting* friendship for Philoctetes has produced *real* feelings of friendship. We are even invited to think at one point that his loyalties have shifted so profoundly that he is in danger of forgetting that hatred for the Atridae is only assumed: his emotional outburst against them 585-8 produces the following confrontation with the False Merchant in *antilabê* 589-91:

> FM   Watch what you're doing, boy.
> N   I've been watching it for some time.
> FM   I'll hold you responsible.
> N   Get on with it – talk.
> FM   I'm talking.

The scene ends in a verbal exchange over the bow – initiating later physical contacts and exchanges (discussed by Taplin, *GRBS* 12, 1971, 27ff.). The extreme respect and reverence Neoptolemus expresses for it, and Philoctetes' generous response are moving. Whatever lies Neoptolemus has told and may still be telling, the two are seen to fulfil each other's mutual needs. Neoptolemus receives permission to hold the bow, although he does not do so yet. This suggests another, nobler kind of transaction to set against the deceitful verbal exchange for profit. Neoptolemus' final speech, when he puns on *Philo-ktetes*, 'Friend-possessor', to coin the phrase '*ktêmatos kreissôn philos*, 'a friend beyond possession' (673), expresses the shift in values of this scene.

Narratives

After offering his impeccable false credentials, the False Merchant proceeds by 'splitting' the simple diegetic narrative of the play so far, which is simply 'Odysseus and Neoptolemus have gone to fetch Philoctetes'. Two parallel false narratives are now temporarily introduced: (1) Phoenix and Theseus' sons have gone to fetch Neoptolemus and (2) Odysseus and Diomedes have gone to fetch Philoctetes.

The split narratives are fictions already in circulation. The theatrical audience are doubtless pleased by these allusions to other versions.[25] In the *Little Iliad*, Odysseus went to fetch Neoptolemus while Diomedes brought Philoctetes. In their dramatic versions, Aeschylus and Euripides had ignored Neoptolemus altogether, and while Aeschylus sent Odysseus to Lemnos, Euripides sent Odysseus and Diomedes there. By sending both Odysseus and Neoptolemus to Lemnos at the start of this play, Sophocles has already interestingly conflated earlier versions. Now the disguised sailor accompanied by another seaman come into view as *yet another* pair of deceitful figures making a sea journey to fetch or manipulate someone. The multiplicity of deceitful journeys creates a kind of narrative *mise en abîme* in which the world seems full of dupers and the duped. This illusory, transient effect of superimposition, in which one story merely mirrors another without an end point, seems to be yet one more of the functions of this particular, highly idiosyncratic loop.

The story of Helenus' capture and prophecy provides some resolution to this endless sequence. Although mentioned last and, because of its narration by a liar, deprived of any absolute truth value, it functions nonetheless as the narrative which is causally prior to all the others, the one which determines all subsequent 'journeys by sea to fetch someone'. Giving such an important narrative so absolutely unauthoritative a position in the play is very much part of Sophocles' subtle narrative strategy. By the end we will discover that the narrative the False Merchant ascribes to Helenus was a true prophecy, and that *peithô*, persuasion (612), which, as subsequent scenes develop seems increasingly impossible, is despite everything the means that is successful in the end.

The situations of Philoctetes and of Neoptolemus are all subtly refracted by the Helenus story. Helenus was forced against his will to use his unique gift to help his enemies; the same fate, it seems, that Philoctetes is to meet, both of them outwitted by Odysseus. Neoptolemus' lying discourse is set against Helenus' prophetic discourse which (despite being here narrated by a liar), *could not lie*. Soon Neoptolemus too will be unable to lie.

Dolos in Electra

Deceit is a traditional element of 'return and revenge' plots, and in the sense that they are not informed of the hero's return, friends as well as enemies may temporarily be deceived. Thus at *Choephoroe* 20-1 Orestes, who thinks he has already seen Electra with the advancing slave women (16-18), nonetheless decides to hide and watch them first. Then, having observed Electra's filial loyalty, he emerges with a speech which immediately declares their relationship (212). In Euripides' version[1] the delay before mutual recognition is longer: Orestes decides to watch the 'slave girl' (108); having recognised her he starts to converse without revealing himself (220ff.): finally the Old Man brings about mutual recognition (578). The extended delay in recognition here is normally attributed to Orestes' unheroic timidity. In neither play is there an explicit policy of exclusion, the feature so very marked in Sophocles' version. At 77 Electra cries out, off stage, 'O wretch that I am!' *iô moi moi dustênos*. The Paedagogus thinks the voice belongs to 'some attendant' (78-9),[2] but Orestes seems to intuit that it is his sister and suggests waiting to hear her lament, exactly as in *Choephoroe*. But his suggestion is put in the form of a question, to which the Paedagogus' resonant answer is *hêkista*, 'Absolutely not' (82). This marked break-off begins what is perhaps Sophocles' biggest *dolos*.[3]

Electra and the chorus are subsequently further deceived by the deceitful narrative of Orestes' death, and this leads, via disbelief in Chrysothemis' true account and Electra's decision to take revenge single-handed, to the superb culmination of the recognition scene when *dolos* drops away. Only then does the traditional action of revenge get under way. In this version then, the traditional story of Orestes' revenge refocuses around Electra, and the entire section 82-1227 comprises a huge loop, largely, although not completely, redundant in terms of the traditional *fabula* of return and revenge.

It is an extraordinary achievement. The forward movement of the plot is handled with great subtlety so as to be almost imperceptible, yet the action does advance, and the suspense created by the prologue remains undissipated. The scenes are theatrically dynamic, not least because of overlapping ludic effects – Electra is *deluded*, the theatrical audience *colludes* with the playwright in the web of *allusions* evoked.

All the same, it is the sense of a past continuing unchanged into the present which is strongly conveyed in the texture of these scenes. On the level of individual words, this is achieved by many 'frequentative' markers,[4] while at the level of scenic structure, each scene (Electra with, successively, chorus, Chrysothemis, Clytemnestra) follows the same pattern, which is that fresh items of news are invariably delayed until *after* there has been a generalised debate on the whole situation of Agamemnon's murder and Orestes' possible return.

For example, it is only at 310 that the chorus, who have been onstage with Electra since 121, make any reference to the present time by asking whether Aegisthus is at home or not. Similarly, Chrysothemis enters 328, the chorus remarking on her entry that she carries *entaphia*, funerary items (326), but even the report of possible walling-up is delayed until 379 and serves largely as a stimulus for more antithetical argument. At last, 404-5, Chrysothemis recalls her mission to Agamemnon's tomb: however, then Clytemnestra and Electra argue the rights and wrongs of their positions 516-634. Each character generalises a good deal, in the present tense, about the other's fixed position. The result is that what we see enacted on the stage is taken as indicative of the entire period of waiting.

Within the loop the stage figures repeatedly focus on the subject of Orestes' return, but none of their information is conclusive. It is made clear in the *parodos* that Electra's entire hopes are centred round his return. News about him is described as 'always frustrated' (169-70). In the first episode the chorus specifically ask for news again, and the ensuing brief conversation (317-23) highlights the ignorance of the participants and, as at 169-70, the gap between word and deed ('He says he'll come. But he doesn't do what he says', 319). Channels of communication are referred to, but to date there has been no authoritative statement either way, just some informal word of mouth coming to Electra, and maybe to Clytemnestra's spies.

Orestes' return is the subject which polarises the relationship between mother and daughter. Electra describes the alteration in her mother's behaviour 'when someone hears that Orestes is coming', 293-4. Waiting for him has significantly affected both women (305-6, 780-2). Electra admits that she would if possible have brought Orestes up to be *miastôr*, avenger, of his mother's crimes (601-5). For both, Orestes' survival and possible return has the status of a life-or-death issue.

Though the loop is completed when recognition finally takes place at 1227, this chapter goes only as far as the messenger speech (680-763). It analyses each narrative leading up to it, looking at its provenance (eyewitness account? divine utterance? unsubstantiated rumour?), consequent authority, and reception, both internal to the play and external to the audience. The messenger speech is the well-prepared climax of an entire series of concealed, abortive or delusive messages which together comprise this play of cheated expectation and show us Sophocles at his most elusive.

Though the opening frame with Orestes encourages us to believe the play is a closed structure, it is not bounded by a matching closing framework in which the deceitful action is clearly understood to be over, and well over.[5] Aegisthus is still alive as the play ends,[6] and there is no clue about the political future of Argos. Nor is there any invitation to the audience to find a distance from the onstage events as in *Eumenides*, or in the plays of Euripides which include a closing aetiology. There are no unambiguous pointers to the future elsewhere either. The only narrative taking us beyond the murders is given to the Paedagogus 1364-6, and is motivated merely by the need for deferral. (On the deadening effect of these predictive words, see Segal, 1966, 519: 'The endless succession of nights and "equal days" points back to the static condition of Electra in her first scene.') At the end, the audience is forced to pick up the burden the characters have just dropped, unable to contemplate with satisfaction 'an action complete in itself'. Like the False Merchant scene in *Philoctetes*, they are left with the disturbing and unconcluded effect *on themselves*.

7.1 Prologue (1-85)

In the prologue we are given a report of an earlier narrative and prepared for a future one: put more concretely, Apollo's oracle gives rise immediately to the creation of a false message. The link between oracle and false message is striking (cf. *Choephoroe* 556ff. where the same elements are also closely juxtaposed).

Orestes' report of Apollo's oracle is extremely brief; the possibly accurate reporting of 36-7 undercut by the casual 'of such a kind' (35, 38). The subsequent details of the *doloi* (37) enjoined by Apollo appear to be Orestes' own, but we have no idea what Apollo actually said – a familiar Sophoclean technique (cf. Robinson, *CQ* n.s. xix 1969, 44f. of the oracle in *Philoctetes*: 'Sophocles at no point allows any of his characters to purport to quote the exact words of the oracle ... *verbatim* and in full, uncut, unexpanded and uninterpreted. This is surely deliberate.') Furthermore, if the extent of the god's involvement is left unclear, the context in which his message is reported is already that of *kairos* and *akmê*, 'the critical moment', and the oracle appears almost outdated and insignificant compared with the details of the *dolos* to be carried out. However, when Orestes speaks of himself as 'impelled by gods' (70), Apollo is certainly implied.

The Paedagogus is invited to listen hard and correct him if necessary (29-31). The imperatives provoke the audience too to listen to the subsequent details of the plot (each element of which is later carried out as indicated here). They also suggest that the details of the false death are Orestes' own idea. At this point the Paidagogus makes no corrections, but certainly does so at 82ff., when he so firmly brackets Apollo with the deed of revenge and makes this the justification for excluding Electra, 'No way. Let us attempt nothing in advance of Apollo's orders ....' In this authoritative statement he is, like Orestes at 70, putting the entire action of the play under the auspices of the god.

Overall then, the provenance of the plan of false report is problematic and indefinite. Apollo, Orestes and his tutor are in different ways all involved in its authorship.

At vv. 59-66 Orestes dismisses any theoretical objection to fabricating a narrative of his own death.[7] This is the the only reflective section of this practical speech and must be considered important; in narratological terms, at any rate, it suggests a general *devaluing* of communication in itself, inevitably attendant on the decision to lie. It points not just to the immediate denial of communication to Electra, but to the ethos of the entire play, which explores a world in which narrative is used for profit, not truth. 'No word is bad that brings gain' (61).

7.2 Walling up (373ff.)

In a passage reminiscent of *Antigone*, Sophocles makes Chrysothemis tell Electra she is soon to be walled up outside the country's boundaries in a vault of some kind (designated by the vague phrase, *katêrephei stegêi*) if she does not stop her laments (379-82). As with news of Orestes, the provenance of this report too is unclear and lacking in much authority (378-9). Clytemnestra and Aegisthus might well have discussed this as an option for silencing Electra. No eyewitness is referred to. The report, however, is a fresh narrative, one offering a potential if fleeting resolution to the impasse between Electra and those in power: she will lament herself to death and then be silenced for ever, properly *shut up*.

On the whole, critics are inclined to minimise the significance of this passage (e.g. Kamerbeek, '... its function is restricted to the narrow limits of the ensuing debate. Apart from the vague menace 626-7 the matter is not referred to again in the course of the play'), as if its function were merely to spark off the stichomythia 385-404 which so well displays the sisters' antithetical positions and Electra's fearlessness at the prospect of death. It is true that the matter is not specifically referred to again (except by Clytemnestra's threat at 626-7); but the idea of death by walling-up, or something similar had already come into the play when at 149-52 Electra compared herself to Niobe, using a similar phrase 'in a tomb of rock', *en taphôi petraiôi*. Both passages predicate a kind of death, an abnormal death-in-life without due ritual, mimicking Agamemnon's wrongful death and ritually-incorrect interment (*maschalismos*, mutilation of his dead body, 445). As so often in his loops, Sophocles enriches various narrative lines by suggestive superimposition, and temporarily invites us to consider this alternative *telos*, suggesting its fittingness for his heroine. Electra's position in the play, as she often reminds us, is a liminal death-in-life (e.g. 141; 185-6; 207-8). Excluded from society (312, 328-31, 516-8, 802f., 817-19), we see her overwhelmingly concerned with Hades and the dead.

7.3 The dream (417ff.)

Sophocles worked within a literary tradition which had always included sceptical comments about dreams (e.g. *Od.* 19.559-68, *Il.* 2.80-3, *Ag.* 274-5, *OT* 981-3, *IT* 1259-84). Euripides omits the dream in his version, and here Sophocles plays it down, in the sense that he does not introduce it early on, as in *Choephoroe*, where its lyric presentation creates the opening brooding atmosphere and context for the developing revenge. Nor does it have *Choephoroe*'s strong functional relevance, where the dream sets up an obligation to carry out apotropaic ritual and so produces the initial entry of the chorus and Electra, and the little scene centred on the onstage tomb of Agamemnon in which her dilemma over the offerings is watched by Orestes in secret, paving the way for recognition between brother and sister.

Instead, the dream element is 'artlessly' introduced. The chorus noted the tomb-offerings, *entaphia*, at 326, but no question of their purpose is raised until 404-5; they remind the audience throughout that something of the standard plot is under way, but in this version the tomb is off stage. Sophocles perhaps teases us with the possibility that Chrysothemis might depart without Electra even learning of the dream – or that recognition of Orestes might be made by Chrysothemis rather than her more valiant sister; and it is in fact Chrysothemis who subsequently finds the tokens (871ff.), producing another twist in the play.

Chrysothemis has not attempted to interpret the dream herself, and she is vague about it.[8] Her position is sceptical and pragmatic. 'The dream is only a new reason why Electra should be cautious' (Jebb, 1894, on 428-30). Like the oracle, it lacks authority being in fact merely a third- or fourth-hand account (reckoning *first* hand as the original eye-witness dream experience of Clytemnestra). The dream was 'shown to the Sun' and at the same time overheard by a bystander who then gossiped about the details. We do not know whether she spoke directly to Chrysothemis, or whether Chrysothemis merely overheard. If the latter, the communication has been overheard, rather than directly communicated, *twice*.

Electra however, responding only to the vague phrase 'a fear in the night', has immediately assumed that the dream has a divine provenance. Her comment, 'A few words have often made or marred men's fortunes' (415-16), emphasises her sense of its significance.[9] The comment also appeals to the audience, but in a more complex way: the words have one meaning within Electra's frame of expectations, another with reference to the forthcoming deceptive words of the Paedagogus.

At *Choephoroe* 549-50 Orestes responded in a similar positive fashion to hearing Clytemnestra's dream. In both plays a dream-message to Clytemnestra warning her of impending murder by her son is *overheard* by a hostile child; Aeschylus had already exploited the ironic possibilities here (see 4.5).[10] The dream was 'adequate' for Clytemnestra, in the sense that it provided sufficient information about her fate, but as a communication to Orestes about his role it ultimately fell short.

The dream, described so briefly 417-23, appeals strongly to the authorial audience because of its complex allusions to other texts. Sophocles departs from the familiar Stesichorean and Aeschylean snake motif.[11] Like a snake charmer, he converts the traditional flexible serpent into a rigid royal sceptre, which Agamemnon then plants in the hearth, with clear sexual connotations:[12] the sceptre now softens again and grows into a huge plant giving shade to all Mycenae.

Sophocles here links together powerful symbols from Homer and Aeschylus. The sceptre is that powerful Pelopid sceptre whose genealogy is given *Iliad* 2. 101ff. Made by Hephaistos, Zeus gave it to Hermes to give to Atreus. It is the major symbol of Agamemnon's power and in the events of *Iliad* 2 it is used to articulate an entire narrative sequence, its impeccable credentials counterpointing the ambiguous nature of the power it wields (see Easterling, 1989). The impossible movement back from artefact to plant, from object of culture to object of nature, recalls Achilles' mighty oath (*Il*. 1.234ff.): 'Now by this sceptre which since it was cut down will never more bear leaves ...' The sceptre is a fitting symbol for the return of Agamemnon from Hades back to the world – an *adunaton* except in supernatural or metaphorical terms.[13]

The dream also contains echoes of *Agamemnon* 958-72, one of Clytemnestra's most lavishly deceptive narratives, uttered as Agamemnon is in the process of walking into the house over the tapestry. Agamemnon is successively compared to a plant producing shade against excessive heat, then warmth in winter, then coolness. Synaesthetic images of fertility quickly contradict and dissolve into one another, dream-fashion, and the audience understand these lurid, unchecked images mean no good to Agamemnon.

Here Chrysothemis finds the dream meaningless but Electra and the chorus give it a positive evaluation. The traditionally ambiguous role of dreams in tragedy, as well as the complex allusions of this one, militate against the audience adopting either of these simplistic approaches. At the same time the dream provokes efforts at interpetation. Sophocles thus builds the dream into his narrative flow to make it yet one more ambiguous communication.

7.4 Stasimon (472-515)

Choral odes regularly offer narratives, or allude to narratives, at a different level from the episodes. Even if, as here, the stage is not empty, during
an ode the audience frequently approaches the position of addressee, and
the generalising tenor of many lyrics specifically invites the audience to
make an interpretation of the action in the play to date.

In this stasimon there is a marked disjunction between the strophe and
antistrophe on the one hand, and the epode on the other. Janus-like, the
ode faces both forwards and backwards in time, the first part optimistic,
the second pessimistic. The second part seems to point silently to a
common feature of tragedy – narrative shortfall.

The chorus, now narrator, first offer a predicative narrative addressed
to Electra, 'child' (477), based on their positive interpretation of Clytemnestra's dream. The temporal distance from the episode is small ('no long
time', 477). Their language is rich in words of prophecy ('seer', 472,
'prophetic', 475, 'prophecies', 498). There are confident future indicative
tenses at 475, 477, 482, 489, 501). Their confidence is further stressed in
various ways, by the noun *courage* at 479, repeated 495; and by emphatic
phrasing ('never forgets', 482; 'never, never', 496). They have confidence
both that dreams have meaning (495ff.), and that the correct interpretation of this dream is that Dikê (Justice) and an Erinys (Fury) are coming
to avenge Agamemnon. Clytemnestra and Aegisthus are definitely referred to (despite the textual difficulties of 492-3),[14] but there is,
interestingly, absolutely no allusion to Orestes himself; it is the Erinys
who is spoken of as about to arrive (489f.). Only in the glancing (and
familiar) link made between dreams and prophecy (499-500) could we
possibly be reminded of Apollo's oracle and see oracle and dream as linked
communications.

A sophisticated audience, familiar with Sophoclean choruses, might
well react coolly to the first part of the ode. The chorus' predictive powers
are frequently fallible. The more they insist on their interpretation, the
wider yawns the familiar tragic gap between opinion and knowledge.
Further, the 'if ... not' formulation of the clauses which open the strophe
and, ring-fashion, conclude the antistrophe, might also be thought subtly
to undercut the very certainty they seem to be expressing.[15] The emphatically Aeschylean echoes created by the language of Dikê and Erinys
remind us of the unexpected outcome of Orestes' action in *Choephoroe*, and
encourage the view that the chorus might be as ill-equipped to predict the
future as the choruses of *Agamemnon* and *Choephoroe*.

All the same, the message of the strophe and antistrophe remains
overtly optimistic. The epode is quite different. As the confident final
phrase of the antistrophe ('will safely come to harbour', 501) fades away,
the chorus adopt a quite different tone.

There is great narrative disjunction at this point, unmediated by any

link. The metre changes to iambo-dochmiac colaria, with their dragging
three long final beats. In the strophe and antistrophe the chorus, as
politides, female citizens, were addressing Electra and giving her support
in an immediate temporal context; in the epode the chorus addresses not
Electra but 'Pelops' chariot race long ago, cause of so much suffering'. They
suddenly acquire an autonomous authority.

Plunging into the past, with a narrative reach quite unprecedented in
the play to date,[16] the chorus abandon thoughts of the immediate future.
We do not know what motivates the change of tack, unless it is their own
mention of *Dikê* and *Erinys*. They focus, with immediate exactitude, on
'Pelops' ancient chariot-race, cause of so much suffering'. There is substantial narrative compression here. The complex story of Pelops' victory over
Oenomaus, and his relationship with Myrtilus are passed over; the spot-
light falls on the moment of Myrtilus' ejection from the chariot and plunge
into the sea (508-12).

After the initial exclamation, a very tight temporal control is maintained from 'for ever since' (508) to 'never yet' (513) and we are dragged
straight over the intervening generations of the Pelopidae until the final
phrase (*poluponos aikeia*, 'outrage, cause of so much suffering', mirroring
poluponos hippeia 'chariot-race, cause of so much suffering', 505) abruptly
coincides with Clytemnestra's entry for the next episode. There is key
vocabulary here: repeated use of *poluponos* tightly binds all the intervening generations together and *aikeia* is used twice more in this immediate
context (486, 511) to describe the deaths of Agamemnon and Myrtilus.

In general this play lacks the expansive and beautiful choral odes of, for
example, *Antigone*, which offer related meanings by providing parallel
narratives in other times and places. This epode is almost the only point
where the 'low horizon' of the play briefly lifts, allowing a conspectus on
the Pelopid family's past.[17] As such, it is tempting to take the epode, with
its great narrative reach and consequent apparent authority, as an indication of how to interpret the puzzle of the play's truncated ending and come
to an overall understanding of it. On a negative reading, *poluponos aikeia*
ironically refers to Orestes' matricide and the phrase 'never yet' is taken
ironically as well to mean 'never yet – and it's not going to now'. The Furies
referred to in the antistrophe, even if they are not presented on stage at
the end, will in some way or other continue to pursue the family (for the
tragic lack of resolution of Electra's position, see Reinhardt, Friis Johansen, Segal and Winnington-Ingram). The perspective opened up by the
epode has set the individual crimes of Clytemnestra and Aegisthus against
Agamemnon and the forthcoming revenge of Orestes into a much longer
family history of *unending* suffering.

However, the ode must be primarily viewed in relation to its ordering
within the sequence of scenes. It comes one-third of the way through a
complex series of communications which all together in due order comprise
the play. The two parts of the ode, however disparate, comprise one lyric,

and one must at least try to find a unified reading for it. In fact the epode's surface meaning can be aligned to the optimism of the first part, especially if the phrase *poluponos aikeia* is taken, by a sort of zeugma, to refer largely to Clytemnestra as she comes on stage. 'Never yet' might be merely an open rather than an ironic judgment. We can restrict too the range of reference of the two items recalled from the distant past, Pelops' wearisome horse-race and Myrtilus' violent ejection from the chariot. Taking the play sequentially, we need look no further than the narrative of Orestes' fatal fall at the Pythian games, prepared for 48-50 and about to interrupt the very next scene. These items could be a simple thematic advance reference, to give the later account more resonance.

This view cannot stand. The *underlying* connection between Pelops' horse-race, Myrtilus' death and the forthcoming narrative about Orestes is *deceit*. Deceit is the characteristic means by which the house of Pelops, generation by generation, has carried out its outrages. (And surely, mirroring its content, the sly compression of the narrative which brings these past events to our attention should alert us to the fact that we are dealing with narrative too that is *dolios*.)

Deceitful narratives create a figurative discourse, one in which the content, lacking a clear referential function, can only relate without restriction to the entire structure into which it is embedded (see Perron, 1989, 529f.) Sophocles does not make it possible to limit the range of possible readings here. So this ode too, contributes along with the earlier scenes into a developing view of the action as a kind of Proteus-like structure in which the audience must try to grasp what is offered, but expect a hundred shapes to appear and disappear between its fingers.

7.5 Electra and Clytemnestra's *agôn* (516-659)

Clytemnestra and Electra confront one another from positions fixed long ago;[18] but once embarked on argument, they react with a fierceness and freshness as if seven or more years had not passed.

Clytemnestra tells of Agamemnon's sacrifice of Iphigeneia. Her speech is full of I-you markers (e.g. 530, 531, 533, 534, 536). There are many rhetorical questions (535, 538, 541, 543, 545, 546), which Clytemnestra answers herself (547) and on behalf of her dead daughter (548). Electra's response (558ff.) takes the same rhetorical form (I-you markers at 558, 560, 561, 565, 566, rhetorical questions at 560, 579; Electra answers herself, 560, 565). As audience we feel sure they are only repeating what has already been said many times; their dialogue is 'reciprocal and potentially infinite' (Winnington-Ingram, 1980, 223). They are equally matched in their ability to narrate and describe their points of view (only one of the many similarities between mother and daughter, for which in general see Kitto, 1961, 133-5; Segal, 1966, 501, 525f; specifically for this scene, see Blundell, 1989, 172). Each woman in her argument makes use of a narrative to incriminate or exculpate Agamemnon, but in the context we are invited to find no real validity on either side. The stories of Iphigeneia's sacrifice and Agamemnon's offence against Artemis seem dead issues. This is discourse which fails to persuade. Lacking a judge, the debate ends in a stand-off. This scene is rich in other aspects of the play's meaning, but as rational communication between two characters, it fails.

7.6 Clytemnestra's prayer (637-59)

A kind of circle is completed as Clytemnestra speaks. The play began with a message from Apollo, and now Clytemnestra offers a message to him. Her prayer gives another interpretation of the dream. We have heard the initially sceptical view of Chrysothemis, the guardedly optimistic reaction of Electra, and the chorus' ode on the subject. Now the proper addressee of the dream narrative addresses Apollo Lycaeus on the subject. The image of Apollo[19] is, naturally, silent.

Apollo is an extremely important figure in the play. As the premises of actantial theory indicate, he cannot be excluded from consideration simply because he is not a stage figure – particularly since his statue gives him a permanent stage presence. He is thus an ironically silent witness to all that occurs, continuously reminding the audience that, having initiated *dolos*, he is the *author* ('the maker or composer of a narrative', Prince, 1987) of the entire tragic action, the playwright's proxy. Apollo's importance cannot be minimised – but his motives cannot be clarified either.

Electra, who throughout the play so far has either been denied information or been treated to second-hand accounts, now merely overhears another communication in silence. All the same, her position is far from powerless at this point: significantly, she has given permission for the prayer to take place at all (632-3), and her continuing proximity forces Clytemnestra into words which are guarded. Clytemnestra's request to Phoebus to hear her 'concealed utterance' (638), with expectations that he will understand even what is not mentioned (657-8), alerts the audience too to listen hard for a sub-text.

Clytemnestra's response to her dream is typical of tragic dreamers. Like the Queen in *Persae*, the Clytemnestra of *Choephoroe* and Hecuba in *Hecuba*, the dream has scared her (636), and inspires her to offer sacrifice and prayer, but she feels open about the outcome: she at least *talks* of it as if it were equally likely to presage good or bad (646-9). Such lack of acuity presages her vulnerability to the Paidagogus' lies and the success of the false narrative.

Clytemnestra's silent prayer is clearly for Orestes' death, and it is this implicit part of her prayer which will appear to be immediately fulfilled. Sophocles uses a very similar *dolos* at *Oedipus Tyrannus* 911-23: Jocasta prays to Apollo for 'a deliverance without defilement' (921) just as Clytemnestra utters 'prayers for deliverance' (635-6), and immediately her prayer *appears* to be positively answered by the entry of the herdsman announcing Polybus' death (although *in fact* the tragic recognition is advanced by his message).

7.7 False messenger speech (660-763)

In contrast to the merely ambiguous communication in the play so far, the messenger speech of *Electra* is an overt *tour de force* of continuous, outright lies, occupying the important dead centre of the play (for the central position of the messenger speech see Brann, 1957 and Segal, 1966, 479-81). It is Sophocles' longest extant message narrative and internally it appears to be the eye-witness, authoritative account denied both Electra and Clytemnestra for so long.

Rather than having Orestes tell his own lies, as at *Choephoroe* 674f., the poet has taken pains in the prologue to flesh out the vestigial figure of the Paedagogus and then reintroduce him here in disguise. As ironically perceived by the authorial audience, on entry he conforms exactly to the norm of the conventional tragic messenger, the anonymous character who dispels all ambiguity by a relation of the facts.

Extended sections of continuous narrative effectively immobilise the onstage narratees, creating a pause in the forward movement of the stage action. Where the narrative is transparent, the pause is compensated for by the creation of *enargeia*, Barthes' 'effet du réel'. But here, given that its narrative content cannot innocently signify, we are forced to view the *rhêsis* from a different, complex set of perspectives.[20] Internally, we see the production of a high-risk fiction in the heart of the enemy camp, one which can only succeed through its sheer inventiveness and rhetorical power. We thus assess the narrative, the acting ability of the Paedagogus, and the theatrical effect naively as narrative audience (will his speech convince?) but also as authorial audience in a more sophisticated way. Since attention is focused on the narrative's special fictive status, we consequently admire the marked-off element 'message speech' with, perhaps, something of the appreciation accorded Homeric similes, which in the same way are marked off as bravura inventions with special status within their context.

At another level we are forced to view the play spinning itself into existence before our eyes, creating illusion as it goes, and playing on the emotional responses of all involved, including ourselves. That we should be moved by what we know in advance is a *dolos* is disturbing. Watching fictional characters watch another fiction – an effect created to varying degrees in all the loops under discussion – in particular reminds the audience of its own naive collusion; a problematic effect.[21]

Behind his mask the Paedagogus has extraordinary and unlimited narrative authority, approaching the role of the poet himself. Normally, first-person narrative such as the messenger's produces two kinds of focalisation, the 'experiencing I' and the 'narrating I'.[22] The eyewitness experience provides the material with which the narrator produces his report, and the words of the report combine the two elements: sometimes the focus is on what was seen, sometimes on the comments or remarks of the narrator, making use of *ex eventu* knowledge. A narrative report of a supposedly actual event is necessarily subject to restrictions of various kinds – restrictions of place, of access and particularly, of understanding. These restrictions are an interesting study in themselves (see de Jong, 1991, 12-29) and are often used creatively by the poets.[23] But here, apart from the Paedagogus' brief of convincing his audience that Orestes has died, there are no restrictions in operation at all: his narrative powers are unbounded.

The complex narrative situation creates tension and a sense of danger, as it did in the other loops. The Paedagogus' narrative is a *dolos* and cannot *innocently* signify. Perhaps because of this, it positively crackles with a range of possible interpretations. According to narrative theory, each new narrative situation is to be 'construed as a revised configuration of the entire sequence up to that point (a set of sets) leading to a revised expectation concerning the outcome' (Holloway, 1979, 106). In that case, the Paedagogus' speech, which shows Orestes galloping towards a fatal *telos*,[24] seems to suggest a disastrous *telos* for the overall action of revenge.

7.7.1 Opening dialogue (660-679)

In this opening section, every conventional element which normally marks off the messenger's account as an infallibly true, eyewitness statement of fact, is included and exploited to create an ironic *verismo*. This is particularly underlined in Clytemnestra's request for 'the truth' producing the Paedagogus' full report, beginning, 'That's what I've come for' (679-80).

At 660 the Paedagogus enters requesting confirmation that he has come to the right place. Such a request is an established convention in messengers who come from outside (cf. *Ajax* 733-4, *OT* 924-6), and so serves to remind us that the Paedagogus is now adopting his messenger role. He flatteringly recognises the queen and puts emphasis on the fact that the words he brings are 'sweet' (667 – as agreed earlier at 56), and that they come from friends (667, 671, 672 cf. 44-6). This too increases his theatrical 'credibility', given stage messengers' notorious anxiety for their own safety when bringing bad news (cf. the guard's comic hesitation at *Ant.* 223f. and particularly 277). Clytemnestra, influenced by her prayer, takes the bait (668).

At 673 comes the headline, 'Orestes has died'.[25] To this announcement there is a unique twofold reaction. Electra expresses despair, Clytemnestra excitement ('What are you saying, what are you saying?'), coupled with the wish to exclude Electra from the communication ('Don't listen to *her*'). The entire sequence of headline and twofold reaction are repeated again at 676-8 (the same technique as at *Trach.* 874-5). Sophocles has polarised the reactions of two narratees elsewhere, e.g. Jocasta and Oedipus on hearing the news from Corinth, but this effect depended on the discrepant awareness of the two narratees. Here, by including Electra with Clytemnestra as duped narratees he has created a different kind of contrast. Mother and daughter, who should lament together, yet again demonstrate their polarity.

Clytemnestra's question 'How did he die?' (679) is another standard feature: request for detail leads in to the full narrative.[26] The answering line (680) with its 'declaration of intention to narrate', is also a standard feature.[27]

7.7.2 Introductory section of speech (680-95)

With the mention of the Pythian Games we know that the Paidagogus is embarking on the account indicated in the *prologos*, 47f. The ludic element of narrative could not be better embodied than in these resplendent games.

As in the other loops discussed, the false narrative sets up complex references to the external world, to other texts, and to the play itself. Taken together, it creates many *dolioi* parallels and glancing possibilities, pleasing the authorial audience and teasing them to make interpretations concerning ultimate outcome. At the same time, the narrative audience follows the account with the keen attention accorded racing commentaries.

Although the scholiasts and (probably) Aristotle felt that the games were an anachronism, we cannot be sure that this was the case for Sophocles or his original audience (see Easterling, 1985, 7ff.). As they were a continuing feature of contemporary life, a possible gamut of contemporary external associations would become activated at this point: not least, the theatrical audience would enjoy the probability that a noble reared in Phocis would enter the lists at nearby Delphi (a point first made by Kaibel). It has been established that as part of the historical procedure the herald called out the name, patronym and origin of the competitors before each race (Finley & Pleket, 1976, 27), so 693-5 would have had a convincingly realistic, as well as heroic, ring.

Of the literary references, some belong to epinician lyric, but the overwhelming, overt reference is to Homer,[28] since in the focal section of the speech, the Paedagogus clearly adapts the *fons et origo* of all subsequent chariot race narratives, *Iliad* 23.262-650.

Orestes is quickly established as a hero whose time of *aristeia* is at hand. He is *lampros*, 'brilliant', *sebas*, 'an object of awe' (685), he wins all the contests for which he enters (690f.) and was 'deemed blessed' (693). He does thus under the gaze of everyone (685) including heralds, umpires and an entire audience drawn from all the communities of Greece. Orestes is presented as the glorious scion of a noble house.

It is interesting that no common features of message narrative are employed which would individualise the figure of Orestes. We have no physical description of him (no hair colour, no gesture), nor does the Paedagogus ever give us Orestes' own words or thoughts, either in direct or indirect speech. This is a unique omission of conventional elements which could provide vividness (*enargeia*) to the account. Direct speech in messenger speeches is very common.[29]

But this Orestes is a temporary cipher with no existence outside the Paedagogus' words, so in that sense he is fittingly blank. Homer famously never tells us even the colour of Helen's hair, and in the *teichoscopia* scene our perception of her is largely focused through the eyes of admiring Trojans (e.g. *Il.* 3.156f.). So here, Orestes is described only as he appears to the multitude, and the view of him is restricted to just so much as could be seen by an average spectator. All the same, the omission of detail is poignant in relation to the two listening women, neither of whom have seen Orestes since childhood. The narrator's focalisation through spectators makes him publicly glorious – a highly desirable son and brother in different, innocent circumstances.

The glorious public space, the open male world of critical speed and definite action towards a defined goal, could not provide a greater contrast with the enclosed, static world of the women. Competing in the individual contests is an activity for which the words *agôn* (682) and *krisis* (684) come into play – key vocabulary of the prologue (22, 75, 85) – reminding us that the performance of the speech to which we are listening – the narrating instance – is itself the first part of the crucial enterprise of seizing power. The competitive content of the games thus mirrors the hidden projected action, and its fictive outcome – disaster – suggests a similar conclusion to the revenge-and-return plan.

7.7.3 Main section: horse race (696-763)

The Paedagogus' 'editing' at 688ff. had produced a very marked *frequentative* stress. By building up a picture of continuous victories he had enhanced the picture of Orestes as a typical hero whose fall is preceded by conspicuous success. This prepares for the significant contrast of 696-7, a bridging maxim (*gnômê*) into the main narrative which is of utmost importance:[30]

> Such were his deeds. But when one of the gods inflicts
> harm (*blaptei*), no man however strong can escape.

At 694-5 the herald's proclamation of Orestes as son of heroic Agamemnon recalled the opening lines of the prologue, and now at 699, the morning time of the horse race recalls the strange phrase (17-19) which evoked the morning time of the prologue when the action first got under way. These echoes from the prologue subtly repeat the invitation to superimpose the horse race, focused on outcome, over the main plot as a predictive model of disaster. At the same time, discrepant awareness makes us realise that to Clytemnestra, having prayed to Apollo to live *ablabêi biôi*, 'a life without injury' (650) the god is now, in his own Games, fulfilling her prayer by inflicting *blabê* on her enemy.

The verb *blaptein* (697), according to Kamerbeek, combines the Homeric and classical meanings of *impedire*, 'to hinder the feet', and *damno afficere*, 'to afflict with a loss'. The lexicon entry distinguishes between references to horses' feet being tripped, disabled, or entangled in reins, and more metaphorical expressions relating to states of mind – distracted, perverted, misled. But *blaptein* from Homer onwards certainly incorporates both concepts, always containing the idea of movement catastrophically arrested by divine agency (see, e.g. *Od.* 1.195, 4.380).

Significant Aeschylean associations intertwine with the Homeric, as *blaptein* and *blabê* (the noun, 'hurt', 'harm', 'injury') form an important part of his vocabulary of *atê* and entrapment.[31] In this play Clytemnestra speaks of Electra as a *blabê* in terms which make her synonymous with an Erinys, 'For she is a greater *blabê*, living in the house with me, continually draining my undiluted life's blood' (at *Cho.* 577-8, 'the Erinys ... is drinking undiluted blood'). *Blaptein* and the Erinys are connected in the play's 'foot' imagery: the Erinyes are 'with many feet and many hands' (489) and 'with brazen feet' (491). Orestes too is associated with an Erinys when the chorus at 1391-2 sing 'For stealthily within the house is being led the *dolios-footed* avenger of the dead below ...'.

The Paedagogus has just resonantly defined Orestes as Agamemnon's son. What more appropriate verb than *blaptein* to describe the family's unending (*aianês*) association with *hippeia*, *doloi*, *Erinyes* and *atê*? The epode had already suggested that the action of the play is operating 'under the sign' of this kind of *blabê*.[32]

There are teasing parallels with the Homeric horse race (*Il.* 23.306ff.) and between the figure of Nestor and the Paedagogus.[33] The non-combatant Nestor frames the Homeric horse race,[34] acting as advisor to Antilochus just as the Paedagogus is advisor to Orestes. Nestor's frequent function of supplying an embedded narrative is matched here by the Paedagogus' temporary licence to narrate. In Homer, Nestor's rather obvious detailed tactics for victory seem to be treated as a somewhat hoary *topos*, and the epic contains no subsequent description of how the contestants do in fact round the turning-post during the race. Sophocles makes the Paedagogus 'choose' the Homeric account on which to base his own – but this time Orestes exactly carries out Nestor's advice about the turning post, with fatal consequences.

Sophocles creates ten contestants from different communities (see Kells and Kamerbeek *ad loc.* for the realistically modern origins of five of the contestants in northern Greece) but lets eight of them crash together, thus concentrating on a flat-out contest for first place between Orestes and his

Athenian opponent. No gods overtly assist them but, with typically subtle *legerdemain*, 696-7 suggest that a god – surely Apollo, author of the oracle, addressee of Clytemnestra, president of the Games and on stage as a statue – presides over the entire disaster.

Homer's race, rich in *mêtis* and *doloi* vocabulary, in one sense thoroughly suits *Electra*. Nestor's advice to Antilochus contains an unusual tricolon on *mêtis* (315-18); Apollo 'cheats' Diomedes and Athena plays a trick on Eumelus; then Antilochus wins – in Menelaus' words, *blapsas de moi hippous*, 'by making my horses stumble' (571). But there is contrast here too, since this Homeric *mêtis* is non-tragic: no one dies, and the *doloi* have no associations of *atê*.

The world of the play, by contrast, seems devoid of any possibility of positive resolution. Sophocles, having created through his Paedagogus a race rivalling Homer's in intensity and excitement, now moves away from his Homeric model to carry out the tragic shaping presaged by 696-7. Orestes hits the post, is thrown and caught up in the reins (the phrase 'twisted in the reins', 746-7, perhaps evoking *blaptein*; see also 836-7 and 863). Three-fold focalisation creates the successive frames through which the narrative achieves closure, moving back from its brilliant fiction to the drabness of the stage world: first, the spectators respond with a splendidly ambiguous cry;[35] then, even to his *philoi* the body of Orestes, disentangled by other charioteers, becomes unrecognisable. Finally the narrator, after introducing some Phocians who are coming into Argos with the urn, closes his account with a modest *sphragis* (coda), in which he himself is one eyewitness among others (762).

The pace of the narrative, with its lengthy background, full description, and speeding up at the end, mimics the course of the race itself. The Paedagogus creates a brilliant Orestes – and then destroys his creation. Through the vivid compression of his narrative, we see Orestes' body now hovering between earth and air, now unrecognisably bloodied, now burnt and the remains compressed into a small urn (cf. *Ag*. 433f.) for immediate delivery to the narratees.

In the rest of this scene and beyond Sophocles explores the effects of this speech on Electra and Clytemnestra. Their reactions are outside the scope of this chapter, which has been trying to explore the intricate narrative ambiguities employed by Sophocles and the complex reactions likely to have been evoked in the audience.

During the Paedagogus' false narrative they seem particularly rich. The audience are on the one hand engrossed by the moment-by-moment description of the race and crushed by the death of Orestes. On the other they admire the appropriateness of the account, the skill of the false narrator and the plurality of references to other texts. If it is all a lie, it means nothing. Yet it is clearly not meaningless, rather it suggests too much, and without restriction. Sophocles forces us to confront the deceitful, extraordinary power of narrative.

Part IV

Euripides

8

Euripides' Narrative Strategy

... the rhetorician and iconoclast of Aeschylean tragedy; the precursor of Alexandrian comedy; the realist who brought the myths down to the level of everyday life; the inventor of the romantic adventure play; the lyric poet ...; the producer of patriotic war plays – and also of plays that expose war's ugliness in dramatic images of unbearable intensity; above all, the tragic poet who saw human life not as action but as suffering.

Knox, in Burian, 1985, 1

... a kind of deliberate polytonality, as if tragedy were now being written in two keys at once.

Whitman, 1974, 113

... dissonance, disparity, rift, peripeteia ...

Arrowsmith in Segal (ed) 1968, 17

... Euripidean tragedy is a kind of tragedy of the genre itself.

Michelini, 1987, 51

8.1 Introduction

These quotations suggest a glaring disconnection between the narrative strategies of Euripides and his earlier rivals. However, although Euripides certainly produces remarkably new kinds of tragedy, broadening out its range to include both 'the untragic and the hyper-tragic', as Segal puts it,[1] these movements inevitably result from a reworking – however radical – of tragedy's traditional narrative resources.[2] His plays show the same underlying concerns with deceit, knowledge, time, and the relationship of man with gods, however differently formulated. If they point away from tradition, they arguably do so by reaching back within its resources. Euripides re-uses narrative patterns which originated in Homer, reworks and develops existing tragic strategies and re-invests in metrical structures, including those from earlier tragedy which had fallen into comparative disuse.[3] To do so refocuses the tradition while remaining within it.

Critics have made typologies of the plays and, at the scenic level, of repeated narrative motifs (supplication, kin-murder and averted kin-murder, recognition, rescue and escape).[4] However, Euripides' most consistent narrative strategy is to present a formal narrative in both prologue and closing section (*exodos*), and it is around this fact that our discussion of his general strategy is focused.[5]

Oracles, dreams, portents and curses tended to arise from within the plays of Aeschylus and Sophocles. They provided a gradual suspense and gave the plays an overall shaping. Characters were shown enmeshed and ultimately overwhelmed by events which began long ago: the play's 'work' was to grasp the meaning of the prediction as it unfolded over the course of time.

By contrast, such proleptic items within the body of a play are a marginal feature of Euripides' strategy,[6] omitted entirely (except, maybe as a glancing reference) in eight tragedies (*Alcestis, Medea, Andromache, Supplices, Heracles, Trojan Women, Orestes, Iphigeneia in Aulis*), and limited to a single scene in three. In two of these (*Heracl.* 381ff., *Phoen.* 834ff.) the prophecies motivate a virgin sacrifice; in the third (*Hipp.* 886ff.) Theseus, having discovered his wife's letter, immediately curses his son.[7] Marginalisation develops into confrontation in *Electra*, where Clytemnestra's traditional dream is entirely absent and the oracle is barely referred to (though see 87) until it appears somewhat tangentially in the stichomythia between Orestes and Electra before Clytemnestra's murder: Orestes speaks of it in the most slighting way ('Apollo, what a lot of folly you prophesied', 971) and Electra's defence of it seems largely designed to bolster his courage. At the end, Castor fails to explain or justify it (cf. 1244-6). The oracle has still nominally shaped the action – but the semi-comic rural setting, the mild and reasonable behaviour of Clytemnestra and Aegisthus, the perpetrators' horror at their own actions, emphatically refuse to make a satisfying religious shape.

The only surviving Euripidean plays which – arguably – make an overall investment in oracles and/or dreams are *Iphigeneia in Tauris*[8] and, to a lesser extent, *Hecuba* and *Ion*.

Instead of oracles and dreams, Euripides' preference is for an introductory narrative which makes a formal frame for the play's action. These prologue narratives may be delivered by a god (*Alcestis, Hippolytus, Ion, Trojan Women, Bacchae*) but are more often given to a human. Given the omniscience of gods, the first group of narratives may appear emphatically and infallibly proleptic ('I shall take revenge on Hippolytus today', *Hipp.* 21-2), in the latter, much less so: human prologue speakers, though able to speak infallibly about past and present, can only point with hope and fear towards the future (like the chorus). The lack of prolepsis is particularly obvious in the plays beginning with a supplication scene: in four out of five of these (*Heraclidae, Andromache, Heracles, Helen*, but not *Supplices*) the prologue-*rhêsis* speaker is the helpless, threatened suppliant whose life (or chastity, in the case of *Helen*) hangs in the balance.

But the distinction between divine and human prologue-*rhêsis* speakers is not as sharp as might at first appear: ambiguity is always hidden behind the apparent clarity of the god's prediction (the subject of chapter 10), since all proleptic narrative contains gaps, omissions, ambiguities – *doloi* – or there would be no suspense. Conversely, human speakers are at least able to point to possible outcomes often expressed in binary form as alternative possibilities (like oracles). Divine and human prologue-*rhêseis* in Euripides all perform the same function as narratives of dream and prophecy in Aeschylus and Sophocles in that they indicate a crisis without fully describing how it will be resolved – even if, with a divine speaker, they appear to do so.

In the *exodoi* of nine out of the seventeen surviving tragedies of Euripides (*Hippolytus, Andromache, Supplices, Electra, Iphigeneia in Tauris, Ion, Helen, Orestes* and *Bacchae*), a god appears and (among other things) delivers a second narrative, this time clearly proleptic, in the form of an *aition* (an account of the origin of a cult). To this group we can justifiably add both the 'demonic' (Dunn, 1996) epiphanies of humans: Medea at the end of *Medea*, Eurystheus at the end of *Heraclidae*, Polymnestor at the end of *Hecuba*, and the 'saviour' figures of Heracles at the end of *Alcestis* and Theseus at the end of *Heracles*. In these five plays human speakers are granted special dispensatory or predictive powers which bring the play to an end and align their function with that of gods. This makes a total of fourteen out of nineteen tragedies which end with divine or near-divine prolepsis.

Dunn suggests that while the final proleptic narrative, set among a whole group of formal, authoritative closing gestures in Euripides' *exodoi*,[9] has the function of guaranteeing that the audience know that the action (whatever point it has reached) is over. The action itself, by the formal artifice of its ending, tends to become problematic; there is frequently little satisfying sense of 'completion'; the god's presence merely establishes, even forces, an end to an otherwise potentially infinite chain of events – and it frequently does so by indicating a sequel.[10]

Euripides tends to resist creating narrative structures that make satisfying sense over time. As de Romilly (1968, 119) insists, for Euripides 'time is the realm of *tuchê* or chance'. This is a difficult but important area which highlights a major distinction between Euripides and his fellow-poets. Narrative theory tells us that events only make sense in a time sequence and that each event has meaning for the whole (narrative is taken to avoid redundancy, as if following the principle of Occam's razor). In the *Oresteia* we saw the 'narrative pendulum' in operation. Aeschylus developed a structure of great temporal complexity containing apparently haphazard events that eventually aligned to make resonant sense from the perspective of closure. In his single plays Euripides can also work in something of the same way. In *Medea, Hippolytus* and *Bacchae* the entire sequence of events can ultimately be seen as having taken place within a unified temporal scheme.[11] The course of these three plays follows a recognisable tragic narrative pattern, peaking in a familiar way (see 2.2.4). No doubt this is part of the reason why they are considered particularly canonical among Greek tragedies.

In many other Euripidean plays, however, this overall narrative shape is not present. The structure of *Phoenissae* has been called 'pageant-like' and that of *Trojan Women* 'actionless'. In a much larger group of plays, on the other hand, the problem is not too little but too much incident. For example, many plays open with an immediate crisis (like the five plays opening with supplication). Such crises, however, have a tendency to resolve a third or half of the way in, and a fresh development is required. In such situations, a Euripidean character may produce a 'statement of intent' *rhêsis*, sometimes so much like a new prologue that they have acquired the term *epiprologos*.[12] This typically Euripidean way of proceeding, in which past events are first neatly disposed of in a chronologically sequential prologue as necessary background only and then, once a first action is over, a supplementary *rhêsis* initiates a fresh action, shows a radically different, apparently more casual approach to narrative time. In some plays, the reframing moves the action into areas arguably not intrinsically connected to what went before, raising the chimerical problem of unity. Such unheralded changes of direction, usually associated with the sudden appearance of a new character – a feature traditionally connected with comedy rather than tragedy – have attracted criticism since Aristotle (*Poet.* 1461b20), as well as apologists to defend the unity of their supposedly bipartite or tripartite narrative structure.[13] However, apparently random movements in a play must be considered the result of a deliberate strategy, reflecting not poor narrative organisation but rather a different way of perceiving the world – one where chance, rather than any coherent divine plan, is the determinant of human affairs.

The foregrounding of chance makes for involving, if occasionally (from some critical standpoints) superficial theatre. Its absolute unpredictability makes either positive or negative movement possible, but entirely unknowable, creating short-term rather than an overall suspense. There is a strong contrast here with the more long-term suspense-arousing strategies of Aeschylus. Euripides exploits chance in a variety of ways: it may chime in with the will of the gods, however bizarre, as when Xuthus 'recognises' Ion after being told by the oracle that the first youth he encounters on leaving the shrine is his son (*Ion* 517f.). It can be manifest in the entry of a rescuer (Peleus, *And.* 545, Heracles, *Her.* 513). In *Iphigeneia in Tauris*, one of Euripides' three 'recognition thrillers' (in Lowe's excellent phrase), chance is manifested at the verbal level: statements and questions eventually bring about recognition and, meanwhile, heighten the significance of every word that is uttered: the stichomythia in such cases is a superb vehicle for this line-by-line type of suspense. The same effect is created in *Iphigeneia in Tauris* and *Helen* when deceit must be practised on the enemy to achieve escape.

The unpredictable operation of chance is frequently given verbal expression:

> O Chance, who changes the fortune of thousands, now to fare
> wretchedly and now again to fare well, what a hair's breadth away
> I was from murdering my mother ... ! (*Ion* 1512-15)

The sense seems little different if 'god' is substituted for chance:

> What an involved and riddling thing is god! (*Hel*. 711-12)

Pylades' encouraging words to Orestes seem to be pointing out that chance can effect a positive reversal in the plot in which they are embroiled:

> Sometimes, sometimes, exceptional misfortune by chance
> takes an exceptional turn. (*IT* 721-2)

It seems that a major advantage of the formal frame of narrative at beginning and end is to open up predictable mythical material to display the unpredictable operation of chance. The framework creates a 'play-pen' within the confines of which a traditional story is liberated to make comparatively free and unpredictable movements – experiments which are uneven in quality and frequently hard to assess. As Dunn, writing of *Helen*, notes, 'accustomed as we are to clichés about fickle fate ... it is hard to appreciate Euripides' originality and seriousness in presenting this issue so directly'. The rest of this chapter looks in more detail at how this strategy works.

8.2 Narrative at the beginning

The prologue consists of everything that precedes the first entry of the chorus.[14] The defining situation of tragedy is chorus plus actors or – occasionally – chorus on its own, never actors alone.[15] All prologue material has a distinct status and by definition contains information denied to the chorus and all other offstage figures. Off-set from the main action, tragic prologues give the audience privileged, specific information as to how the ensuing action may be understood.

Aeschylus and Sophocles tended to minimise the separate status of prologue material. Euripides stresses it.[16] His opening *rhêsis* immediately orientates the audience to novel aspects, bringing everyone up to the same level of information – a vital process when the play has a largely invented or unconventional plot-line. The person of the prologue speaker may embody an aspect of the novelty *per se*, like the Farmer in *Electra*, the slave-wife Andromache in *Andromache*, the virtuous Helen of *Helen*, the still-living Jocasta in *Phoenissae*. The exposition is lucid with an apparently transparent function to communicate. Since only speaker and audience are present, the audience is overtly put in possession of what feels like *the facts*.[17]

But the *rhêsis* is only the first part. Formal *telling* is, in the second half of the prologue, replaced by a second scene of *showing*. This subsequent scene (or scenes), usually a dialogue at the main narrative level of the play, appears to initiate the action and contrasts with the formality of the opening *rhêsis*. But in the absence of the chorus, these second scenes too are still as much creating a frame for the play as developing its action (it is easy to forget this while reading, or watching an informal production). The function of these second scenes (of which *Hippolytus* is an outstanding example) is specific to its context in each play, but frequently is to set up complex foreshadowing effects and to initiate themes which will be developed later.

In Euripides, the subtly combined sections of the prologue, with their juxtaposition of narrative and dialogue (or sometimes monody) are an extremely economic and effective way of transferring necessary background information and creating early and complex manipulation of audience expectation. Since Euripides so regularly framed his very diverse output by this kind of prologue, he must have found it a reliable technique which could be re-worked every time to serve the purposes of each play. The Euripidean prologue is a bridgehead into the rest of the play and a vital part of his strategy.[18]

8.3 Narrative at the end

At the other end a god's narrative, set among a 'flourish of formally persuasive gestures' (Dunn, 1996, 7) may or may not render the preceding action intelligible or satisfying – but at any rate, brings it to an end and marks it out (or, if there has also been a divine prologue-*rhêsis*, reconfirms it) as having taken place under divine auspices, however ambivalent and questionable. As with the prologue narratives, the concluding section of each play deserves the thoughtful analysis now projected by Dunn. As a repeated means of closure, Euripidean tactics here make an interesting comparison with the subtly open endings of Sophoclean drama.

The strategy of placing an authoritative narrative framework at beginning and/or end has a variety of consequences. (One result, in the case of divine prologues, is to leave the humans on their own in the middle, ironically ignorant of their predicted fates – the appearance of Lyssa and Iris in the middle of *Heracles* is the exception.) The major narratological advantage is that a new story has been very quickly established, leaving the large central space of the play proper available for the development of new narrative trajectories which can – theoretically – be cut off at any point by formal gestures of closure which, since they come from 'outside' do not have to be effected from within the plot (although it is only in three tragedies (*IT* 1437f., *Hel.* 1642f., *Or.* 1625f.) that the god actually puts an end to the action with the cry, 'Stop!'). Required to adhere to traditional characters and to retain at least elements of their traditional stories, Euripidean tragedies can by these means nonetheless launch off into new directions.

8.4 Narrator and narratee

Tragedy was by now a thoroughly established genre, operating within its own well-understood conventions.[19] Euripides could appeal – at least to a sophisticated section of his audience – with extreme ease: Burnett writes convincingly of 'a unanimous trained emotion and a wealth of predictable associations' (1971, 16). A brief mythical reference could swiftly evoke a complex story. Ancient audiences clearly appreciated new variations on familiar themes – and ancient tragedy was restricted to exactly this by the defining context of the festival (the interaction of Sophocles' *Electra* and *Philoctetes* plays with earlier play versions was considered earlier). Euripides wrote two *Hippolytus* plays and reworked the Orestes story three times in his last decade, with *Electra*, *Iphigeneia in Tauris* and *Orestes*. If the task was to provide continuity, but at the same time find new story lines and new strategies – or develop old ones – so that suspense and *ekplêxis* could be freshly aroused and if, as Winnington-Ingram remarked (1969, 36) 'audiences were perhaps tired of always knowing what would happen', Euripides fulfilled his brief.

His narrative innovations are bold, though not unprecedented. Plays may be set not in Greek cities but Egypt, the Black Sea, the ruins of Troy, the remote countryside or seaside: they may not begin until after the traditional story has ended (the 'aftermath' plays) – an obvious way of creating a new narrative. They may conflate traditional chronology: in *Heracles*, Heracles now kills his children *after* completing his labours; in *Phoenissae*, Jocasta and Oedipus are still alive when their sons kill each other. In *Electra*, Electra has married a farmer, puts a waterjug on her head and rejects the traditional tokens out of hand. In *Orestes*, Orestes' immediate fate hangs on the verdict of a democratic debate rather than an aristocratic assembly. *Helen* is founded on the variant myth that Helen never went to Troy. These 'alternative' plots at the most extreme can feel like 'deformations'.

The 'deformation' of the plot tends to liberate the characters from their traditional heroic roles, and they may manifest unheroic 'soft' qualities – cowardice, indecision. They may become further removed from their heroic background by anachronistically employing rhetoric with a strong contemporary ring. Called *tragikôtatos* for his psychologically acute portrayal of human suffering, Euripides nonetheless abruptly pulls his audience away from its involvement in humans suffering to the contemplation of those same humans engaged in forensic debate (the classic example of this is

Hecuba in the scene in *Tro.* 895-1059). All these features are productive of a certain 'polytonality' (see Whitman's quotation at the head of this chapter), a quality underlined at the level of narrative progression by the increasingly distinct juxtaposition of its various component parts – *prologoi*, *agônes*, *rhêseis*, *stichomythia* (whether in iambic trimeter or trochaic tetrameter), and lyric (see n. 3). The 'hard edges' of these elements (which Sophocles had 'softened' to create a more naturalistic flow) produce an effect of disjuncture, so that the plays in effect have not just one formal opening frame (the prologue *rhêsis)*, but include a succession of secondary reframings along the way – an effect which previously, only choral odes were likely to have created. Semi-comic realism gives way to lush lyric or to horrific murder. The juxtaposition of such elements, with their oddly sequential appeal first to narrative and then to authorial audience, seems deliberately disconcerting. Euripides can seem in almost Brechtian revolt against total submersion in a fictive world.

Doloi can reach new levels: the normal pattern of the 'lure-murder' (2.2.3) is subverted in both *Hecuba* and *Orestes*, where the intended victim is not, after all, killed. In *Orestes* false clues are scattered: Helen's death is plotted, she goes inside, and we hear the standard offstage cries, 'Menelaus, I'm dying' (1296 and 1301). The slave's extraordinary monody brings us to her death ('she's dying, she's dying', 1461) – but the chorus then disrupt his narrative by asking a distracting question. He returns to the point at 1490f. to describe Hermione rushing in 'upon the ground-falling murder of her mother', *epi phonôi chamaipetei matros*, where *epi* can ambiguously mean either 'on the point of' or 'directly after' (Arnott, 1973, 145). All this points to her death and yet the audience must wonder, how could Euripides deviate so far from Helen's traditional story? Finally we learn that she suddenly disappeared (1493f.). False clues are similarly scattered in *Electra* in the description of the murder of Aegisthus (774f.). The messenger mentions 'a trail of possible murder weapons' and at each mention the audience wonders if this will be the one to strike the fatal blow.

In the same way, existing stage conventions continue to be exploited to create a sense of *ta exaelpta*, 'the unexpected'. The chorus markedly fail to arrive in their expected position at *Iphigeneia in Tauris* 61-6; nor does the messenger at *Electra* 759: in *Orestes* the expected messenger is a Phrygian eunuch who *sings* (1369f.). The inexorable, obtrusive entry of the chorus, clearly unwanted at Orestes' sick-bed is mocked (*Or.* 140f.).

The extent to which any of these strategies suggest themselves to be metatheatre, parody, or the fruit of a retaliatory raid on comic territory must always be debatable, varying now as then from spectator to spectator and production to production.[20] In the particularly elusive case of parody, genre studies suggest that parody arises spontaneously from within an evolved form, and owes nothing to external influence.[21] Without adding to the debate, it is just descriptively useful, in the case of Euripides' narrative strategy, to say that where it is unpredictable and paratactic, there is a resemblance to comic strategy, and to note that some of his new plot lines resemble comedy's licence to create a new fictive world in which, on a temporary basis, almost anything can happen.

In the second half of Euripides' writing career, the narrative of his plays becomes increasingly complex, exhibiting chains of incident turning on chance which are particularly well-suited to theatrical exploitation for their temporary effects of emotion and suspense. Burnett's phrase 'mixed and multiple reversal' is useful shorthand for plays containing some or all of the following elements:

characters in ignorance attempting to murder their kin
characters threatened with imminent death
characters crippled with indecision
characters helplessly longing for news or rescue
characters overwhelmed with joy or grief
characters recognising their kin after an extended recognition sequence
characters concocting and pursuing a plan of revenge or escape

The first six of these tropes form part of complex recognition. None of them are new in themselves: they can be traced back to the *Odyssey* and are found already in tragedy. New, however, to tragedy is the multiplication of characters involved and the plethora of such motifs, each leading to reversal, within each play.

Beside this fecundity, Sophocles' loops fade into invisibility. Both poets, however, seem to reflect increasing pressure to create complexity and surprise within the limits of a single play, and do so by engaging both theoretical aspects of the audience: while the narrative audience shares the stage figures' shifting emotions and is embroiled in the suspense of the moment, the authorial audience is granted the pleasurable awareness of the play's theatricality and (particularly in the case of Euripides), is engaged in working out how this particular narrative can ultimately achieve conformity with tradition.

However, the differences are also great. Sophocles' temporary alternative outcomes, I suggested, acted largely as an ironic foil to reinforce the ultimate validity and authority of tradition. In Euripides' non-tragic plays, the twists and turns have broken free and can be exploited in a number of new ways.

The following chapter looks at the structure and function of Euripidean recognition sequences, discussing first the general significance of recognition in all narrative. It then contrasts the treatment of recognition in *Iphigeneia in Tauris* and *Helen*.

9

Recognition

Yes, there's a god at work in recognition (*theos gar kai to gignôskein philous*).
Euripides, *Helen* 560

Slow, complex recognition began with the second half of the *Odyssey*. Long after his return to Ithaca, Odysseus avoided recognition not only by enemies but also by loyally-waiting family and supporters. Homer's narrative lingers on the prolonged ignorance of those waiting, exploring their grief, loyalty and helplessness and even their ineffectual attempts to resolve the situation alone. Strong effects of irony are developed: the disguised hero encounters those who wait for him and holds lying discourse with them, talking of himself as dead or fantastically involved elsewhere. There is constant suspense: the danger of premature recognition always looms, which would abort Odysseus' plans. But frequently Homer's narrative delays recognition without clear motivation and for no better reason, one might think, than to delight in its own exuberant subterfuges.

This epic material was a gift that lay waiting for transformation into drama. Delay is not a particular feature of the first surviving tragic recognition, *Choephoroe* 165ff.,[1] but later tragedies drew on the greater complexity of the epic model, giving the key role to the waiting heroine and making the recognition process a more central element.

Recognition, whether of kin, god, or more abstract or inward forms of knowledge,[2] is present in all narrative, reflecting its essential concern for knowledge. Its processes operate like those of narrative itself: by initial hiding and concealing, by making use of ignorance, lies, secrets, disguise and delay to create effects of irony, pathos, suspense and shock which ultimately give way to profound (or less than profound) satisfaction when recognition is ultimately achieved.[3] Fictional characters struggling towards recognition mimic the hermeneutic activity of the external audience or reader; re-cognition, *ana-gnôrisis*, is etymologically inseparable from the activity of the reader, the *ana-gnôstês*. Tragic recognition finally occurs in exciting minutes of present stage time, but the figure of 'knowledge recovered' necessarily includes the movement back towards lost beginnings – for which the great analepsis triggered by Eurycleia's recognition of Odysseus' scar (*Od.* 19.392-466) provides an epic example – as well as forward towards fresh narrative possibilities.[4] In this way, recognition mirrors the analepsis and prolepsis inscribed within narrative. Recognition is a model or microcosm of the narrative process itself.

Aristotle grasped the centrality of recognition in narrative, understanding its importance for his ideas both of plot and of mimesis,[5] and considering both emotional impact (*Poetics* 1452b) and logical probability (1454d12). We may suppose that ordinary theatre-goers as well as philosophers had already been discussing the subject: elaborate recognition sequences presuppose an audience attuned to appreciate variation on the familiar patterns of this theme.[6]

In an important article, which contributes to and develops Aristotle's views on plot, A.J. Greimas and J. Courtés (1976) located four positions which between them, they claim, cover the entire range of cognitive possibilities in all narrative. The fact that they are strikingly relevant to tragic recognition demonstrates again the way that recognition functions as a model for the entire narrative process. The four abstract positions (with changed numbering) are:

1. Secret (existing + not appearing)
2. False (not existing + not appearing)
3. Delusion/lie (not existing + appearing)
4. True (existing + appearing)

The relationship between these positions can be expressed diagrammatically in a figure called the veridictory square:

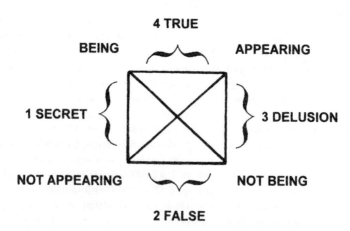

The movement between the different positions marked on the veridictory square is said to cause a release of 'transformative power': news of death, for example, moves the narrative into lament, while the most climactic transformation comes with final recognition.[7]

The scheme is of course too simple to convey the ambiguities of actual dramatic situations. Furthermore, the question of whose cognition is at issue is not addressed – whether that of protagonist, of another stage figure or of audience. Nonetheless, movement around the positions helps show how a simple narrative may achieve complexity and stature, accruing its own history as it goes. It shows how temporary possibilities, narrative loops, can be created. The scheme springs to life if it is read from the point of view of protagonist seeking kin, as it shows the underlying position at any point in a complex recognition sequence.

Recognition between kin occurs in many forms in Euripidean narrative.[8] We are concerned here, however, with a particular formal type which consists of a scene or sequence of scenes presenting two relatives through speech recognising one another:[9] *Electra, Iphigeneia in Tauris, Helen* and *Ion*. In the first three, recognition is followed by plots of revenge or escape whereas in *Ion* recognition is set up in the prologue to be the goal of the entire action and, as the play progresses, a series of partial, false or incomplete recognitions leads to the final one.[10]

Electra, Iphigeneia in Tauris, Helen and *Ion* may all be roughly mapped according to Greimas and Courtés' scheme. The desired brother/husband/son, designated *philos*, is first merely absent (position 1, all plays). Then a report may bring news of his supposed death (position 2, all plays except *Electra*).[11] The two meet, but at first the true identity of the *philos* is concealed (position 3, all plays). The concealment may be either voluntary or involuntary, providing opportunities for marked irony and added complexity if both characters conceal their identity. Either character may 'split' into two, talking of themselves in the third person, but notwithstanding, through sympathetic identification, a kind of intuitive recognition may operate between the characters. This occurs despite the fact that during the same phase murder in ignorance may be attempted, giving rise to the possibility that final recognition will be that of the *philos* dead (*Iphigeneia, Ion*). Finally, full recognition takes place (position 4), its establishment sometimes hindered by the very success of the previous deception.

In all plays recognition is made dependent upon the tritagonist (third actor), thus increasing the variety of verbal exchange and possible reaction: the Old Man in *Electra*, Pylades with his letter in *Iphigeneia in Tauris*, the messenger with news of the phantom in Helen, the Pythia with her cradle in *Ion*. Recognition is marked by a duet in *Iphigeneia, Helen* and *Ion*, and by a brief dochmiac ode from the chorus in *Electra*. Once recognition has been accomplished the scheme is complete, and so the narrative moves either towards closure (*Ion*) or a fresh one is begun (*Electra, Iphigeneia in Tauris, Helen.*)

Cave (1990, 224f.) proposes two essential types of recognition in Western literature, both of which occur in ancient tragedy: the Odyssean, which results in the recovery of wife and property, and the Oedipal, resulting in violent transgression of kinship lines, and loss of kingship. Both types of recognition are predicated on severance from origins but, whereas Odysseus always knows who he is, Oedipus has lost the knowledge of his own identity, creating the conditions for profound inadvertent transgression. In Cave's terminology, *Electra, Iphigeneia in Tauris* and *Helen* are Odyssean (in their recognition, as in other ways), while *Ion* incorporates the Oedipal into the Odyssean.

Chance

In these four plays Euripides uses recognition to explore his fascination with the operation of chance and contingency. Frequently he begins by setting heroines in the most remote and helpless situations over which they have little or no control (Electra married and in a cottage on the frontier, Iphigeneia and Helen marooned on the unpredictable edge of the world). Reintegration to a life where 'normal rules' of society and society's logic might apply can be achieved only after identification of the *philos* (who is himself in some marginal condition), and Euripides turns the phases by which this comes about with further examples of the operation of the contingent. Chance manifests itself variously. In *Iphigeneia in Tauris* it is most intricately structured with Pylades' apparently irrelevant anxiety about fulfilling his oath (for Aristotle's admiration of this see *Poet.* 1455a11), whereas in *Helen* there is an abandonment of plausible development – the premise of the action is, after all, an *adunaton*, an impossibility – and benign chance operates in the grossest, almost shockingly careless way, exemplified by the sudden disappearance of the phantom Helen.

Chance and tokens

Cave (1990, 242ff.) makes a strong claim for the significance of tokens. He argues that they function like the signs by which a skilled hunter reads the narrative of a beast's passage (by footprints, droppings, broken twigs, etc.), and also like the signs used by a seer (bird flight, inspection of animal entrails, etc): the hunter reconstructs an analeptic narrative, the diviner a proleptic one. The skills of both are opposed to those of the mathematician or logician because they use inductive rather than deductive reasoning and require 'an unquantifiable internalised ability to select significant detail on the margins of perception and make capital out of *chance* occurrences' (Cave, 251; my emphasis). Such skills, he argues, are the property of *mêtis*, the cunning intelligence of the individual struggling with his environment.

Cave's account accords well with Aeschylus' *Choephoroe* 164-245, a recognition focussed entirely around tokens. In stichomythia with the chorus, Electra first finds the lock of hair, which arouses hesitant hopes. Can it be a sign of Orestes? Her hesitant *mêtis* is shown clearly in operation in the *rhêsis* 183-211 (she cannot quite exclude the possibility that Clytemnestra left the lock). Then she finds and analyses Orestes' footprints, setting her feet in his tracks and so so tracing him to his hiding-place. Orestes then confirms his identity in two ways: by matching the lock to his own hair and hers, and by showing Electra a piece of tapestry she once wove for him. Electra explodes with joy. Solmsen (1967) has well analysed the emotional and dramatic tensions of this recognition which uses tokens in two ways, first for 'tracking' and then for proof.

Composing some fifty years later for a more sophisticated audience, Euripides' response to the token tradition is highly varied and deserves careful study. Recognition-by-tokens can be the crux of the recognition process but it can also be emblematic of the conflict between one kind of reasoning and another. The scene of *Electra*, in which the heroine rejects recognition-by-tokens in advance and subjects the Old Man's hopes to withering logic seems a caricature of the disapproving view Aristotle was to adopt on the subject.[12] In her insistence on the implausibility of traditional tokens as proof Electra doubtless mirrors some contemporary debate.[13] As critics note, however, her rigidly logical mind-set is implicitly criticised: the narrative ironically shows that the Old Man, employing his *mêtis*, did after all make correct inferences. Furthermore, the clinching proof of Orestes' identity is yet another traditional, rationally inconclusive token, the scar on his forehead.

Elsewhere, Euripides certainly understood that little is more engrossing to an audience than following the *mêtis* of a character whose future, like that of Odysseus, entirely depends on their precarious ability to read signs, to grapple with chance. In *Ion*, tokens have great ritual and civic as well as the usual hereditary significance. Hidden in the Long Rocks, the cradle and its tokens have their own history, which repeats that of the Earth Born Erechthid family: they confirm not only individual identity (Ion) but a birthright (Ion, king of Athens). Their state of preservation is miraculous (1435-6). However, the narrative employs them in a new way (as if making the participants play a new game with an old set of cards). The cradle is produced at a moment of crisis when both parties are still in ignorance of the other's identity and Ion is threatening to kill his mother. Creusa instantly recognises it (1398f.), but her approaches to Ion are repelled with the revulsion he earlier accorded Xuthus. Ion then uses the individual tokens in the cradle as a test of Creusa's claim to be his mother: she must correctly list each item from memory – whereupon Ion holds it up to the audience.

Helen avoids tokens altogether,[14] but tokens are included in *Iphigeneia in Tauris* and will be discussed later.

Recognition of kin – on which the social system is based – is precarious: get it wrong, and the possibility of catastrophic transgression rears its head, a danger both threatened and actual in tragedy. The un-tragic Odyssean recognitions in these plays have been anachronistically designated 'melodramatic' or 'romantic'– pejorative terms in comparison with recognition of the Oedipal kind. Such labelling obscures Euripides' continuing investment in epic narrative patterns and the ongoing project of both epic and tragic poets to portray humans in crisis, beset by ignorance, deceit and unpredictable gods – forced to grapple with the vagaries of chance.

The phases of Euripidean recognition are developed in a loosely predictable sequence of scenes, using narrative elements which can be seen schematically as exploitations of the various phases of the veridictory square. This framework allows comparisons to be made in the treatment of recognition. Two plays are discussed here, whose similarities have often been noted (see, e.g. Platnauer, 1938, xv-xvi, Lattimore, 1973, 3-5), but which exhibit marked differences in their treatment of recognition, especially when analysed in the light of Greimas and Courtés' scheme. *Iphigeneia in Tauris* contains a long, intense, familial recognition which uses every potential element of the scheme, while *Helen* avoids or confounds most of them, creating a new recognition which lightly explores the problems not only of recognition but of cognition itself.

Both plays are followed under similar headings up to the point when the narrative of recognition gives way to a narrative of escape.

9.1 *Iphigeneia in Tauris*

Opening (1-66)

Iphigeneia presents a new story in her opening narrative. For the purposes of comparison with *Helen*, I note here only that, despite narrative novelty, she makes her *captatio* to the audience as a conventional family daughter.

Presentation of philos (with friend, 67-123)

The simplest strategy is to present the heroine's *philos* separately in the second prologue scene: thus Orestes and Pylades here (just as in *El.* 82-112). The technique of making the audience momentarily expect the chorus (61ff.) adds immediately to the sense of the random. Apart from this feature, however, the interplay of Orestes' anxiety and Pylades' encouragement is as conventional as the presentation of Iphigeneia.

Supposed death of philos (kommos with chorus, 123-235)[15]

The *philos*' supposed death is a frequent feature of complex recognition and, if this false belief is sustained right up to final recognition, a great transformative movement from death to life takes place (position 2 to 4 on the scheme), creating moments of profound cognitive amazement on the stage and intense audience involvement.[16] Thus in *Ion*, Creusa has come to believe that her son has died, so that the eventual opening of the cradle with its tokens symbolises both the opening of a dead child's coffin and the child's miraculous resurrection as a beautiful youth. The language conflates these ideas (1440-4):

> Creusa: I hold you in my arms, you whom I thought to dwell below the earth with Persephone.
> Ion: Yes, and in your arms I am made visible, dead and not dead.

The imagery of rebirth is then applied to the royal house when Creusa says, 'Erechtheus is grown young again, the earth-born house no longer looks upon darkness but looks up to the rays of the sun' (1465-7).

Given the intense transformative power of a staged 'resurrection', it is interesting that both *Iphigeneia in Tauris* and *Helen* initially invite, but then avoid, an *anodos*-type recognition. Both establish the *philos'* supposed death (Iphigeneia narrates her dream which indicates, as she thinks, the death of Orestes (42ff.) while Helen hears from Teucer that Menelaus is 'spoken of as dead throughout Greece', 132). However, in both plays the false news is overtly 'corrected' before recognition itself takes place. Iphigeneia learns from the disguised Orestes that her brother is still alive at 569 (although the recognition itself does not take place until 827) while Helen, taking the chorus' advice, finds out from Theonoe that Menelaus is alive and in the vicinity at 528f. (final recognition not until 622). It is interesting that Orestes' interjection when Iphigeneia at last gives her name expresses little more than extreme surprise: 'Alive? Where is she? Has she died and come back again?' *katthanous' hêkei palin*? (*IT* 772).[17]

Why does Euripides turn the narrative in this evasive, less than profound way, engaging it with death only to disengage it again? Certainly, as narrative loop rather than narrative event, the supposed death of the *philos* provides temporary occasion for tragic lament and (in the case of *Iphigeneia* dramatised ritual action). It also provides a movement which aligns with both plays' overall narrative trajectories away from grief and despair (both have family and Trojan War deaths as their background) into a world of renewed life and positive action. Behind this may well stand the influence of Homer and his elaborate exploitation of delayed recognition in the *Odyssey*.

Both *kommoi*, whose emotional burden the audience know to be falsely based, are marked out as operatic events (as often in Euripides) with self-reference to their musical activity (*IT* 143-6, 179-85; Helen's *prooimion* invokes the Sirens and Persephone and the chorus' response alludes at length to the sound of her voice, *Hel.* 167-78, 184-90); however, in Iphigeneia's case what she sings is a true lament, focussed on Orestes, the 'fact' of his death, and her plight as chief mourner: note *thrênos* (144, 182); the chorus make an appropriate antiphonal response (*antipsalmous ôidas*, 179); Orestes is addressed directly (170-7) and receives ritual offerings

(159-6). She develops her own woes (203-28), but explicitly draws a line under them: 'Now let me forget that and weep for my brother dead in Argos' (229-30). Her significant last word is 'Orestes'.[18]

Course of recognition (467-642)

Iphigeneia in Tauris contains the fullest extant recognition. All possible cognitive positions from Greimas and Courtés' scheme are present, clustered together into the first 430 verses of the great second episode. The *philoi* start at the greatest possible level of ignorance, each initially believing the other dead and, moreover, concealing their own identity (position 2). However, Iphigeneia soon discovers that her *philos* lives (position 3). The potential murder of the *philos* is a theme present from the start, partly averted (578-96) then restored and lengthily developed (579-718), All this occurs in dialogue between brother and sister, uninterrupted by the chorus. In this emphatically family play, Pylades is made 'virtual' kin as well in various ways – by Iphigeneia's misidentification of him as Orestes' brother, by his forthcoming marriage to Electra, and by his imagined role of supervising Orestes' tomb in Argos. The participants receive no outside assistance or hindrance, whether human or divine. Recognition is put into the realm of chance in a particularly heightened, verbal way. For the audience, it is like observing a hunt-the-thimble game which the players do not quite know they are playing: the characters are sometimes 'warmer', sometimes 'colder': only the audience know that recognition is the issue. Under these conditions, chance words are fate, random emotional response is destiny. Some details of this phase deserve noting:

First reactions

Euripides likes to make an ironic play with the first reactions of kin meeting each other as *xenoi*, strangers. At one pole, instinctive admiring sympathy triggers a flow of information about the past which gradually paves the way to recognition, while the audience still enjoys its discrepant awareness and the unconscious ironies of the speakers.[19] Iphigeneia's first sight of her Greek victims, whom she takes initially for siblings, immediately evokes thoughts of their family, and especially a possible sister, 'deprived of such brothers' (472f.). Sisterly sympathy continues to release information. Later, when Orestes chooses to save Pylades' life in preference to his own, Iphigeneia cries admiringly, 'I pray that the one man left of my family may be like you – for I too have a brother' (611). The feature gets reversed: on hearing how his corpse will be disposed, Orestes says, 'Alas, if only my sister's hands could wrap my body' (627), referring to Electra in Argos – not the unknown sister before him who now offers to perform such rites.

Potential killing of the philos[20]

'Sacrificial' kin-murder is a continuous thread of the history of the Pelopid house and so very appositely fills the 'potential murder' slot in the recognition process here. Iphigeneia is priestess of an Artemis cult in which all foreigners are sacrificed. In preparing the victim she is the 'virtual' murderess, and in doing so now for the 'two Greeks', she would coincidentally take revenge on the entire Greek race which agreed her sacrifice long ago: the false dream-news that Orestes is dead leaves no avenger but herself (an idea perhaps taken from Sophocles' *Electra*). This idea is developed in the soliloquy before the recognition scene (342-91, see esp. 348-50). In the recognition scene itself, kin-murder is a running thread and delays the outcome, since his future sacrifice (as he believes) keeps Orestes silent about himself (502, 504). Iphigeneia offers Orestes the chance of life if he takes her letter, but Orestes transfers the privilege to Pylades. Arrangements for burial ritual are explored at length: Iphigeneia offers to tend his grave; Pylades agrees to build his tomb in Argos.

The nobility of all three characters is amply displayed and (apart from elegant interplay with the traditional myth) seems to be a major function of this theme. Neither authorial nor narrative audience are likely to fear that fratricide is a real danger. This is due in part to the total absence of other temple authorities to force her to it (the only staged Taurian to date is a humble cowherd). Iphigeneia herself seems to have total discretion as to her victims. Even more, her established warm heart and unshaken piety[21] seem already to have rendered her psychologically incapable. If Orestes' earlier supposed death created ironic pathos rather than intense tragic grief, his possible murder by his sister creates only temporary and unrealisable possibilities rather than real suspense. The stage figures' insistent criticism of Artemis and Apollo (569-75, 711-15) keep reminding the audience that these gods have different fates in store for their human protégés. The major function of the narrative of Orestes' potential death is – like Odysseus' deceitful narratives in the *Odyssey* – to create a delay in the course of recognition.

Final recognition

This is achieved by complex use of Iphigeneia's letter. The letter, which initially raises audience hopes, then only confirms their doubts when Orestes transfers the *sôtêria* it offers to Pylades. Orestes is now again set on a death and if recognition looks a hair's breadth away, it seems again likely to be Oedipal rather than Odyssean.

The letter spawns the oath which adds nothing. Neither does Pylades' legal quibble that, if the letter were lost at sea, the oath could not be considered binding. Yet (mixed metaphors permitted) it is by logically pursuing the details of the problem created by the letter down this apparently blind alley that recognition finally comes about. When Iphigeneia decides to resolve Pylades' anxiety by reading out the letter (so that he can memorise its contents) what was secret is immediately revealed (770-1), 'Tell Orestes, Agamemnon's son that Iphigeneia, sacrificed at Aulis sends this – the living Iphigeneia'. Then Pylades completes the mission he is under oath to do: he hands the letter to Orestes.

Like the moment when Sophocles' Electra puts down the urn or Admetus puts his hand on Alcestis' wrist in the bridegroom's gesture,[22] the act of delivery marks a moment of deep satisfaction and rest for the audience, who have followed the complex manoeuvres of recognition through to the end. The binding power of the oath, which previously seemed irrelevant, now reveals a function as it underlines the authority of the gesture, making it an even more potent symbol for the transformation of identities taking place below the level of words.

Tokens (808-26)

To the extent that the letter contained proof of Iphigeneia's identity it too operated as an unusual token. More traditional tokens are now used to prove Orestes' identity and, like *Ion*, they function as a memory test – in fact they have no existence as stage props, only as part of the shared memories of the participants. Iphigeneia asks for evidence of identity (*tekmêria*) and Orestes tells her to ask questions but she (perhaps out of courtesy, as Platnauer suggests) prefers the passive role of 'learning'. This complex introductory frame suggests that Orestes might employ a range of quite new proofs, but the first three items – ritual objects and tapestry – seem wholly conventional.

The precariousness of recognition is interestingly cast here. Proof depends entirely on Orestes' ability to find in his memory items which will match whatever may be stored in Iphigeneia's memory. The *mêtis* at work takes the form of correct guessing. Euripides is careful to show Orestes (a baby when Iphigeneia disappeared) referring not to what he himself knows, but what his older sister Electra has told him. Items are carefully pegged to important phases in their family history: the tapestry woven by Iphigeneia which showed the Golden Lamb and the sun turning back; the lustral water her mother sent for her wedding to Achilles; the lock of hair she sent back from Aulis for her mother to put on her empty tomb. These three items are unadventurous, referring to segments of Iphigeneia's public history. A false Orestes could safely invent them. Only the final item does Orestes claim to have seen for himself: Pelops' spear, inexplicably kept in Iphigeneia's bedroom: not only a prime symbol of the family's troubled history but also just the thing a small boy wandering over his parents' palace would have noted. This public token kept in a private place is a genuine secret (*kekrummenên*, last word, 826), now brought to light and completing recognition.

Recognition duet (827-99; see n. 4)

The earlier phases of recognition turned on chance, *tuchê*, and the characters used much *tuchê* language (both noun and verb).[23] Now *tuchê* language is the pivot on which the duet moves from consideration of past and present to the future, and into the play's second half. Iphigeneia calls herself fortunate (*eutuchousa*, 837) and Orestes wishes that they may always be so (*eutuchoimen*, 841). Then he distinguishes their *tuchê*: they are fortunate in birth, but unfortunate in incident (*eutuchoumen ... dustuchês*, 850-1); once Agamemnon all but sacrificed Iphigeneia, now Iphigeneia has all but sacrificed Orestes. Iphigeneia sings (870-4): 'By how slender a thread you escaped unholy destruction, from being murdered at my hands! On these terms, what ending can we expect? What will *tuchê* bring now?' Recognition is completed and the play moves into the narrative of escape.

*

No analyst could fail to admire the geometrically elegant recognition phases of *Iphigeneia in Tauris*, whose themes of suffering and human sacrifice dovetail so intricately with the background myth. All the same, to modern tastes (if not to Aristotle or Goethe), the thin setting deprives the situation of any convincing sense of danger, while the characters fail to develop attributes more complex than the virtues of their respective sexes, a feature enjoined on them by the complex outer narrative, which has to show brother and sister at last 'redeemed' by right action. Consequently the moral choices they make are predictable.

Lacking the profound depths of Oedipal recognition, the recognition of *Iphigeneia* also lacks the capacity to arouse deep aesthetic surprise. However intricate its structure and cleverly delayed its dénouement, it ultimately has no greater function than the prototype tragic recognition of *Choephoroe*; that is, to reunite kin who will then go on to defeat the enemy. The emotions aroused in the audience by the temporary suggestion that Orestes is dead or that Iphigeneia will kill him seem trivial indeed compared with the profounder ironies to be found in Sophocles' loops. The original novelty of this play and of the recognition sequence within it – despite the latter's dazzling display of the operation of chance – cannot now prevent the feeling that as a narrative structure the play founders in its own ingenuity.

9.2 *Helen*

In *Helen* the versatile Euripides has reworked much similar material to very different effect.

Opening

As in *Iphigeneia*, protagonist delivers prologue-*rhêsis* setting out the new story (*IT* 1-66: *Hel.* 1-67). However, her *captatio benevolentiae* takes a very different form. Helen establishes a startlingly new *persona* for herself[24] which expunges the usual Helen's wicked nature. Her narrative exonerates her from all blame for the Trojan War.

This is a particularly outrageous move on Euripides' part (his own *palinode*?), since his stage figures elsewhere regularly reflect with hatred on Helen's guilt.[25] Helen is now virtuous – but this does not exhaust her qualities. When she casts doubts on the Zeus-as-a-swan tradition of her paternity (17-22, and 227-29 if these lines should not be excised), she shows a delicate scepticism about her own ontological status. Engaging in itself, her doubt undermines the very myth and mythical figures embodied in the play and sheds a mocking light over the future warped process of recognition, encouraging the audience to feel a slightly detached amusement. However much re-characterised as a faithful Penelope, the new Helen (a unique character in ancient tragedy) is as much embodiment of paradox as credible stage figure. The phases leading up to recognition are also shaped to explore paradox.

The audience may sense the operation upon themselves of the protagonist's *acting* to achieve such a bold *captatio*. Any adoption of a new *persona* by a stage figure gives pleasure to both narrative and authorial audience by its manifest display of acting, and this can achieve a number of effects. Ironic gaps between impersonator and impersonated may emerge – as here, with great complexity, between the two Helens – productive, in this case, of humour, some bitterness, and intellectual entertainment. Onstage disguise tends to produce a (manic) surplus of performative energy,[26] highlighting the actor as actor and possibly creating a locus for questioning traditional ideologies:[27] here, contemporary debate about the conflict of appearance and reality, reputation and truth[28] finds dramatic embodiment in the paradoxical Helen. Throughout the recognition sequence, Helen's problematic existential status and her acting skills – inseparable features – are foregrounded to great ironic effect. Her acting is convincing: she acts with Teucer in the second prologue scene to stay alive (and acts again to achieve the escape); but when, on first meeting Menelaus, she stops acting, the result is disastrous: she is dogged throughout the first half of the play by her *alter ego* the phantom-Helen, from whose wicked reputation she can hardly free herself.

Helen is a figure of metatheatrical and epistemological novelty and delight. She also undeniably raises psychological questions in being so radically 'split'. Splitting is a consistent minor feature in recognition: characters already afflicted by huge spatial and temporal separations with plausible motivation regularly create further impediments to recognition by evading direct answers to direct questions and denying their own identity, in a sense reinforcing at the human level the divine substitutions which have already split them once.[29] Thus Iphigeneia says of herself that she died in Greece long ago (541), and Orestes too, reluctant to give any information to a supposed enemy, refuses to give his own name: 'you'd be right to call me Unfortunate' (*Dustuchês*) is as far as he will go; 'you will sacrifice my body, not my name' (500, 504).[30] He talks of himself in the third person as 'Agamemnon's son' (556, 558, 560). Helen does the same with Teucer. But Helen is far more radically 'split'. Other characters temporarily project a false *persona* until recognition restores their original unity of identity. Helen, by contrast, seeks recognition as a means of deleting her *alter ego*.

In Kleinian theory the individual responds to experience by alternate processes either of integration or of splitting, which involves projection. These continuous activities (which may be normal or otherwise) are presumably creatively at work in poets' imaginations and, while the genesis of the split Helen in Euripides' mind is unknowable, it may be connected with psychological reactions in Athens following the devastation at Syracuse. The innocent Helen does seem to be a feverish projection created out of some extreme pain, a figure 'begotten by Despair/ Upon Impossibility'.[31] The effect of a newly-innocent Helen on the audience is also unknowable but, arguably, in accepting the fantastic premise of Helen, Euripides creates for them a temporary space in which losses may be disowned and guilt abandoned. The relief is only partial, however: not only because the play shows that the projected Helen can barely sustain her own innocence, but also because her innocence itself involves further pain – the abandonment of the idea that the Trojan War had any meaningful, let alone heroic, purpose.

Presentation of philos-substitute

The narrative development here is more complex than in the *Iphigeneia* because a different exploration is under way. By giving Helen an exact double, 'a breathing likeness composed of air' (34), Euripides deliberately sets up a situation in which recognition has become a logical impossibility. The entry that now takes place encourages the audience to enjoy the prospect of this impasse. As if rethinking and giving a new, separate role to the *philos*' traditional companion, the second prologue unexpectedly introduces a new Greek hero. Teucer, wandering the sea from Troy, is a doublet for Menelaus[32] like Helen's phantom double and, as Segal (1971, 563) understood, Euripides uses him to demonstrate the dangers and difficulties that arise when a Greek *sees* Helen, the most hated woman in the world, giving Teucer the same visual terminology later used by Menelaus: Helen is an *opsis* (vision/apparition, 72: 557); the likeness between the two 'Helens' is extreme (74: 669).

Teucer encourages the audience to imagine the greater problems that lie ahead in gaining recognition from Menelaus. Now, for example, Helen can deflect Teucer's murderous inclinations (71-7) by concealing her identity and talking of herself in the third person (79, 99, 115, 117, 123). But her ultimate goal is return to Sparta having achieved, not avoided recognition and, given her evil reputation, she cannot do this without Menelaus' help (277f.). What *captatio* will work on Menelaus, who has been living in unquestioning daily contact with the phantom for the last seven years (112, 116)? Helen begins to probe the problematic evidence of 'sight' and 'eyes' in the question-and-answer stichomythia of 117-22 (Dale would delete 121-2 with Ribbeck), asking if Teucer's 'seeing' of 'Helen' were not 'an imagining (*dokêsis*) from the gods' (119): later she will unsuccessfully plead with Menelaus to stop imagining, and place his trust in the evidence of his eyes (118, 122: compare 576, 578, 580). But the premise of *Helen* is that visual evidence can provide no proof.

Menelaus' own entry is delayed until the stage has been emptied, giving him a separate, prominent introduction. The great hero of Troy (as he insists) is, ludicrously, almost naked as he delivers a second prologue speech (386-436) and he is further 'publicly' humiliated in his encounter with the Old Woman.[33] Menelaus' problem with his identity is a minor version of Helen's: he is not projecting a false *persona* to save his skin (although this will be required of him for escape) but unsuccessfully seeking to establish that he is who he says he is – despite appearances to the contrary. From the Old Woman he gets perplexing news of Helen which forms the basis of a further monologue, 483-514. As in the scene with Teucer, the difficulties of recognition – which in this play most especially require logically disposing of events which defy logic – are again highlighted. His concluding rationalisations (497-9) look disastrous for recognition, if he will indeed resolve his confusion by the partly logical belief that there could be two Helens, Zeuses, Spartas and Troys.

Supposed death of philos (kommos, 167ff.)

This heading is not so appropriate for *Helen*. Helen has received many more items of bad news than Iphigeneia and sings a lament both more general and more self-centred – and certainly far less focused on her *philos*. Mention of Menelaus' supposed death is merely sandwiched between those of Leda and of her brothers (200-11). The second strophe adopts a general lyric theme, the search for the *archê kakôn* (prime cause of suffering), and locates it in the hand that felled the pine for Paris' ship (like the Nurse at *Med.* 3-4). A certain sense of irony is maybe created here in the authorial audience, given that in other tragic lyrics Helen is herself the *archê kakôn* (a tradition which begins at *Ag.* 681ff.). She blames 'deceitful, murderous' Aphrodite and Hera, ending 'my good name by the streams of Simois has an empty reputation'.

The tone of the lament has been interpreted very variously, from Dale

(76), who comments that the 'words must not be expected to bear too close a scrutiny of their meaning' to those who read the play and this lyric as a tragic comment on the disastrous Sicilian Expedition (e.g. Podlecki) and emphasise its pacifist character. The fantastic remoteness of the setting, fantastic plot and fantastic nature of its central figure, as well as the early guarantee of a happy outcome (56-9) seem to debar a strongly serious tone at any point. If there is pain, it is muffled by distance, as a comparison with the extreme immediacy of *Trojan Women* shows.

The lyric's content is recycled in Helen's following speech (255-305) which develops cogent arguments to show why her own misfortunes are unparalleled. Menelaus' death is referred to again (277-9, 287-92) not to explore grief but the difficulties thereby created for herself. Emphasis is placed on the fact that her evil reputation is undeserved (270, 280-1), her beauty a curse rather than the blessing it should be (261ff., 304-5). Is it possible (especially if 299-302 are retained), to find here echoes of the specious Helen who speaks at *Troades* 914ff.: *qui s'excuse s'accuse*? In this metatheatrical play the effect will depend on the acting.[34] The speech explores her situation for our metaphysical pleasure, not to move us or present her in any profound way as a victim.

Course of recognition (541-96)

The first reactions of Helen and Menelaus on meeting are at the opposite pole to those of Iphigeneia and Orestes. Helen and Menelaus' initial encounter (like the earlier one with Teucer) startles both of them: Helen fears that Menelaus, looking wild and ugly, has been sent by Theoclymenus (*Hel.* 541), while Menelaus is utterly astonished (549) – an emotion which turns to revulsion when Helen tries to touch him (567).[35] Omitting the features from the scheme which extended this phase of *Iphigeneia*, the scene quickly comes to an end. Recognition *fails* and produces a new trope, non-recognition: a unique coup towards which Euripides was demonstrably working from the first. The narrative disintegrates, leaving the audience with no idea what will happen next. The religious frame of *Iphigeneia* had created a discrepant awareness between stage figures and audience so that audience never doubted that recognition would ultimately come about; the obvious manifestation of a developing recognition sequence added to that certainty. Here, the vaguer religious framework, though still pointing to some positive outcome, leaves the audience at this point no wiser than those on stage.

Final recognition and new extension: the Slave (597-750)

Into the impasse he has created, Euripides sends the Slave-messenger, a figure who essentially takes over the recognition and is then single-handedly responsible for an extra development arising from it which cannot be plotted on Greimas and Courtés' scheme and is not part of the subsequent 'escape' narrative. This gives his character and his words a unique significance.[36]

The Slave's arrival is grossly fortuitous.[37] As already noted, chance in this play is quite differently cast from the carefully developed, painstaking progression of contingent detail in *IT*.[38] The Slave reports that the phantom Helen has just disappeared with explanatory parting words (608-15). It came from Zeus and has now gone, since 'it had stayed on earth the length of time appointed by fate. Helen herself is innocent.' This report, instantly and miraculously removing all obstacles to recognition, almost entirely deflates the transformative power of the moment and sidelines hero and heroine, who are both as surprised as the audience.

The emotions springing from traditional recognition continue to be avoided. Instead of the expected joyful duet, the Slave, still centre stage, sets eyes on the onstage Helen for the first time, and now disbelieves his own message (thinking that the phantom Helen was merely lying, and has in mockery transported herself here from the cave). The *sight* of Helen continues to confuse and a new, false recognition temporarily endangers the anticipated true one, again diverting attention from husband and wife.

Recognition duet (625-97)

The duet, in *Iphigeneia* a bridge between the play's two halves, here moves the narrative back, not forward. It begins with joy and ends in renewed expressions of grief.[39] Menelaus recalls the happy occasion of their marriage (637f.) and both at first feel intervening suffering can be discounted (644-9). But the past is not so easily disposed of: Menelaus asks about the circumstances under which Helen left Troy and she sinks into incoherent lament (661-2), recalling the details of her wretched history.

The Slave now takes the initiative again, wanting to understand what has happened. To critical bafflement,[40] he dominates the stage for another fifty-seven lines before the narrative turns to escape (gradually achieved in the subtly-characterised dialogue, 761ff.). He delivers two more speeches which use the completed recognition as the basis for further reflections. In both speeches the Slave reflects on the problem of knowledge, thus, as Zuntz (1960) noted, paving the way to the central entry of Theonoe (865ff.), who is 'knowledge personified'.[41] Both slave and priestess at their different levels introduce a moral tone into the play. In Zuntz's words, 'they impersonate the paradoxical ideal of a piety without identifiable gods of righteousness, who speak with no certainty of reward'.

In the first speech (711-33), beginning, 'Daughter, how involved and riddling is god' (for god we may well substitute *tuchê*), the Slave's *gnômê* is a comment on the blind operation of chance in his masters' case – no new subject. Then he recalls their wedding in Sparta and is moved by the memory to conclude: 'Base the man who shows no right feeling for his masters by sharing their joy and sorrows. Though slave, I am noble (a familiar Euripidean oxymoron) and my mind is free if not my name.'

In his elliptical way, the Slave is talking about the impossibility of knowledge in the face of chance, and about his own ambiguous status which, at the bottom of the social scale, mirrors the grand paradox that is Helen. Set against unknowable world and unacknowledged identity is the importance of right feeling.

The second speech has prophecy for its subject (744ff., 'I see now how mean and riddled with lies prophecy is ...') and springs from the painful realisation that acknowledgement of Helen innocent is also acknowledgement that the Trojan War was fought *matên*, for nothing.[42] The tenor of his thought, however, is the same as before. Calchas and Helenus, the great prophets of Greece and Troy respectively, did not let it be known that the war was pointless. If the reason for their silence was that the god did not wish humans to know, then why consult prophets? Again, knowledge seems unattainable. He concludes that it is better to offer the gods their appropriate sacrifices and otherwise to rely on *gnomê*, one's own judgment, and *euboulia*, common sense – those qualities Theonoe, on her transcendent plane, will herself employ.

*

In *Helen* Euripides puts recognition to new use by creating two Helens and investing in a fantastic exploration of the problem of knowledge itself. But however remote his Egypt, it is nonetheless tainted with war, death and futility (as many critics, notably Wolff, 1973, have explored). In an extraordinary narrative manoeuvre, recognition is first denied then, at its climax, taken away from Helen and Menelaus,[43] to be focalised and then extended through the cliché-ridden mouth of an insignificant and unheroic character. Yet perhaps, as 'man in the street', uncompromised by heroic ambiguities, he is the figure with whom the audience can most readily identify and put their trust. Another late play, *Bacchae*, more sharply contrasts the superior *aidôs*, moral sensitivity of ordinary people (see Dodds, 1944, 123) with the arrogant mental confusion of their rulers.[44]

The Slave draws more lengthy conclusions from recognition than we find anywhere else in Euripides and, despite his incoherent formulations – another of Euripides' deliberate paradoxes – he delivers a significant moral message. Chance operates blindly and makes knowledge impossible, personal identity unacknowledged and rationally-based action futile: nonetheless, the slave asserts that there is a right way to conduct our lives.

10

Gods as Prologue-Speakers

10.1 Introduction

The amount of *future* information given in a prologue-*rhêsis* superficially appears to turn on Euripides' decision to make the prologue speaker human or divine. Humans, after all, can do no more than describe the crisis they are in and whatever attempts they are making to resolve it. *Iphigeneia in Tauris* contains predictive material of a sort – Iphigeneia's description of her dream and her reading of it – but this is quickly proved wrong. By contrast, gods have potentially unlimited narrative authority to relate the entire action of the play, and it is this power which Euripides may appear to grant to his prologue-speaking gods (and to the ghost of Polydorus in *Hecuba*). However, the conviction that gods in prologues convey *all* relevant future information is a Euripidean *dolos*. Euripides capitalises on the supposition that gods are omniscient; the opening position of the divine *rhêsis* with its lucid iambic trimeters reinforces this effect, as does the choice of the narrative medium itself, since (as we considered in 1.4) it is a property of narrative to have appear to have overall definiteness, to offer a full and objective truth. On close examination, the divine prologue *rhêsis* in fact underlines the way continuous narrative can exercise a total and deceitful control over its material.

In terms of narrative typology, divine prologue predictions are proleptic narratives hardly distinguishable from the dreams or prophecies embedded within the body of the plays of Aeschylus or Sophocles, except that the god speaks directly in the unmediated first person, rather than through a human agent, and his delivery is expository rather than oracular or oblique. An opening divine prediction naturally obviates the need for further proleptic narrative. The total absence, or restricted or largely critical presence of dreams and oracles in Euripides' plays confirms this.[1]

In fact Euripides imposes different kinds of limitations on his gods' ability to relate the future. Authority may appear total: for example, Aphrodite unequivocally states, *timôrêsomai Hippolyton en têid' hêmerai*, 'I shall have my revenge on Hippolytus today' (*Hipp.* 21-2), and at *Alc.* 64-71 Apollo emphatically foretells the future rescue of Alcestis, beginning *ê mên*, a formula for oaths and other incontrovertible utterances. However, the authority of this prediction is diminished by giving Thanatos the last word in the scene, and Euripides frequently characterises the prologue god as one apparently *not* entirely in control of events and *not* able – or willing – to speak of the future with authority. Thus Apollo in *Alcestis* has been *latris*, servant, to a mortal and appears unable to dispose of Thanatos; Hermes in *Ion* is another *latris*, mere agent of his brother Apollo; Poseidon in *Trojan Women* has been worsted by Hera and Athena and has no plan of his own. None of these prologue gods has the totally impressive authority of Aphrodite in *Hippolytus*, but even here Euripides has designed into the structure an opposing, equally authoritative goddess, and is at pains to describe the compromise established between them, a permanent stand-off enforced by Zeus which allows each of them only a restricted independence within their own sphere (1328ff.). The divine prologue speaker's authority is too often treated by critics as if it existed in a vacuum; Euripides usually reminds us that this is a polytheistic universe in which many powers may oppose or cooperate.[2]

This deals with one apparently disastrous problem with the divine framework – the removal of suspense. Divine prologue *rhêseis*, like dreams and prophecies elsewhere, are in fact a potent cocktail of authority and ambiguity, ultimately producing in the audience much the same involvement in a hermeneutic process as before. Apparently infallible prologue information will after all turn out to contain gaps, ambiguities, slips of detail and small inversions of ordering just as dreams and prophecies do. Euripides conceals *dolos* in clarity. The opening presentation of fact in combination with these omissions and inversions – unrecognised as such at the outset – are an important strategy by which he tightly controls audience reception of the ensuing action and manages to create, despite an initial surface appearance of flat omniscience, his own precisely-defined fictive world to which audiences can after all respond with shock, surprise and astonishment, and with powerful intellectual and emotional engagement.

The divine framework creates a whole range of different effects. Initially it encourages a distanced view on the action. We might be aware that the drama has been arbitrarily sliced out of an originally larger whole. The action is presented as 'a design made for human minds to inhabit' (Michelini, 107) and make what sense of they can. The god is *didaskalos*, the poet who directs the actors, with the power 'precisely to shape and control the action of any particular play' (Easterling, 1993, 80), an effect most powerfully created in *Bacchae*. The prologue god draws attention to the play as a multi-faceted, technical medium for exploring dilemmas and contradictions in human life, juxtaposing divine and human perspectives, determinism and free will. Whether the god is characterised as weak or powerful, the subsequent action is 'under their sign'. The first appearance the human stage figures make is, as it were, on the god's cast list, deprived of autonomy.

In subsequent scenes, Euripides abandons his divine framework, leaving the mortal characters to play out their crucial scenes on their own.[3]

Euripides is a master of psychology, and we become deeply involved in the humans as they respond to a series of acute dilemmas. At the same time, relieved to some extent of the basic problem of *what* will happen, we are free to observe the detail of *how* exactly the predicted events work out at the human level. In this exploration the passions and dispositions of the characters become extremely important, as does the intellectual discussion of the issues, often evaluated in the terminology of the contemporary *polis*.

Lacking oracles and dreams to work on, the stage figures have no possibility of understanding the divine will: understanding comes about only after their unassisted human actions have been disastrously completed, via another divine narrative at the end. Here, at last, the stage figures see and hear the god (as the human audience did earlier), in an ultimate interaction which is often a moment of mutual reproach and bitter understanding. However visually elevated by appearing on the roof of the stage building or on the crane, the concluding *deus* is not, as at the beginning, at a higher narrative level: but the meeting on the same level usually comes too late.

The placement of gods in the prologue invites the audience to criticise their role in human affairs. Human suffering is set in motion by individual gods characterised as they appear in Homer – partial, jealous and vengeful. If they mutually cooperate, as Poseidon with Athena in *Trojan Women*, it is for individual advantage. (*Ion* is different – but Apollo attracts criticism there too.) Criticism may be verbalised explicitly by stage figures: *Hipp.* 120, 'Gods ought to be wiser than mortals'; *Bacch.* 1348, 'Gods should not become in anger like mortals'; and even from one god to another: 'Why do you gad about in different directions at different times, hating and loving to excess and at random?' (Poseidon to Athena, *Tro.* 67-8).

If gods cannot suffer or die and thus cannot attract our sympathies the way the human stage figures do, the chorus may nonetheless remind us that their power in the universe fulfils vital needs or offers humans desirable gifts. While the first stasimon of *Hippolytus* (525f.) sang of the destructive power of Eros, citing the fates of Iole and Semele and building towards Phaedra's fate, the fourth (1282f.) uncritically celebrates the power of love for its universal influence over the whole of creation (cf. the Nurse, 439f.). Throughout *Bacchae*, the vengeful Dionysus is celebrated for his gifts of ecstasy, joy and freedom from physical pain. These tragedies can exploit the hymn-like tendencies of lyric to create a rich disjunction between the anthropomorphic, dictatorial presentation of gods speaking in iambic trimeters at the beginning and/or end of a play, and their depiction in lyric sequences where they are spoken of as eternally fulfilling human needs.

In *Hippolytus*, *Ion*, and *Bacchae*, a deus closes the action as well as opening it. Human drama is thus sealed off at either end with a formal narrative in which the gods' 'directorial' role to define and determine mortal life is doubly emphasised. While *Hippolytus* and *Bacchae* open and close with narratives of divine punishment, a quite different, gently ironic unity is created by the proxy benevolence of Hermes and Athena at each end of *Ion*.

Both *Hippolytus* and *Bacchae* begin and end with the epiphany of a god bent on revenge, and contain a powerful and horrific religious message. The action in each is in essence the destruction of a virginal youth, who rejects worship of the prologue god, by the divinely-inspired passion of a (step) mother. Both plays bring the broken body of the youth onstage at the end. Both are intensely concerned with the contradiction between reason and passion, social norms, social aberrance and shifting *logoi*. However, there are significant differences in prologue strategy.

10.2 *Hippolytus*

Hippolytus is an excellent place to begin, since we know that Euripides dramatised the same story twice, and that one of the major changes made was the addition of a divine prologue speaker to his second version.[4] In Euripides' earlier version Phaedra very probably spoke the prologue herself (Halleran F443 = A Barrett). Euripides presented in unmediated form a woman who shamelessly made an attempt to seduce her stepson and then falsely accused him (according to the familiar 'Potiphar's wife' myth pattern found also in the stories of Peleus and the wife of Acastos and of Bellerophon and Sthenoboia). This version, for its immodest woman, met with disfavour and Euripides, according to Aristophanes, reworked the story in a way to minimise Phaedra's transgressive nature: 'It is evident that [the *Hippolytus* we have] was written second, for what was unseemly and worthy of condemnation has been corrected in this play.'

Given the new virtuous, silent Phaedra (whom even Aphrodite calls *eukleês*, 'of good report', 'noble', 47), Aphrodite's prologue-speaking role is now – apart from anything else – simply a structural necessity so that we can know of her victim's unvoiced passion. However, the effect of Aphrodite's presence and her speech goes far beyond this. A higher-level narrative of divine revenge is now firmly superimposed onto the traditional 'Potiphar's wife' story, and as a result two new and important dimensions unavailable to the first version open up. First, the huge gap between human and divine: as Knox (1968, 90) wrote, 'in no other Greek tragedy is the predetermination of human action by an external power made so emphatically clear'. Second, a view emerges of Phaedra as now *externally* afflicted by passion, struggling to stay *within* the norms of society, a figure whom the audience cannot, as before, reject for her immorality.

Aphrodite (1-57)

The stage on Aphrodite's entry probably displayed two statues, one of herself and one of Artemis. Aphrodite refers to her universal powers and declares that, while she benefits those who give her worship she 'brings down' (*sphallein*) those who show her insufficient respect. Gods enjoy receiving honours, *timê*, from mortals. She will exemplify the truth of this (9). Now she begins naming the characters, linking them into the preceding sentence with a consecutive 'for' (*gar*). The frame is set: the stage figures will demonstrate the working of divine revenge.

Time scales are now drawn; she will take her revenge on Hippolytus today (21-2); her plans are already well advanced; Phaedra became infatuated earlier in Athens when Hippolytus had visited to celebrate the mysteries. At that time she had set up a temple to Aphrodite known as '*Hippolytôi d'epi*' (32).

The language here, as always in Euripidean prologues, is limpidly clear and simple, but the meaning is elusive. The plurality of possible translations show how readily ambiguity may be created. Is it, as Barrett thought (1964, 5 and commentary), '*over* Hippolytus', in the *topographical* sense or in terms of the *power* relationship between them or, given that the shrine is a testimonial to Phaedra's love, does it mean '*named for*' Hippolytus? (Goff, 1990, 113f. and Dunn, 1992, 105-6). Halleran (1988) understands it causally, '*because of*' Hippolytus. For the contemporary audience the phrase was perhaps most simply understood in a topographical sense, since in the fifth century the precinct of Hippolytus which contained the temple to Aphrodite was situated on the south-western side of the Acropolis, right near the theatre (the proximity is emphasised in the phrase 'the very rock of Pallas', 30). The nearness of the building to the audience, together with the phrase *katopsion tês gês*, 'overlooking this land', gives Barthes' *effet du réel*: but it seems typical of Euripides to combine concrete detail with ambiguous phrase in this way.[5]

> The wretched women is dying in silence, and none of the household knows of her disease. But her love is not at all bound to turn out in this way. I shall reveal the matter to Theseus, and it will be brought to light. And the father will kill the young man who is hostile to me with the curses which the sea god, Lord Poseidon, gave Theseus as an honour, that he could pray to the god three times and it would be fulfilled. Phaedra, though she keeps her reputation, nonetheless dies. (39-48)

There is much that does and does not point accurately forward to the scenes of the play in this prediction. *In silence*: as Knox first explored (1952), this has thematic importance for the structure of the whole play: not just the first scene between Phaedra and the Nurse but every scene, in fact, is articulated around a choice between speech and silence, a choice which abundantly reveals the predispositions of the individual characters as it hastens on their fate. *I shall*, etc.: but we do not expect Aphrodite herself to appear again during the play. Who then? The passive '*it will be brought to light*' takes us no further. Here Euripides conceals the role of the Nurse and Phaedra's tablet discovered on her dead body – two innovations in this version.

Furthermore, the smoothly presented information disguises the fact that the sequence is not right. The ordering here conforms to the traditional storyline (which Euripides himself used in his earlier version) in which Phaedra kills herself *after* the death of Hippolytus when her shameful love is discovered. The only glancing anomaly presented now is that Phaedra should somehow die *eukleês*, with her reputation safe. Euripides hides his narrative re-ordering of the story line and his own innovations. The narrative gaps and deceitful temporal inversions, disguised by Aphrodite's authoritative presentation, allow after all for genuine suspense and surprise. By this means Euripides will dislodge us from our omniscient position so that both authorial and narrative audience become intensely involved in the characters' quest for knowledge.[6]

Hippolytus and the huntsmen (58-120)

Aphrodite gives way to Hippolytus and the huntsmen. It is appropriate that the exclusive, virgin youth should be presented in this exclusive early scene, before being embroiled with other, sexually-charged characters. This complex second scene begins the threatened exemplification. The discrepant awareness created by the prologue *rhêsis* starts to have its effect on us. The hymn, prayer and garlanding, devoted exclusively to Artemis, are highly disturbing, while Hippolytus' concluding wish to end his life as he has begun it is painfully ironic.

Counterpointing this anxiety is pleasure in the description of the beautiful, untouched meadow which, in its suggestion of an actual *temenos* (sacred area) belonging to the goddess, creates a ready, sympathetic image for Hippolytus himself. However, it is also a warning, as many commentators have noted.[7] The meadow where the virgin (Korê, Creusa, e.g.) gathers flowers is a known erotic *topos*, its innocence inviting violation.

In a brief passage of stichomythia (88-107), one of the huntsmen timidly attempts a warning. Throughout, he focuses our own reactions. The huntsman draws an analogy between human and divine pride, and the adjective *semnos* is used four times (93, 94, 99, 103). Barrett's commentary (1964) explores the way Euripides makes the huntsman innocently exploit the word's range of meanings, from 'august' and 'dread' in the divine sphere through to 'arrogant' and 'unapproachable' in the human. The effect is deliberately confusing, isolating the whole question of *semnotês* (the noun 'dignity', solemnity'), whether a property of god or human, and making it problematic. Both the huntsman's manifest fear of his master and his analogy set up an implicit comparison between the goddess and her victim, both of whom possess the ambiguous property of *semnotês*.

On Hippolytus' exit the huntsman turns to Aphrodite's statue, offering a brief prayer that Aphrodite might forgive Hippolytus (114f.), suggestively repeating his slave/master, men/gods analogy (88: 115), and ending with a statement that is almost a plea: 'gods ought to be wiser than men'. His wishful, humble piety acts as a foil to Hippolytus' arrogant certainty, and this pathetic prayer, like his earlier failed *peithô*, acts out a last chance to avert catastrophe. Our knowledge that it is already too late is painful and disturbing.

The second section does not advance the action, but suggestively exposes the beauty and dangers of Hippolytus' exclusive worship of Aphrodite by juxtaposing the blithely doomed Hippolytus and the anxious huntsman. Our sympathies and fears are already shaped in complex ways. The complexity, even instability of *audience* response is something that happens also to the *characters* during the play. The prologue displays the inexorable fixity of divine purpose. At the same time it sets up unstable and problematic concepts which are successively argued, inverted, contradicted and re-defined by all four characters throughout this tightly-constructed drama. The concepts refuse to remain stable.[8]

The prologue had indicated that the play concerned Aphrodite's revenge, brought about at the human level by a 'Potiphar's wife' story line. But there are, probably, *two* statues on stage and in the prologue the two goddesses are paired – Aphrodite appeared and Artemis was hymned (in fact each received a prayer (Aphrodite, 73-87; Artemis, 114-20). The pairing is repeated again at the end: Aphrodite is hymned at 1268-81, then Artemis appears at 1282-439. A three-fold repetition is also at work: the prologue showed first Aphrodite (1-57), then Artemis (58-87), then an attempt at reconciliation (88-120). This tripartite arrangement too is repeated and brings the play to an end (see Dunn, 1996, 87-100).

After the messenger has reported Hippolytus' death, the chorus sing of Aphrodite's power (1268f.). Although they sang of love earlier (the *Erôs* ode 525f.), to do so now is in itself a surprise: Aphrodite's most obvious victim, Phaedra, is long dead and the audience's thoughts are far away from the goddess by this time: they have been concerned with the power of Poseidon's curse, the bull, and the death of Hippolytus. This brief ode reminds us of the prologue and that the theme of the play is Aphrodite's revenge on Hippolytus; her agency stands behind the entire action. At the same time, however, its calm, uncritical, hymn-like celebration of her universal sway, looking neither forward nor back into the play,[9] induces a more distant perspective on recent events and indeed, of the entire action. It becomes possible to see Hippolytus' death not so much as raw divine *revenge* as an expression of eternal law. The ode paves the way towards closure.

That this ode to Aphrodite should be followed by the immediate onstage presence of *Artemis* is far greater surprise. Yet the juxtaposition mirrors the opening and begins a closing frame to balance the beginning. First, Aphrodite appeared and Artemis was invoked; now Aphrodite is invoked and Artemis appears. The scene contains many details and verbal echoes of the prologue and helps point up the action as a cycle completed. Artemis 'teaches' Theseus how events have occurred in accordance with Aphrodite's plan (*ekdeixai*, 1298: *deixô*, 9). Although he will receive pardon, her inhuman coldness matches Aphrodite's (1290f., 1297, 1313-14: esp. 48-50). The unusual verb *prokoptein* is repeated (1297: 23). She restates Aphrodite's remarks that the gods let each other alone (1328-30: 20), grant polarised favour and disfavour to mortals and destroy those who ignore them (1339-41; cf. 6-7). Hippolytus can sense but not see Artemis (1391-2: 86). Theseus repeats the verb *sphallein* to describe his fall (1414: 6).[10]

This revenge is completed, but a mirror action will follow beyond the frame of this play. At 1417 *Artemis* expresses her intention to take revenge (*timôrêsomai* placed emphatically at end of 1422: similar emphasis 21). Adonis (probably – the youth is not named) must die and so *mutatis mutandis* a beautiful youth devoted to Aphrodite will be destroyed by Artemis. The two goddesses are mighty opposites, governing sexuality and virginity, polarised aspects of life; Euripides suggests that their operation is not only polarised but also identical and infinite. The structural symmetry of this second version offers a profound message about the workings of the divine universe.[11]

Like Aphrodite, Artemis too gives an *aition*, again for a Hippolytus cult but this time in Troezen (1423f.: 29-33). Hippolytus, who began as a figure in Aphrodite's narrative, now re-enters narrative (as Zeitlin noted) as the subject of the brides' song. So does Phaedra. Artemis confirms Aphrodite's declaration that Phaedra's love will not be a matter for silence (1430: 39f.). Her final tones are softer and go beyond Aphrodite's prescription: she suggests reconciliation between her favourite and his father. Aphrodite left Hippolytus as good as dead (56-7), Artemis does the same (1162-3) and now Hippolytus does indeed die.

There is an exclusively human focus in the final moments of the play. It has been well observed (by e.g. Taplin 1978, 135) that Hippolytus' death-pangs mirror Phaedra's symptoms of love-sickness. But however human in his death, he also expressly fulfils (in reverse order) Aphrodite's final prologue predictions. She said the gates of Hell were open and he was seeing his last day's light (56-57); at 1444 Hippolytus says that darkness is falling across his eyes; at 1447 he sees the gates of the Dead.

10.3 *Bacchae*

Dionysus (1-63)

Compared to the fairly restricted features of the traditional Hippolytus story, Euripides could draw on a much broader background for a play about

Pentheus. There were many previous tragic renderings of the advent of
Dionysus in which Pentheus, Lycurgus, Orpheus or the daughters of
Minyas received punishment for their rejection of the god.[12] From these
plays various elements survive, either in fragments or from secondary
sources, which are familiar to us because they also occur in *Bacchae*:
Dionysus' effeminate costume, his and his supporters' capture and miraculous release, the shaking of the royal palace, madness and *sparagmos*
(tearing apart) of the *theomachos* (god-opponent), either by Bacchants
and/or a mad parent, a nearby mountain.[13] If some elements were specific
to one individual (obviously only Semele is blasted by lightning), others
were general, inherent possibilities of the Dionysus myth (representing,
as Seaford has shown, aspects of Dionysiac cult practice and/or initiation
ritual) potentially available for inclusion by the versatile Euripides in this
Pentheus play. However, it is not clear whether any previous version began
with Dionysus himself speaking the prologue.

Euripides gives Dionysus the most *dolios* prologue-*rhêsis* of any surviving play, no doubt arousing and subverting expectations about the details
of *his* version. The extent of innovation or appropriation is hard to plot
with any exactitude.[14] However, if the largely unknown but certainly rich
background material available makes it particularly difficult to pin-point
audience expectation at the outset, it does not mean that the prologue's
uniquely circling, cat-and-mouse strategies – entirely characteristic of
their speaker – cannot be explored in their own right to illuminate
Euripides' technique. Only as the *rhêsis* progresses do we start to understand the speaker's *parole* and so develop insights into the meaning
behind his words.

Dionysus refers to his change to human shape at 4 and again 53-4,
creating a ring. Within the ring he refers to his manifestation as a god with
increasing frequency (22, 42, 47, 50). The opposition disguised/manifest
becomes a *leitmotif* which manages to remain unexplained.

The prologue is shaped like the play itself in that it begins innocently
and becomes cumulatively threatening. It never unconditionally states
that there will be a future catastrophe, nor does it do more than ambiguously hint at what form it might take, leaving the audience to project
possible outcomes from its knowledge of myth, cult and previous tragic
versions. One striking omission is any mention of Agave.

Between *hêko* 'I have come' (1), and *êlthon*, also 'I have come (20) ... to
be a manifest god' ... through to 26, Dionysus presents himself in neutral
terms merely as spreading his cult. The blasting of Semele is attributed to
Hera's *hubris*. No human *hubris* is suggested at this point. Indeed, Dionysus has 'approved' Cadmus for making a shrine of her tomb, giving it the
Dionysiac token, the ivy cluster (10-12). (The idea that Cadmus has
become a Bacchant merely out of family policy is very faintly suggested
here.) Having spread his joyful worship in Asia, he has set the Theban

women dancing and given them too the tokens of his cult. All this seems a mark of favour.

At 23-54 Dionysus returns to the opening idea, his arrival in Thebes, and now explains it hypotactically. With the conjunction at 26, *epei*, 'since', a shift begins. His choice of Thebes is not merely due to the fact that it is his birth city. More specifically, it is due to the fact that his mother Semele's sisters did not believe that Zeus had fathered her child, *toigar*, 'and so' (32) he has sent them out of the city as bacchants. The language becomes violent: 'driven to a frenzy with madness ... they are deranged ... I compelled them.' The whole city must *ekmathein*, 'learn to the (bitter) end' *even if it is unwilling*; in defending his mother he will be a 'manifest god to mortals' (42).

Our understanding alters in complex ways here: Dionysus has not *just* arrived (as the verbs at 1 and 20, coupled with his entry seemed to imply): he has been here long enough to send the Theban women out to Cithaeron. We gather that the Theban bacchants are not, as initially presented, similar to the Asian women since this time they worship under compulsion. The city has not been initiated into his rites. We also learn that somehow Dionysus' *disguise* is part of a project of *punishment*.[15]

In a new section marked off by the transitional particles *men oun*, 'well now ...' and using the rare verb *theomachein* (45), 'to resist a god' (cf. 325, 1255-6) we learn that Pentheus refuses to accept Dionysus. Then these lines follow:

> *That is why* I shall show myself to be a born god to him and to all Thebans. I shall move off to another land when I've established things here, revealing myself. But if the city of Thebes seeks in anger with weapons to lead my bacchants from the mountain, I shall, as general to my maenads, join (with them). *That is why* I have taken on mortal shape and changed my appearance to the nature of a man.

The complexities of this deceitful, almost Machiavellian prologue prediction, contrasting with the clear programmatic prediction of *Hipp.* 42-8, have failed to receive the attention they deserve. Here we have a sequence of vaguely delineated events in which (1) Dionysus shows himself. Talk of moving away then distracts us. (2) The city under arms might attempt to bring the women back. (3) Dionysus will then oppose them, also in arms (*sunaptein* with *stratêlatôn* gives a military colouring here).

To explore the problems, starting with syntax: there is a heavily stressed causality ('That is why', *hôn hounek'* at 47 and 43) which, despite its emphasis, does not readily create a logical sequence of events for the passage. Then too, (2) and (3) are not statements but the protasis and apodosis of a conditional sentence. The interruption between (1) and (2) is remarkable.

Next, the content: (1) In what following scene or scenes does Dionysus show himself to be 'a born god' and how does this reference to manifestation relate to his disguise? (2) Why mention the *city of Thebes* with *weapons* when eventually we see only *Pentheus unarmed* going to his doom? (3) Why the suggestion of the unmilitary Dionysus involved in military conflict?

Although the need to interplay with other versions is certainly an (unfathomable) issue here, *suggestio falsi* can be only a partial answer to the difficulties. When Euripides is writing at this level, it is to be supposed that his prologue strategies not only create subsequent opportunities for suspense and surprise but also demarcate areas for our special attention and begin to arouse a specific set of responses to them. Even if, in the event, something suggested here does *not* later happen, the false suggestion remains important for what it tells us about how we are being invited to read the play. There is no second prologue scene to do this.

The first *hôn hounek'* is superficially coherent: Pentheus does not worship him and *that is why* Dionysus needs to make a demonstration of himself as a god. Divine epiphany proves existence. But when exactly in the play would the original audience consider this prediction fulfilled? The conventional Euripidean epiphany takes the form of the god's formal appearance *ex machina* or from the *theologeion* at the end. From this position the god often quashes human doubts and criticisms, which would be appropriate here. But, although Dionysus does finally appear in this form, Pentheus is by then spectacularly dead.

The repetition of the *hôn hounek'* clauses (which Dodds, 1944, found 'rather clumsy') is perhaps better understood as deliberately problematic. Rather than forging logical links in a sequence of events, they have the effect of forcing together the opposed ideas of Dionysus disguised and Dionysus manifest. Dionysus *has* disguised himself (54) and he *will* reveal himself (47). This oscillation underlies the entire prologue speech.

Oscillating, paradoxical manifestation lies at the heart of the god's nature, Dionysus being a god who *manifests* himself in *disguise*, by shape changes and 'doubling' in various ways. He can talk of himself in the third person. More precisely for this passage, Dionysus' current *disguise* takes the form of effeminate human youth (as we see him speaking these lines; the audience is distinguished from all the stage figures by knowing that it is, in fact, a form of the god himself). The disguise which masks his godhead symbolises his double, deceptive speaking which affects his victims' vision: Pentheus sees double (918-19), Agave sees her son as a lion. There is also a conceptual overlap between the stage figure's *disguise* which is a theatrical *manifestation*, and subsequent *manifestation* not in human form at all but as bull, snake or lion. Dionysus is in the wine, he has mastery over nature and effective control over fire, thunder and lightning. He controls vision and can be 'whatever he wants' (478).

Given this confusion, which scene or scenes of the play fulfil 'showing as a god' predicted here? Hamilton is the most definitive of critics to take the lines to refer to the 'palace miracle' scene and its following trochaic tetrameter account of Pentheus' reaction to Dionysus' miraculous escape 576-641. Seaford follows this, heading his discussion of this section 'The Epiphany of Dionysus'.

I think this is right, but it is not without difficulties. Two sections need to be taken together. In the first (576-603), Dionysus is off stage but he declares himself a god, 'the son of Semele, the son of Zeus' (581). The chorus confirm this: 'Dionysus is throughout the halls' (589); 'the lord, the off-spring of Zeus will come upon these halls, turning them upside down' (602-3). However staged, (on which see Goldhill, 1986, 277-84 and Wiles *GR* 1987, 136-52), what matters is that the chorus 'see' a leaping-up of the flame around Semele's tomb (597f.) as if in confirmation of the fact that it is 'still living' (as described in the prologue, 8). Dionysus' voice invokes Earthquake; the chorus 'see' the lintels of the house move apart. They fling themselves to the ground in extreme fear.

In the second section (604-41) Dionysus himself enters – in his effemi-nate disguise. The chorus do not identify the god (whose manifestation they have just attested) with the youth who continues to lead their *thiasos*; and the disguised god keeps up his disguise, talking of himself in the third person (605, 623, 629, 632), as in trochaic tetrameters he describes how Pentheus tied up a bull thinking it was himself, attempted to put the fire out around Semele's tomb thinking that it was his house on fire, charged at a light with his sword and thought his house was dashed to the ground. By these means Euripides encourages a picture of simultaneous super-natural effects occuring throughout the palace (on and off stage) while Dionysus freed himself from his bonds.

Certainly then, this is the major episode of Dionysus showing that he is 'a god born' in Thebes; but hardly so to 'all the Thebans' and at this point Pentheus himself, on stage for so much of the play, is merely described, rather than shown, reacting to it.[16] Narratives describing miraculous effects (admittedly on Cithaeron, but reported in Thebes) are delivered to Pentheus both before and after this 'epiphany', at 447-8, 704-13, and 734-64, each time concluding with the speaker's advice to Pentheus that a god is at work. Depending on individual production, the 'palace miracles' are not necessarily a major 'event' in the play. Finally, they do not create an immediate turning point in either direction. Perhaps the prologue's teasing counterpoint of disguise and manifestation should be understood largely in general terms: Euripides indicates that Dionysus is a god to be recognised specifically by disguise and that every scene will be infused with ideas of *shape-change, dressing up* and *transformation*.

At 48 Dionysus breaks off to talk of departure: it seems that simple manifestation is all that is required in Thebes. Earlier (13f.), a narrative sequence, later building up to mention punishment, was also broken off by mention of worship elsewhere. The apparently innocent distraction cre-ated by the intrusion of 'elswhere' becomes extraordinarily sinister the second time around. The god's discourse now characterises him as one disguising an inflexible purpose in light and easy speech.

The second *hôn hounek* (53-4) has been suspected and some (most recently Willink, 1966), propose deletion: 'the only deducible implication is that Dionysus would not have taken on mortal form but for the prospect of a clash of arms – which is absurd' (30). Against this view are two related points; first that Euripides is here manifestly rounding off the entire prologue speech and so the antecedent to the relative *hôn* is, depending on delivery, to be taken as referring to the entire situation in Thebes described in the previous verses. The second point: the structure of all these closing lines mirrors 26-33 with its similar causal emphasis (*epei* 'since', *hôn … hounek'* 'that is why', *hoti* 'because', *toigar* 'and so' …). The earlier passage was a clear account of insult followed by infliction of madness. When we reach this one, we understand that Dionysus uses such causal conjunctions exactly when he is meditating *punishment*. The concluding verses then allusively sum up the theme that the whole prologue has been cumulatively developing: his presence in disguise in Thebes is for punishment, and *revenge* is the subject of the play.

To consider the *suggestiones falsi* of 47-54 in turn:

(1) *If the city of Thebes* … this leads us to expect Pentheus (named 44) at the head of the Theban army and may refer to another version. Although plays of this date frequently explore the problematic relationship between ruler and city (and Thebes is a city frequently chosen for this exploration), this play – especially given the choice of chorus – leaves little room for this issue.

A muted process of conversion of the Theban populace takes place during the play; only Teiresias and Cadmus go to Cithaeron in the first episode, but subsequently a series of messengers, representative Thebans, are seen to be won over. Euripides shows Pentheus increasingly isolated from his city and finally emphatically alone in continuing to resist. Pentheus: 'I am the only man to dare this deed.' Dionysus : 'Alone you labour for this city, alone' (962-3). It is not hard to read into the irony here the idea of king turned *pharmakos*, scapegoat for his community. But the main reason for the stress on city in this prologue must be the narrator's desire for concealment (see below).

If what is suggested here is false, its conditional form relieves it of being an outright lie. Furthermore, 'if' might suggest a real chance to acknowledge Dionysus in time to avoid disaster. Yet, though Burnett (1970, 26-7) stresses the element of 'fair chance' offered Pentheus, it would in fact be unique in revenge tragedy for the outcome to be made truly dependent on the behaviour of the offender – punishment has always been inflexibly decided on in advance. Here, although it is not until 810 that Dionysus begins to 'draw Pentheus into his net' (see 848), the pre-maddened bacchants are already there on the mountain, ready and waiting. The condition, in my view, merely gives a painfully ironic edge to the scenes showing the *theomachos* increasingly overwhelmed with evidence that Dionysus cannot be resisted, and remaining ever more ludicrously entrenched in his resistance.

(2) *With weapons*: Pentheus' desire to use weapons against the maenads is certainly *suggestio falsi* but it does introduce a motif which has significance in the later narrative development. As Hamilton and Erbse show, Euripides flags 'weapons' here, and 'weapons' are to be the specific turning point in Pentheus' relationship with Dionysus, the pivot from which he falls to his ruin. Despite clear evidence from a messenger that arms would have no effect (758-64, confirmed by Dionysus 798, who reminds Pentheus it would be 'shameful' to use weapons against maenads: see Hamilton, Erbse and Buxton for the 'fulfilment' of this prologue motif in the messenger speeches), Pentheus is persistently determined on an armed attack (780, 794-5). At 809 he says 'Bring my weapons out here and stop talking' and Dionysus then utters the *extra metrum Ah* (810). Even at the end of this scene Pentheus is still considering weapons. His exit line is, 'Either I'll proceed under arms or I'll yield to your advice' (845-6).

(3) *I shall, as general to my maenads, join with them* (*xunapsô*, 52): taking verb and participle in conjunction with the previous two lines creates the false idea of a pitched battle between citizen army led by Pentheus, and their bacchant wives and daughters led by Dionysus. But, taking 52 separately and treating the military language as metaphorical, it becomes an exact prediction.

When the maenads destroy Pentheus, Dionysus is acting as their general or leader, not on earth but from heaven (1079-81, 1089). Furthermore the verb *sunaptein* (in essence a neutral word; *xunapte*, 'take my hand', says Teiresias to Cadmus, 197), has true proleptic force independent of its context here. The verb recurs at the important moment when Cadmus explains to the newly-sane Agave what has been happening (1302f.): '[Pentheus] was similar to you in not honouring the god. That was why [Dionysus] joined all together (*sunêpse*) into one destruction, you and this man.' *Sunaptein* makes explicit the connection between killer and killed, Agave and Pentheus, the mother and son so artfully separated in the prologue.

Agave is the prologue's major *suppressio veri*. She is one of Semele's sisters, who have already been mentioned as a group driven mad (32ff.), and Pentheus the *theomachos* has been mentioned too as 'Cadmus' daughter's son' (45). Agave's name, which would naturally arise in either or both contexts and link mother and son together, is deliberately omitted. The prologue lays stress on *polis* in order to conceal mother and son within their gender groups: 'all the women of the city' (35-6) conceals Agave, and 'all the Thebans' and 'the city of Thebans' (48, 50) conceal Pentheus. *Sunaptein* (1303) finally joins them.

From hindsight a position similar to that in the prologue of *Hippolytus* appears. In both plays the god's revenge operates in two stages. To punish

Hippolytus, Aphrodite had already made Phaedra mad with love before the opening of *Hippolytus* and the play itself dramatises the important second half of the revenge process (i.e. Hippolytus, believed to have sexually assaulted Phaedra, is destroyed as a result). In *Bacchae* Dionysus has already made (Semele's sisters and) Agave mad, and the play itself dramatises the second half: the process by which Pentheus comes to be torn apart by her.

With a suppression worthy of Aeschylus (cf. *Septem*'s suppression of Oedipus' curse), Euripides conceals Agave and holds her in reserve for the end, concentrating in the interim on the fascinating encounters between Pentheus and Dionysus. Where Phaedra dominated the first part of the play but had died by 776, Agave's entry is delayed until 1169, after the fatal killing. Onto her, the mother, is focused the movement back from madness to sanity which reverses the movement made by her son. Euripides lays the ground for a great scene of *anagnôrisis* and *peripeteia* to precede her more conventional *mater dolorosa* role.

The prologue hardly makes the future action clear, and the onstage action of the play up to 846, for all its fascination, lacks any definite forward movement towards a particular *telos*. Only a slight change comes about with Pentheus' new susceptibility to Dionysus (811-46). It is only after this that Dionysus' following speech clarifies and completes the plan of action that was withheld or merely adumbrated in the prologue (847-61, reversing 847 and 848 with Dodds and Seaford). He speaks openly for the first time of Pentheus' madness, transvestism and tearing apart by his mother. Although addressed to the chorus, this brief speech functions as a completion of the prologue.

Closing the prologue, the unusually long entry speech (55-63), takes the form of an invocation of Dionysus' personal *thiasos* (group of revellers) from Lydia. The *chorodidaskalos* brings on his *choros*. These drumming, musical fellow-travellers, settling like gypsies on different cities in turn, strengthen the description Dionysus has given of himself as an essentially mobile, transient god (13-22, 48-50) whose enacted arrival marked the beginning of festival time.

As this Lydian *thiasos* enters, Dionysus himself leaves for the Cithaeron *thiasos*, and the Lydian chorus take over the Theban space abandoned by the Theban women. The cross-over that goes on here at their moment of entry is an extraordinary tactic, adding enormously to the play's world of superimposition, doubling and substitution.

As they enter, Dionysus worship is immediately, visually established in the centre of Thebes – though the play will show the Theban characters ultimately leaving the city to join the other group on Cithaeron. Dionysus moves effortlessly between the two places, creating paranormal effects in the heart of mundane Thebes as much as on the mountain. As Dionysus indicated, the play presents a whole world that is magicked, whether visible *here* or invisible offstage *elsewhere*: in their lyrics the Lydian chorus invoke Phrygia, Crete, Cyprus, Pieria and sheer wild nature as well as Cithaeron, binding them all into the Dionysiac experience. Cithaeron itself and the women on it, merely an unnamed mountain in Dionysus' prologue account (23-42), is developed in a succession of vivid narratives (215-25; 434-50; 660-774; 1043-152: see Buxton, 1991).

At the beginning of the exodos (1165f.) Agave, representative of the Theban troup on Cithaeron, enters to the chorus bearing the head of Pentheus (probably the actor's mask) on the end of her *thyrsos*. At this moment the two groups of Maenads in a sense merge. Madness and ecstasy have visibly done their work, and the Lydian group gradually change character now merely to convey the sympathy and horror of a typical female chorus.

Later, Dionysus appears from the machine or *theologeion*. An unknown number of lines (but at least 50 according to Dodds, fewer according to Seaford) are missing from the beginning of his speech which would have delivered predictions relating to the future fates of Thebans, Agave and her sisters, and presumably given an *aition*. The existing lines predict wretched and protracted fates for Cadmus and Harmonia, ultimately alleviated by removal to the land of the blessed – a dispensation produced by no weakening in Dionysus' continuing revenge, but by the intervention of Harmonia's ancestor Ares. Nor is Cadmus spared, though Dionysus approved him in the prologue.

The god's appearance seems almost redundant. Cadmus' speech at 1301-26 was already conclusive in tone; he had already predicted exile (1312), ending with an emphatic statement that the events revealed the existence of god (1325-6); the chorus had then commented that Pentheus' fate was an *axia dikê*, a just punishment (1327-8). Cadmus now reproves the god (in terms recalling *Hippolytus* 120: 'gods should not continue in anger as mortals do'). Dionysus answers by alluding to the insults he received, and to the power of *anankê*, necessity (1350). It is not absolutely clear if he leaves *before* the wretched *exodus*. In either case, the final human farewells are less uplifting than in *Hippolytus*.

Euripides' prologue brilliantly conveyed the vagrant, polymorphic nature of its disguised narrator, and began to unfold the exotic, magical world of the play, one idealised by the chorus, but always dangerously unstable even though the exact, horrific form Dionysus' revenge would take was left inexplicit until 847f. At the end we are left with the knowledge that bleak punishment will continue long into the future. Post-festival hangover is magnified into acute suffering. Dionysus the god revealed has none of the alluring, shape-shifting qualities of Dionysus the festival god disguised.[17] He represents only cruel necessity.

*

It seems remarkable that a group of play texts, produced for a limited festival context in a small community twenty-five centuries ago, should continue to exert any power today. Analysis of narrative patterns, however, reveals the presence of specific strategies which help to account for our continuing and complex engagement with tragedy's staged stories. Many of these are inseparable from tragedy's intrinsically hybrid and paratactic form; its potent juxtaposition of song, chant and metrical speech, of narrative and dialogue; tragedy adapts and recreates Homer's already potent combination of 'showing' and 'telling' in a range of new ways.

The tragic medium can also enlarge on Homeric foreshadowing, using lyric, oracles, dreams or divine prologue-speakers to give religious perspective and extensive time-frame to the brief performance time. Foreshadowing, which frequently gives rise to discrepant awareness between different stage figures as well as between stage figures and audience, creates a range of disturbing, ironic effects which are further assisted by the ambiguity naturally arising from tragedy's disjunctive form. Given the original audience's familiarity with the story-lines of the plays, it is not surprising to find many strategies employed to create ambiguity, uncertainty, and shock. Tragedy is rich in *doloi* of many kinds, sometimes blatant, sometimes concealed.

All stories, however slight, offer meaning and in all cultures they are ideologically powerful and important; as soon as children can understand language we start to tell them stories as a kind of indoctrination into the human condition. Deceit, *dolos*, is present in many of them, but seems to be particularly characteristic of tragedy. Perhaps tragedy's most characteristic *dolos* (the deceitful bait to which we remain attracted) is that it tantalisingly suggests – in moments of revelation when a cloud of unknowing temporarily lifts – that we might gain knowledge about ourselves as humans in the world.

Notes

1. Theoretical aspects

1. Genette's pioneering work on narrative time in Proust (1980) remains very influential. For important work on focalisation see Bal, 1981, 202-10 and 1985, 100-14.

2. Esslin, 1976, 89: 'It is in the actor that the elements of reality and illusion meet: have we come to see Othello as played by Olivier or Olivier as played by Othello?' Ibid. 91: 'We get our pleasure on two levels at the same time: in watching Othello we are deeply moved by the misfortunes of the hero, but at the very same moment when tears come into our eyes at his downfall, we also, almost schizophrenically, say to ourselves: "How brilliantly Olivier held that pause!"'

3. When the Muse is asked to sing in the present tense, the temporal reference is to the narrating instance, not the past time of the narrative itself.

4. Cf. Esslin on Dickens' public readings: 'Clearly his vocal characterization of his fruity ... characters amounted to "acting". And as to the purely narrative, descriptive, dialogue-free portions of the text: Dickens, in reading these, in a highly emotional and subtly differentiated voice that painted the mood and the scenery, was still an actor: he acted the role of the character "Charles Dickens", the compulsive story-teller' (Esslin, 1987, 24).

5. The nineteenth-century novel, home ground for narrative theorists, always included sequences of character discourse to balance those of the narrator, and we should recall that it was universal practice until the seventeenth century for all texts to be 'mouthed', if not read fully out loud.

6. Cf. Pfister, 1988, 59: 'Traditionally ... dramatists have tended to create mediating communication systems ... whether in the guise of the chorus in classical tragedy, the objective self-descriptions of the allegorical figures of the mediaeval morality plays, the numerous examples of direct contact between stage and audience in plays ancient and modern, or Brecht's epic theatre.'

7. What Stanzel, 1984, 66f., has to say about the junction between narrator and character discourse in the novel is also true of the episode/lyric alternation in tragedy: 'many of the specially interesting phenomena ... are located right at the border-line between these two different types of discourse.'

8. cf. Ionesco, 1962, 185 (quoted by Pfister, op. cit., 13): '... mon texte n'est pas seulement un dialogue mais il est aussi "indications scéniques". Ces indications scéniques sont à respecter aussi bien que le texte, elles sont nécessaires.'

9. On how this interaction was achieved, see Ley and Ewans, 1985, 75-84: on the basis of acoustic evidence, practical experience of teaching classical drama and the experimental findings of the Greek Theatre Project, the authors show that the actors were more likely to have used the orchestra space (especially along the radius from the centre of the orchestra to the middle of the stage building) than a supposed separate stage. The manifestly close range of interactions between stage figures and chorus to be found in the text accords very well with these findings. Chorus and stage figures could have readily intermingled. See also Rehm, 1992, 34-6 for the close physical interaction between the two.

10. The scene (*Cho.* 734-82) is unusual because it contains only the chorus and a minor character and they are shown involved in what is, in terms of the trilogy, a very small detail of the plot overall. It is also unusual in (a) having the chorus intervene directly in the plot, and in (b) characterising in some detail a messenger figure whose speech about nursing Orestes seems to owe as much to comedy as to tragedy (but for three good reasons why the nurse is developed as she is, see Garvie, 1986, on 730-82, pp. 243-4).

11. For the origin of the useful concept of discrepant awareness Pfister (1988, 49f.) quotes the Shakespearean critic Bertrand Evans, who discusses the 'dramatist's means and ends in the creation, maintenance and exploitation of differences in the awarenesses of the participants and of differences between participants' awarenesses and ours as audience'.

12. The opening dialogues of *Antigone* and *Philoctetes* and the opening speech of *Oedipus at Colonus* (1-13) spring to mind as examples of masterly conveyance of information which is perfectly 'naturalised' by being motivated by the needs of the stage figures. The opening of *Prometheus Bound* combines interesting action and multiple points of view at the same time as it sets up the basic situation of the play.

13. Michelini, 1987, 67: 'The formalisation of the messenger scene in Sophocles and especially in Euripides is part of the process by which an original element in the tradition gradually passes into a position of higher relief, by contrast with its changed surroundings.'

14. Cf. the prominent role of Pheidippides, sent by the Athenians to give news to Sparta before the battle of Marathon (Hdt. 6.105) or the story of the dead Talthybius' anger at the Athenian and Spartan treatment of Darius' messengers (Hdt. 7.131f.)

15. The problematic nature of knowledge in *Oedipus Tyrannos* is explored by Buxton, 1996, 38f., who defines as 'a feature of many plays called "tragedies" … the sense they convey of a metaphysical structure informing and conferring significance on events, combined with a sense both of the failure of humans to grasp that structure, and of the inadequacy of that structure to be a comforting and sustaining element in human life' (42).

16. This is not, of course, to say that the narrative was not in itself enacted in a dramatic fashion by the speaker, or that the silent reactions of the onstage audience were not important. One thinks of the contrasting listener roles of, e.g. Electra and Clytemnestra during the Paedagogus' false speech in S. *El.*, or Medea's wordless reaction to the messenger's account of Creusa's grotesque death, an account which includes vivid descriptions of her own husband and children.

17. There are two places in *Poetics* where Aristotle implies that narrative is not part of drama. Neither passage has been totally integrated into the rest of his thinking on the subject. In the first, at 1449b (discussed by de Jong, 1991, 117), tragedy is famously defined as that which operates *drôntôn kai ou di'apangelias*, 'by dramatic enactment, not narrative'. In the second (1460a), considering Homer, he writes, 'the poet should speak as little as possible, since when he does so he is not engaging in mimesis (*ou gar kata tauta mimêtês*). Halliwell reasonably argues that in these passages mimesis is now re-interpreted as something which has to be dramatic or dramatising; but I feel de Jong finds the real solution to the difficulty here. In her view, Aristotle actually means the assumption of the role of narrator *by the poet*, and the modern understanding of the poet's 'I' as a fictional/

dramatic construct, always to be distinguished from the poet's *propria persona*, helps resolve this problem.

18. A slight problem here is that Plato makes no distinction between the actual author or poet and his metonymic representative – the theoretical narrator projected into the the text – as we would do today (see n. 17). It makes no difference to the points at issue, however, if for Plato's 'poet' we substitute 'narrator'.

19. At its most extreme these views have endorsed novels composed completely of dialogue, such as the works of Ivy Compton-Burnett or the very different David Storey. The 'novels' of Beckett are interchangeable as dramatic texts. The idea that 'showing' is better than 'telling' is still a basic tenet purveyed by creative writing courses.

20. The unities of place and time are not apparent in *Poetics* however: their first prescriptive appearance is in Castelvetro's manual, *Poetica d'Aristotele vulgarizzata e sposta*, Basel 1576.

21. The chorus leave the stage at *Eum.* 232; *Aj.* 814; *Alc.* 746; *Hel.* 385. These exceptions are discussed by Bremer, 1976.

22. See Bremer (42). De Jong surprisingly does not dissent from this view (de Jong 1991, 118).

23. De Jong, 1991, 118 n. 4, gathers the scattered evidence for this view. I note also the large number of messenger figures illustrated on vases (see Trendall and Webster, 1971; Trendall and Cambitoglou, 1978-82; Prag, 1975). It is noticeable in modern performances today that restless school children settle down to listen when the messenger starts to speak.

2. Narrative time in tragedy

1. Rehm, 1992, 52 expresses this dialectic as a series of oppositions: actor/ chorus; rhetoric/lyric; individuated/unindividuated; narrative or argumentative/ imagistic; rational or logical/emotional or musical.

2. In the final antistrophe of the ode (Euripides *El.* 699ff.), it is the chorus itself who, after telling the story of the golden lamb, cynically comment that aspects of their narrative carry 'little credibility' (737-8) – but all the same, frightening myths have a salutary effect (743-5).

3. The way oracles and dreams functioned in fifth-century society is outside the scope of this study. For oracles see Fontenrose, 1978 and studies of Herodotus by e.g. Crahay, 1956, also Roberts, 1984. For dreams see White on Artemidorus, 1980, and van Lieshout, 1980. The earliest written evidence for dream interpretation goes right back to *c.* 2000 BC (BM papyrus 10683). The dreams are divided into two groups according to whether they denote good or bad outcomes. Fifth-century opinion on the validity of dreams is very difficult to ascertain but it may well be that, as now, there were attitudes across the complete spectrum, from downright sceptics through those accepting rationalisations of dreams, to those adopting positions of extreme faith in their prophetic power. Herodotus lists 33 dreams and makes great play with the inevitability of their outcome, but this is part of his narrative strategy. Thucydides has none. In Aristotle *Politics* 9, 512a we find the statement, 'Dreams originate in man's material part: it sees and yearns after it knows not what, it remembers the past, discerns the present and foresees the future.'

4. A small, subtle example of the way proleptic elements can be used to probe the gap between stage figure and audience understanding comes at *Ag.* 577-9. The Herald merely gives his imagined wording of a dedicatory inscription that will be put up to celebrate the victory over Troy. Painting the future like this seems not so much false as merely quite irrelevant to the sinister direction events in the play are taking. The chorus' total failure to challenge the rosy picture the Herald paints makes us question – yet again – the reliability of the onstage narrative transactions in the play.

5. The use of emotion also qualifies Garvie's description of early tragedy. Emotion is used in both lyric and trimeter sections to heighten tension and urge on the audience to interpret the action. Emotion also creates *performance* of various kinds: prayer, invocation, supplication, lament. In general terms fear may be associated with *desis* and grief with *lusis*, but this is too simplistic a formulation. More often, as in *Agamemnon* we see a complex interaction between hope and fear as the action progresses; similarly grief and relief can be closely interwoven, as at the end of *Septem* where the women are relieved that Thebes is saved while they mourn their dead.

6. Mythical analogies may work in the same way. When a choral ode refers to another story or stories, such as we find in the Danae ode, *Ant*. 944-87, or an ancestor such as Io in Aeschylus *Supp*., it is setting up at a different narrative level a suggestively parallel story which tempts the audience to accommodate the new information to the main one. Prayers too point to a desired end which may or may not come about. All these elements can be thought of as (sometimes teasing) coordinates plotted on the learning curve of the play.

7. Major Sophoclean messenger speeches: *Trach*. 734-96 and 899-946, *OT* 1237-85, *Ant*. 1192-243, *El*. 680-763, *OC* 1586-1666. For a list of Euripidean messenger speeches see de Jong, 1991, Appendix A.

8. Although the messenger speech was of course identifiable enough by contemporaries to be satirised in comedy; see Ar. *Birds* 1119f. There is a likely parody of *Or*. 866f. in the fragments of Menander's *Sic*. 175f.

9. Cf. Buxton, 1991, 39-48. He is absolutely right to insist on the important difference of perspective and precise context of the utterances of Dionysus, Pentheus, Servant, Cowherd and Newsbringer, all of whom deliver narratives describing the Bacchantes on the mountain (*Bacch*. 23-42, 215-25, 434-50, 660-774, 1043-167).

10. Descriptive scene setting occurs at *Trach*. 750f. and 900f., *OT* 1241f., *Ant*. 1196f., *El*. 681f., *OC* 1587f. Direct speech is given at *Trach*. 797-8, 920f., *OT* 1271f., *Ant*. 1211f., 1228, *OC* 1610, 1627, 1631, 1640. Emotional aftermath: *Trach*. 930f., *OT* 1282f., *Ant*. 1240f., *El*. 757f..

11. Cf. *Trach*. 190-1, also *OT* 1004-6; *Phil*. 551ff., *El*. 772.

12. Since the playwright rarely provides any motivation for this group of messengers, explanatory reference to the basic psychological need (cf. *The Ancient Mariner*) to tell over horrible events is often made by critics at this point; in our society this might be done under analysis, and a modern name for some messengers might be 'disaster victim'. The reactions of messengers are in fact interestingly diverse: I note that the messenger of *Ant*. prefaces his account with as many as seventeen lines of gnomic reflection, whereas the Exangelos at *OT* 1223-31 is concerned only to express an idea of the sheer magnitude of what he has witnessed.

13. At 719f. she imagines a noble death *with* her husband (*tautêi sun hormêi ... sunthanein*).

14. Eurydice's death in *Ant*. is also the unpredicted result of hearing a message, but it does not create the same problems. Eurydice is not so fully presented in the play; and it is the content of the message, not in any way her relationship to the messenger, which brings about her death. After the striking effect of the messenger virtually having to start his message for a second time on her account (*Ant*. 1190), her fate is quite seamlessly subsumed within the overall action and her corpse is straightforwardly added to Haemon's (*Ant.* 1293).

15. See Winnington-Ingram, 1969a for Hyllus' entry from the stage-building rather than with the procession. As Easterling remarks (1982, ad loc.), 901-2 show that Hyllus did intend to go to meet his father – but his mother's suicide has obviously overturned this plan. This interpretation is clearly better than supposing that Hyllus has had the time to leave off lamenting by his mother's body and go to join the (offstage) procession.

16. See Loraux's discussion (1986, 54 and 65-9): Athens traditionally offered protection to the Heracleidae when they were harassed by Eurystheus and his Peloponnesians.

17. Audience response is not likely to be uniform then or now. Some might find grounds for comfort, thinking perhaps that, despite present sufferings the future will be glorious; the son suffers now but in fact he will be an honoured progenitor. Roberts, 1988, however, finds a clear ironic twist: 'Hyllus cannot know that the marriage that now makes him wretched will lead to a glorious line of descendants ... Hyllus is marrying his father's woman, Hyllus' descendants will bear and perpetuate Heracles' name, not that of Hyllus.'

18. That is to say, there is no indication of another speaker in the text; but it would certainly be within the director's discretion to allow incoherent cries to be heard before 1408 if he wished. cf. *Trach.* 863ff.: the chorus talk of a *kôkutos*, wailing, they hear before the Nurse enters.

19. Commands for silence, *Hipp.* 565, 567; *El.* 1399. Questions and further commands, *Hipp.* 571-3, 576, 580, 585ff., *El.* 1400, 1402, 1406, 1410.

20. But for a slightly different view see Barlow, 1971, 77: 'Unlike monody or lyric the messenger speech is not primarily a mode of feeling ... The messenger's report ... permits first a factual assessment which contributes to the understanding ... The full emotional impact ... is not released until the pitiable appearance of the survivors complements this preceding account.' However, I think the messenger's presentation of 'the facts' is in itself highly moving and our pity for e.g. the blinded Oedipus is already aroused before we hear his groans or see the mutilated mask.

21. See Hester, 1979, 12-17. He discusses the creation of false alternative outcomes in three Sophoclean plays, here in *Trach.*, at *Ant.* 365-75 and at *OT* 873-82: his point is that an antithesis is created but the outcome will incorporate *both* alternatives (i.e. Heracles will die by coming to the end of his labours). He might well have looked to the false antithesis used by Aeschylus in Apollo's oracle in *Cho.* for an earlier example of this technique. False prophetic antitheses are frequently employed in tragedy.

22. Were Alcmena to be present: like Thetis for Achilles, she is necessarily the most concerned in her son's fate.

23. We might contrast the veiled treatment of death here with the much more detailed but still mysterious account of the death of Oedipus in *OC*.

24. Stinton's discussion (1986, 67ff.) interestingly follows Easterling (1981, 56-72) in her survey of the historical development of the tradition of Heracles' apotheosis, but he seems to believe that the merest suggestion of apotheosis would spoil the end of this play. He seems to equate ambiguity with confusion and openness with dramatic failure – as though the endings of all the rest of Sophocles' plays produced clear, unequivocal readings. See Roberts, 1988.

3. Narrative deceit: *dolos*

1. 'Even the design of the poem seems affected by the indirect and deceptive methods of the hero. Its structure is more complex and intricate than that of the *Iliad*. Not only do we begin *in medias res*, but much of the hero's experience is related in a retrospective narrative recounted by himself (books 9-12), and the poem contains many other tales with a tale, told by Odysseus and others .... The poet also, like his hero, delays events, prolongs the suspense, and even defers the actual introduction of his hero for four books .... The poet also seems occasionally to deceive or misdirect his audience, leading them to expect a development which he then frustrates. This literary sophistication is paralleled in the self-conscious-ness of the poet concerning his own poetic creation and the deceptive power of poetry in general. Poets (Phemius and Demodocus) figure in the cast of characters, as they did not in the *Iliad*. Odysseus himself is more than once compared to a poet (19.203), particularly when he is telling his supremely persuasive lies, which regularly include substantial elements of truth' (Rutherford, 1992, 7). For some recent discussion see Murnaghan, 1987; Peradotto, 1990; Goldhill, 1991, 1-68.

2. Very attractive is Russo's reading of the problematic motivation of the entire sequence 19.535-20.121, in which he tentatively puts the view that it is best understood in psychological terms: recent events have produced an enormous stimulus to Penelope's subconscious (an excellent, fair discussion in Russo, Fernández-Galiano and Heubeck, 1992, 7-12 and 102ff.).

3. See Holt, 1989.

4. See Garvie, 1978, 64-7; only *Septem* might be considered to contain the sort of recognition and reversal prescribed by Aristotle for a complex plot (*Poetics* chs. 10, 11, also 13 and 14).

5. Propp's actants, derived from Russian folk tales, are: (1) Villain (2) Donor (Provider) (3) Helper (4) Sought-for person (and her father) (5) Dispatcher (6) Hero (7) False hero. Souriau's extraordinary cosmological actants: 1. Lion: the orien-tated thematic Force 2. Sun: the Representative of the wished-for Good, of the orienting Value 3. Earth: virtual Recipient of that Good (that for which the Lion is working) 4. Mars: the Opponent 5. Libra: the Arbiter, attributor of the Good 6. Moon: the Rescue, the doubling of one of the preceding forces.

6. A micro-universe is a discrete unit of any part of the semantic universe. It may be technological, legal, literary etc.. However, 'the semantic micro-universe can be defined as a universe, that is to say, as a signifying whole (*un tout de signification*), only to the extent that it can surge up at any moment before us as a simple drama, as an actantial structure' (Greimas, 1983, 199). Further, 'utter-ance is a drama (*spectacle*). In traditional syntax, functions are only roles played by words – the subject is "somebody who does the action", the object "somebody who undergoes the action", and so forth – a proposition, in such a conception, is only a drama which *homo loquens* produces for himself' (ibid., 198).

7. The exact force of Destinateur/Destinataire is not easy to render: Desti-nataire corresponds to the English word 'addressee' (as on a parcel), but Destinateur is not to be found in a standard French dictionary. It presumably corresponds both to the postal idea of 'addresser,' the one who sends the communi-cation as well as the notion of 'fate', 'will', from its association with the verb *destiner (à)*, 'to intend (for)', and the noun *la destination*, 'purpose' as well as 'destination'.

8. These two tragic actants are identical in New Comedy: see Wiles 1991, 26ff., who finds that in fact Menander has an invariable model for the first four actants.

9. The fragments of Aeschylus' *Lycurgus* tetralogy seem to confirm that Dionysus had the same double actantial role here too: see esp. fr. 72 Mette (schol. Aristoph. *Thesmoph*. 174): 'Lycourgus in the *Edonoi* says to the captured Dionysus, "Where's this effeminate from?" ' See also frs. 75 and 85. (The presence in *Xantriae* of Lyssa (fr. 368) makes it less likely that Dionysus' ambivalent role was a central part of that play's plot structure.)

10. It is interesting that this doubling-up of Subject and Receiver in one identity is the folk-tale pattern Propp described, except that there the actants coincide in an individual (The Hero), not a community. Perhaps we are looking at a necessary shift made by Aeschylus or his predecessors to adapt myth/folk tale to the different ideological and sociological context of tragedy.

11. The maintenance of an open view about the future, despite evidence which strongly suggests a negative outcome, is a delaying narrative technique which may be seen in *Pers*. as well. In psychological terms it is a thoroughly plausible human characteristic, as exemplified by those who 'refuse' to believe bad news, such as imminent war, until hostilities begin.

12. See Mikalson, 1991, 10ff. for the playwrights' licence to transform traditional religious views. He concludes (ch. 6) that Aeschylus' 'theology' makes him the most innovative adaptor of all three playwrights, the one who makes the greatest move away from the practised religion of his time.

13. Taplin, 1996, 196f., compares this positive closure with Aristophanean endings, and contrasts it with the 'open, cracked and unhealed' closures of the single tragedies of Sophocles and Euripides. For a metareferential view of *Eum*. see P. Wilson and O. Taplin, 'The "aetiology" of tragedy in the *Oresteia*', *PCPhS* 39 (1993) 169-80. For a response, see Gredley, 1996, 211f.

14. Aeschylus' concern for the community in the *Danaid* trilogy overall can perhaps be assumed from the extensive treatment of Pelasgus' consultation with the Argive assembly (*Supp*. 365-709). On several projections, these Pelasgian Argives would have constituted an on-stage chorus at the end of the trilogy.

15. The folk-tale patterns taken up by lyric and dramatic poets have their own 'inevitability' or 'shaping': there are repeated motifs of mistaken identity, dangers to be overcome, exposed children to be found. Some of these motifs cannot be deleted or avoided, and Aristotle suggests limits here: 'Now one cannot alter traditional plots (I mean, Clytemnestra's death at Orestes' hands, or Eriphyle at Alcmaeon's) but the individual poet should find ways of handling even these to good effect.' (Arist. *Poet*. 1453b10: Halliwell's translation). All the same, modifications are inevitable: the medium of tragedy is essentially different from folk tale, exploring moral, religious, civic and personal issues shaped into a dramatic context. At the same time, the regular competitive festival context creates a requirement for innovation, for a renewal of *to thaumaston*.

16. Easterling notes, however, two features which make it untypical: Antigone's emphatically frustrated desire to see the place of her father's death, and the insistence of both the chorus and Theseus in bringing the lament to an end (1722, 1751, 1777). The play 'ends in a refusal of ritual' (Easterling, 175, in Silk (ed.), 1996).

17. These verses have the function of neatly disposing of family members who would be extraneous in the closing stages of the play. We are entitled to wonder, however, whether Alcmena, who enjoyed Zeus' favour herself, might not have her own divine information to relate.

18. Cf. two other extremely powerful and painful father-son scenes in Sophocles – Creon and Haemon in *Ant*. and Oedipus and Polyneices in *OC*. See also the relationship between Neoptolemus and his two surrogate father-figures in *Phil*.

19. Although we might read a little ironic mitigation into 1270, 'The future is hidden from us' – it will, after all be a glorious future. Cf. Roberts, 1988. Perhaps Heracles' final speech 1259-63, with its adjective *epicharton*, 'to be rejoiced over' (1262), also lightens the tone.

4. Narrative shaping

1. The play is of doubtful authenticity but is generally agreed to be in some way under Aeschylus' influence. For a survey of the evidence see Griffith, 1977 and 1984.

2. See e.g. the discussions of Fraenkel, 1950, vol. 2, 97-9; Denniston and Page, 1957, xxiv-xxvii.

3. Cf. de Romilly 1968, 72-3: '... quite often Aeschylus keeps for the center of his play the most distant "flashback" as we should say now, and joins it there with an anticipation and prediction about future events. So that the whole sequence of events stands there in the middle, as one great unity, where time's continuous course is gathered into a legible pattern.'

4. The phatic function of communication is that which stresses 'the psycho-physiological connection between narrator and narratee' (Prince, 1987, 71. See Chapter 5, n. 2).

5. In converting from epic to tragedy, Aeschylus could (theoretically) employ from Homer not only overall narrative strategies such as the order of presentation of events, omissions, delaying tactics, advance notices of the end and so forth, but also adapt direct speech narratives put into the mouths of heroes at various points (e.g. Nestor). In fact, narrative techniques could not help being also 'cut off' with the slices that Aeschylus took from Homer's banquet. For an inevitably generalised discussion of Aeschylus' debt to Homer see Herington, 1985, 138-44 who, surveying the table of Aeschylus' works arranged according to mythological theme by Welcker and Mette, believes that Aeschylus may have set himself the task of attempting to reproduce in tragedy the entire corpus of cyclic poetry (135ff. and 139 with notes).

6. Reach is defined as the temporal distance between the story time covered by an anachrony and the present moment (or moment when the chronological re-counting of a sequence of events is interrupted to make room for the anachrony) (Genette, 1980, 40). An example of this would be the temporal distance between the present time of Eurycleia washing Odysseus' feet and the earliest moment in the famous digression which culminates in the boar hunt. In fact there are several linked anachronies in this digression and the earliest one is the account of Autolycus' relationship with Hermes (*Od.* 19.396-8) which precedes even the account of his visit to Ithaca and the naming of his grandson. Extent, on the other hand, does not include the 'present' or narrating moment at all and is defined as 'the duration or amplitude of an anachrony or the story time covered by it' (Genette, 1980, 48. See also Prince, 1987). Using the same example, extent simply covers the entire series of anachronies from the earliest period of time just mentioned right up to the latest, which is Odysseus' return from the hunting trip to Ithaca and – delightful ending – his *narration* of his adventures at the boar hunt to his parents (462-6). The narrative *extent* of the digression is thus at least nineteen years shorter than its *reach*.

7. Glaucus (of Rhegium?) in the Hypothesis to the *Persians* (= Phrynichus, fr. 8 in Snell, *Tr GF* 1). Else, 1967, 142 n. 69 states that the outside chronological limits of the play must be 478-473.

8. For attempts to anatomise story patterns see e.g. Propp, 1968, Lattimore 1964. Much of the work of Greimas was devoted to an attempt to establish structures which make narrative universally comprehensible: see e.g. Greimas and Ricoeur, 1989, 551-62.

9. Cf. Easterling, 1991, for an analysis of the subtle interplay in *Hipp*. between the theatre and drama worlds.

10. The anxiety and tension expressed by Aeschylus' choruses sometimes seem deliberately calculated to arouse and mimic the emotions of the narrative audience. *Pers.* 8-11, *Ag*. 179-81 and 975-83 seem to describe the effects of excess adrenalin (see Thalmann, 1986, on the faculties of *phrenes, thumos* and *kardia*).

11. In his *Apology for Poetry* (1595) Philip Sidney asserts the fictional nature of poetry against the claim that poets are essentially liars: 'Now for the poet, he nothing affirms, and therefore never lieth .... What child is there that, coming to a play, and seeing *Thebes* written in great letters upon an old door doth believe that it is Thebes?' And yet, of course, an audience both does and does not believe. To give an example of this paradox, Shakespeare's Chorus to *Henry V* appears to appeal to the audience's suggestibility directly: 'Suppose that you have seen .... Play with your fancies; and in them behold ... hear ... behold .... O, do but think You stand upon the rivage and behold .... Follow, follow .... Work, work your thoughts and therein see ... behold .... Suppose ...' (Act 3 Prologue). In fact, Shakespeare's direct appeal to the audience to pretend and imagine – largely the function of the *narrative* audience – is, by a typical paradox, a distancing effect which makes a strong appeal to the knowing *authorial* audience, the one well able to appreciate the ardent bravura and cumulative imperatives of this highly rhetorical speech.

12. Herington, 1985, 141: 'Where Aeschylus differs radically both from Homer and from the subsequent tragedians is in the enormous proportion of the *there and then* that he is capable of incorporating into his poem, largely by lyric means. For example the *here and now* of *Ag*.'s action is a mere pinpoint compared with the great spheres of time and space opened up in the choruses and some of the speeches too ... yet all of these converge on Agamemnon's death-cry.'

13. For dust as harbinger of news see also *Ag*. 494 and *Sept*. 82.

14. I would cautiously connect the use of delay here with that in *Pers*. where false expectations about entry are also deliberately created. First, at 529ff. the Queen tells the chorus to look after Xerxes if he should arrive before her own return – but he does not. Then at 849-51 she tells them that she is going to meet her son with fresh clothes before his return – but we never see the Queen again, and Xerxes returns in rags. See Taplin 92ff. on the technique of false or counter preparation with other examples, and his adoption of Nikitin's solution, which is to transpose 529-31 to after 851 and change *kai paid'* in 529 to *humeis d'*. However, the comparison of *Pers*. with *Supp*. seems rather to suggest a deliberate narrative strategy at work, making emendation unnecessary.

15. Herodotus could create the same convergence: cf. Croesus' downfall, predicted by an ancient Pythian prophecy, three oracles to Croesus himself and a portent (Hdt. 1.13, 53, 55, 85, 78).

16. It is interesting that Anderson (*G&R Studies: Greek Drama*, edd. McAuslan and Walcot, 1993, 29-37) is tempted to believe that Darius (despite saying farewell, *chairete*, 840) does not in fact exit but remains onstage in silence throughout the final scene, thus turning the symbolic figures of Atossa's dream into onstage reality.

17. At S. *El*. 645 Clytemnestra refers to *dissoi oneiroi* (i.e. dreams of double meaning). I note that Euripides introduces some variants to Hecuba's interpretation of her dream: before the tragic revelation she twice poignantly *guesses wrong*, supposing the identity of Polydorus' sheeted corpse to be first Polyxena, then Cassandra (*Hec.* 671, 676-7).

18. Garvie ad loc. tells us that 'Orestes does not mean to imply that Apollo is likely to tell lies in the future', but as he himself notes, Apollo's veracity will be called into question in *Eumenides*.

19. See Knox, 1979, 41-2 on Aeschylus' brilliant use of a third actor speaking to create 'this dramatic explosion ... it is the voice of Apollo himself'. Roberts, 1984, 46, reminds us that Pylades comes from Crisa, and is therefore closely associated with Delphi.

20. The varying use Aeschylus makes of predictive narratives shows that we should be wary of shaping whole scenes or arcs of action from missing plays around items such as Laius' oracle or Oedipus' curse. As we shall see with Eteocles' dreams, there is the possibility that such elements serve a temporary purpose rather than a larger structural one.

21. Tragedy is in fact studded with significant expressions of recognition concerned with the eventual understanding of some prophetic narrative (or even single word) earlier heard but not fully understood. With the confirmation, can come the idea that the hearer has all along been a prophet, as at *Sept.* 808ff. where the chorus say 'Alas, I'm a prophet of disaster', *oi'gô talaina, mantis eimi tôn kakôn.* Sophocles is undoubtedly calling on the tradition created by Aeschylus in *Cho.* when he creates the exchange between Orestes and Aegisthus *El.* 1479-83. See also Heracles on hearing of Deianeira's potion *Trach.* 1143-5, 'Alas now I understand', *oimoi, phronô dê* .... See also *Ajax* 353-4, 950-1 and *OC* 64-5, 299-301. For the same tactic in Herodotus, see e.g. the account of Cambyses' death, 3.61ff.: Cambyses, on hearing the name Smerdis, recalls a *dream* in which Smerdis sat on a royal throne with his head reaching the sky; leaping onto his horse to go to Susa to fight Smerdis, Cambyses accidentally gives himself a fatal wound in the thigh: on asking where he is, he is told Ecbatana. 'After the mention of the name, the double shock of his wound and of Patizeithes' rebellion brought him back to his senses. The meaning of the *oracle* became clear, and he said: "Here it is fated that Cambyses, the son of Cyrus, should die" ' (Selincourt's translation). Again, this tactic derives from Homer: see *Od.* 9.507-21; 10.330-2; 13.172-8.

5. Three major narrative scenes

1. It is interesting that at the deep structure level both Cassandra and Io scenes are redundant to the main action of the individual plays in which they occur: their significance is best understood as (a) thematic and (b) in relation to the development of the entire trilogy.

2. In Jakobson's communication model for dramatic language (Jakobson, 1960, 350-77), there are six positions: sender, receiver, content, message, channel and code, for each of which there is a corresponding communication function. Thus: *sender*: emotive or expressive function (reveals nature of sender); *receiver*: conative/ appellative function (e.g. commands, persuasion); *content*: referential function (e.g. teichoscopy, messenger report); *message*: poetic function, reflexively linked to essence of sign, e.g. rhythm; *channel*: phatic function (used to create and sustain communication between sender and receiver); *code*: metalingual (focussing on language, verbal games etc.). For further definitions of the phatic function see Prince, 1987, 71, Pfister, 1988, 113ff., de Hoz, 1979, 153ff.

3. Griffith's view, however, is that the extant Prometheus play comes between *P. Purphoros* and *P. Lyomenos*.

4. Useful readings of the Redepaare scene include Cameron, 1970, 95-118;

Taplin, 1977, 149ff.; Garvie, 1978, 63-86; Zeitlin, 1982; Vernant and Vidal-Naquet, 1988, 273-300 Winnington-Ingram, 1983, esp. 30-1. Most recently Wiles, 1993, 180-93.

5. The numerical ordering of the Argive heroes is heavily marked; after Tydeus comes Capaneus (*hod'allos*, 'this other'), says the scout at 424, and Eteocles begins his response with *kai tôide*, 'and for this one', 437. We have *tritôi ... tritos palos*, 'for the third man ... the third lot' (458) introducing Eteoclus; *tetartos allos*, 'the fourth, another' (486) for Hippomedon; *pempton ... pemptaisi*, 'a fifth one for the fifth gate' (526-7) for Parthenopaeus; Amphiareus is *hekton*, 'sixth' (568); Polyneices *ton hebdomon ... hebdomais pylais* , 'seventh ... at the seventh gate' (631). Each Argive attacks a named Theban gate to which the previous ceremony of the lot assigned him: all these details reinforce the structure.

6. See Taplin, 1977, 142-6 who suggests the lines may be interpolated or displaced. However Hutchinson refers to *Pers*. 521-31 and considers both as examples of useful preparation and deception combined.

7. Wiles ingeniously suggests that, just as the Argives cast lots at 55ff., so now in this scene do the Thebans. The variation in tenses is explained by relating each verb to a throw of the lot just made or just about to be made.

8. For literature on *clêdones* see Peradotto, 1969; Cameron, 1970, 95-7; Roberts, 1984, 14ff. and Goldhill, 1984, 21-4. The latter's discussion of mantic prophecy, Ricoeur's hermeneutics of metaphor, Aeschylean *griphos* and the 'sliding sign' applies as much to this scene of *Sept*. as to its primary target, the *Oresteia*.

9. Language has an intrinsic potency: 'word and name do not merely have a function of describing or portraying, but contain within them the object and its real powers. Word and name do not designate and signify, they are and act' (E. Cassirer, *Philosophy of symbolic forms II: mythical thought*, translated R. Mannheim, New Haven, 1955, quoted by Peradotto, 6). This metareferential view of language, as a potential, possibly dangerous signifier is expressed sporadically throughout Aeschylus in various ways: the desire to avoid unfavourable language (e.g. *Ag*. 1247); calls for silence (Eteocles' struggles with the women); apotropaic formulae (e.g. *Sept*. 5); *griphoi*; finding meaning in names (in *Ag*. 'Apollo, my destroyer', *apollôn emos*, 1081; the famous tripartite epithets of Helen punning on the *hel*-syllable, as *helenas, helandros, heleptolis*, 'ship-wrecker, man-wrecker, city-wrecker', 689-90). In our scene, Amphiaraus finds Polyneices' name (perhaps, 'much-quarrelling') resonant with meaning (576ff.: see Hutchinson for a discussion of the difficulties of the text at this point). Fear that a name might turn out to be all too *epônumos* is frequently expressed.

10. Although the chorus' reactions remain hesitant; see Winnington-Ingram, 1983, on this. I note it is only after the fourth disposition that they state *pepoitha*, 'I'm convinced' (521).

11. See Fraenkel, 1950, Denniston and Page, 1957, Taplin, 1977 and Goldhill, 1984. Fraenkel's concluding discussion on this scene (vol. III, pp. 623-7) is acute and sensitive; Denniston and Page, 164-6 offer an extremely clear breakdown of its complex structure; Taplin's wizardry with the full meaning of the exits and entrances in the scene produces excellent insights (1977, 316-22), and Goldhill, 1984, 81ff. highlights the narrative and linguistic dilemmas of the play at this point.

12. Clytemnestra's *eisô komisdou*, 'come inside', 1035, is important in providing the overall frame of movement in the Cassandra scene; more clearly than with Agamemnon, we experience her final movement into the reeking house (after three hesitations) as a movement into death. She actually says, 'I address these doors as the doors of Hades', 1291. See Taplin 317ff.

13. Although we see that her silence has to do with Clytemnestra's presence. She starts to move and speak when Clytemnestra departs and the chorus disassociate themselves from the Queen's sharpness with their gentle words (1069-71). Sustained reluctance to speak or engage in conversation is a fairly common dramatic feature. See, for example, Teiresias' reluctance *OT* 316ff., and Oedipus' *OC* 1169ff.; as Kraus reminds me, all these three have prophetic powers.

14. '... Nowhere else has the combination of the two elements produced such a marvellous effect as in the Cassandra scene. All that is characteristic of either of the two forms seems here to have found its most powerful expression, and where the limits of the one are reached, the other assists and supplements it so as to provide the whole scene with immense scope and depth' (Fraenkel, 1950, 623).

15. Does Aeschylus create the prototype of frenzied prophetess here in this play out of the thematic requirements of this drama? It is impossible to know. *Il*. 13.366 and 24.699 know her only as Priam's daughter. Her early sighting of the returning Priam is not cast as a vision. Cf. Schol. Hom. Ω 699 (V 632 Erbse): *ou gar oiden autên mantin ho poiêtês*, 'for the poet does not know her [Cassandra] as a prophet'. However in Proclus' *Argumentum* to the *Cypria*, Cassandra as well as Helenus utter prophecies when Paris sets sail (Bernabé, 1987, 39, l. 11), and Pindar *Paean* 8a (fr. 52i [A] Maehler) confirms Cassandra as a prophetess, although, in both cases, not necessarily one gripped by *mania*.

16. For tragic pain cf. Io, *PB* 566ff., 598ff., Philoctetes, *Phil*. 732ff. and Heracles, *Trach*. 983ff.

17. E.g. delay: Prometheus is prevented from prophesying his future by Oceanus' unexpected arrival at 284.

18. *chrêisdein*, 'to desire' and compounds referring specifically to the chorus (not merely Io, who as a direct participant naturally feels strongly) at 641, 701, 787; *pothein*, 'long for', 785; *prothumeisthai* 'be eager for', 786.

19. I note that the embedded figure of Hypermestra is also faced with a choice between two courses at 867.

20. Griffith argues that the variant *oduromai* is more psychologically appropriate; either way, an emotion is expressed.

21. Two of his lists are geographical, the third genealogical. The tone is strongly prophetic and each speech finally gives an aetiology (732-5, 813-15, 839-41, 846-73).

22. Griffith notes the continuing importance of the verb *ekpesein* (= be deposed from power) for the rest of the play (see his note to 755-6).

23. His major speeches describe the battle with the Titans, 197ff., 340ff., benefits to mortals 436ff.). Prometheus releases information about the future in a more gradual, puzzling way. At 168-71 he predicts that Zeus will need his help; at 188-92 that Zeus will be compelled to seek reconciliation; at 256-9 he says that he will be released when Zeus says so. Then at 507-25 the question of Zeus' fall is openly raised, but Prometheus refuses to be explicit, in fact he asserts that it is in keeping silence that he will be able to escape (524-5).

24. In his strong speech following the Io scene, Prometheus refers for the first and only time to Cronos' curse on his son when Zeus deposed him (910-12). This curse, as Griffith remarks, receives no further mention in the play nor do references to it exist elsewhere in ancient literature. (It could of course have been already described in the earlier *P.Purphoros*.) Its unique appearance is paralleled by Eteocles' bald mention of his dreams at *Sept*. 709f. (see above). In the context of Prometheus' unbounded prophetic ability a confirmatory dream or portent would have little validity; confirmation from Cronos supplies more weight, but no great significance.

6. Sophocles and narrative 'loops'

1. See Detienne and Vernant above and *passim*, but particularly 29-35 in their discussion of Oppian's *Treatise on Fishing*, and the pseudo-Oppian *Treatise on Hunting*. That these works were composed in the second century AD confirms the remarkable persistency of these ideas.

2. Cf. for example *Trach*. 225 when Lichas re-enters after a joyful ode celebrating the Old Man's news, or *OT* 1110 when the Corinthian shepherd enters after the same.

3. For an explicit conjunction of these two notions of time in lyric, see the paradoxical words of Apollo to Admetus, Bacchylides 3.78-84 (Snell-Maehler): 'In your mortal condition, uphold twin opinions, both that you will only see tomorrow's light, and that you will live for another fifty years in prosperity.'

4. Vidal-Naquet's discussion of the 'langage des images' in the iconography of Ajax's suicide (1988, 476ff.) prompts the thought that the ironic/tragic conjunction of frozen moments of time and the continuing time-world inhabited by the viewer/audience (precisely what Keats explores in 'Ode on a Grecian Urn') apply here.

5. A somewhat similar duo, the pair of shepherds, appear again in *OT*. At 924-1046 Oedipus receives the true but incomplete information from Polybus' shepherd that Polybus is dead and Oedipus is not his son. This is followed by true information from Laius' shepherd that Oedipus is the son of Laius (1123-81). See Longo, 1978, 79-80. Reinhardt's comparison of the scenes from the two plays (43-4) is marred by his excessive emphasis on Sophocles' stylistic development.

6. Tender emotion, such as love or pity, giving rise to disastrous consequences seems to be one of Sophocles' favourite ironies – e.g. the fatal pity of Laius' servant causing him to disobey the order to expose the infant Oedipus (emphatically positioned *katoiktisas*, 'out of pity', *OT* 1178).

7. Dei-aneira possibly = 'husband-killer.' Davies reviews the inconclusive evidence and scholary opinion (1991, xxx-xxxi).

8. Winnington-Ingram, 1980, 75ff.: 'One might say that the rhythm of the first half of the play is the rhythm of Deianeira's fears.' See also Easterling, 1968, 58-60.

9. The presentation of Heracles' situation is interestingly parallel to Ajax's (*Ajax* 749ff.): both have reached a potentially fatal either/or day of crisis which the audience readily understands as co-extensive with the action of the play. A similar parallel is the evocation of an emotional off-stage crowd (188-9 and 193-9; cf. *Ajax* 721ff.).

10. For a review of the evidence, see Easterling, 1982, 15-16, Davies, 1991, xxii-xxx. As Easterling notes, however, several of the details have been guaranteed earlier in the play.

11. See Davies, 1991, xxiii for 'The Sack of Oechalia' as a folk-tale with the contest for a bride as its original, now suppressed motif.

12. In some stories Omphale bore sons to Heracles who were forbears of Gyges and Croesus; Roman iconography represents him as besotted with Omphale, exchanging clothes with her and sharing her spinning. Fifth-century evidence is less clear.

13. This parallelism is developed throughout, eg. at 464-5 Deianeira says of Iole, 'Because her beauty has destroyed her life.'

14. The most recent editors (Easterling, Davies, and Lloyd-Jones and Wilson) all follow Hermann in attributing the next line of uncertain response to the Old Man rather than, following L, the chorus – 'And shall we wait? Or what ought we to do?' (390). Of course, no one does leave because just then Lichas himself spontaneously reappears for commissions. But possibly Sophocles teases the audience not only at 333 but also 390 into momentarily expecting the chorus to exit.

15. See Easterling, 1978, 27f. for a discussion of the piecemeal and ambiguous release of crucial information, especially concerning the prophecy; as she points out, the lack of crucial information required for full understanding is hidden behind a dramatic technique that always makes the motivation – superficially at any rate – extremely lucid.

16. *Oratio* 52 is a somewhat disappointing comparison of the three Philoctetes plays, while *Oratio* 59 is a prose paraphrase of Euripides' prologue. Mette frr. 249-57 and 787-803 add a little more.

17. See Easterling, 1985, Bain, 1987. *Hamlet*, a play of the self-conscious Renaissance theatre, makes an interesting comparison. There we find the same exploration of role-play, but the purpose of the scene can be pointed up much more clearly. Hamlet asks visiting players to perform *The Murder of Gonzago*, a play which mirrors his father's murder and thus tests his uncle's conscience ('I'll tent him to the quick', 2.ii.593), setting up a similar idea of *dolos* as a kind of test. In fact the performance of the play is not thoroughly conclusive to Hamlet of Claudius' guilt. Earlier, however, Hamlet gets the First Player to recite a speech 'he chiefly lov'd' from another play – a dramatisation of Aeneas' tale to Dido of the fall of Troy in which the agony of Hecuba, 'the mobled queen' is graphically described. The player's passionate identification with his subject ('Look whe'er he has not turn'd his colour, and has tears in's eyes') prompts Hamlet's soliloquy with its famous Hecuba reference in which he contrasts the powerful emotions released by acting 'but in a fiction, in a dream of passion' to the 'cue for passion' demanded by the moral requirement to avenge his father's death. Here, in this narrative loop of *Phil.*, Sophocles, bounded by different theatre conventions, leaves us to *guess* that a similar 'tenting' of Neoptolemus takes place.

18. Ignorance is extensive in this play, within and without. Masaracchia, 1964, 82, perceptively points out that it is only after getting Neoptolemus to investigate the cave that Odysseus gives him his instructions: 'Neottolemo lo ha seguito senza conoscere forse la meta del viaggio.' In this telling of the story, we do not know whether Odysseus rigged votes to get the arms of Achilles. We do not know whether Neoptolemus was treated honorifically and given his father's arms when he came from Scyros. When Neoptolemus pretends ignorance of Philoctetes' identity he is certainly lying, but how are we to read 339-40 or 431-2, for example?

19. One might compare the ambiguity here with Medea's tears in her scene with Jason 899f. and 922f: the reasons she gives him for weeping are not the same as the true reason, but as audience, how are we to interpret them? Are they really for her children? Are they genuine at all? Are they aimed at the chorus?

20. The emotional effects of improvisation are attested by modern therapeutic work, which harnesses painting, dance and drama to help the mentally ill. Dramatherapy (originating in the work of J.L. Moreno in the field of psychodrama in the thirties in America) is increasingly used with e.g. criminal offenders, who are encouraged to act out both criminal and victim roles. See S. Jennings, *Dramatherapy: theory and practice for teachers and clinicians*, London, Sydney and Cambridge Mass., 1987.

21. Fate of Achilles, 332ff.; other Greek heroes, 410-52. See below. Cf. Winnington-Ingram, 1980, 340-1. Roberts, 1989, 168-70 offers a different reading of this earlier scene. O'Higgins sees a failure on the part of the conspiratorial narrators to contain the effects of the past. The barriers between living and dead heroes limit Neoptolemus' authorial control.

22. The phrase has been understood in various ways. It might mean 'as I have got into the same situation as you', i.e. in being anchored at Lemnos (so Nauck, Radermacher and Webster; 546 is taken to support this reading). The parallel suggested by *ta isa* would then operate at a general level. However, the phrase has far more edge if it refers to the *charis* owed a messenger (so Jebb and Kamerbeek, supported by 557-8).

23. The story followed here is not the Iliadic version but that found in the epic cycle and Pindar *Pyth.* 6.28ff. where Antilochus is killed by Memnon while saving his father Nestor.

24. Huxley (*GRBS* 8, 1967, 33-4) suggests that the audience is meant to think that Neoptolemus is lying – the *Aethiopis* has Thersites killed by Achilles.

25. The earlier part of the scene also seems rich in references to earlier play versions. According to Dio, Aeschylus' version included false stories about Greek heroes – Agamemnon dead and Odysseus put to death. In Euripides' version (cf. Dio 59 8ff.), Odysseus pretended to be a friend of Palamedes, exiled from the Greek camp when Palamedes was accused of treason. Dio gives Philoctetes' reaction: 'O he who does not refrain from any of his bitterest enemies, Odysseus, the most villainous man in word and deed!' Sophocles' Philoctetes reacts very similarly: 'I know well that he would lend his tongue to any base pretext, any villainy, if thereby he could hope to accomplish some dishonest end' (Jebb's translation of 407-9).

7. *Dolos* in *Electra*

1. Short of a papyrus discovery, whether or not Euripides' version precedes Sophocles will always be unclear. Evidence for dating is reviewed in Cropp, 1988, 50-1. Burkert has recently proposed a date of 420 for Euripides' play (*MH* 47.2, 1990, 65-9).

2. Sandbach (*PCPhS* 23, 1977, 71-3) suggested attributing 80-1 to the Paedagogus and giving Orestes 82-5, a proposal approved by Winnington-Ingram (1980, 229 n. 40). This idea is properly squashed by Lloyd-Jones and Wilson, 1990, 44. Apart from their excellent arguments, I would add that, with the attribution as it stands, 80-5 creates a distinct echo of *Cho.* 899-902, in which Pylades forcefully intervenes to prevent Orestes 'softening', just as the Paedagogus does here.

3. In the creation of such an extended deceit, Sophocles is certainly indebted to the second half of the *Odyssey*. (See Davidson, 1988, for a general discussion of Homeric influence in this play.)

4. Frequentative markers taken only from the parodos, 121ff. (but very much present elsewhere, particularly in Clytemnestra's opening speech, 516-30): 'always howling' 122-3; 'insatiable' 123; 'always lamenting' 141; 'always Itys' 148; 'Unwearyingly awaiting ... I continually live' 164-5; 'Much of my life has already abandoned me without hope' 185-6; 'I shall never cease from my sufferings, with my unnumbered laments' 231-2.

5. The three final choral lines, 1508-10, have been very variously interpreted (see Segal's discussion 1966, 474ff.). It is hard to restrict them to their surface meaning. Segal argues convincingly, 530ff., that *sperm'Atreôs*, 'offspring of Atreus', is a patronym referring to Electra, and that the phrase *sperma ... teleôthen* recalls the vocabulary of *telein* (to fulfil, accomplish) and *terma* (goal) and so suggests fulfilment – in this case *disastrous* fulfilment, since the verb *teleioô* continues the language of biological growth and life (*blastanein, thallein, phuteuein*) which is used consistently through the play to convey the 'moral rottenness' (ibid. 487) of Mycenae.

6. Roberts (1988, 185-6) writes of 1497-1500: 'Those critics are surely right who argue that Aegisthus' reference to the future misfortune of the family suggests more than his own death; this is made plain precisely by Orestes' attempt in his reply to limit the significance of Aegisthus' remark. It is not, of course, that Aegisthus himself in 1497-8 means anything beyond a vague threat, but Orestes' own short-sightedness (itself stressed by Aegisthus in his reference to Agamemnon's lack of foresight) encourages us to read these lines as referring to his future difficulties. The play, then ends on a note of triumph and completeness, but we are made to think of events in a future beyond this play; familiar with the Aeschylean story, we may imagine Orestes' pursuit by the Erinyes.'

7. These verses are variously interpreted in the light of superstitious scruple (see Eur. *Helen* 1050-2 and Dale's commentary ad loc.), a contemporary *topos* on 'profit' (see Kells 6 and note ad loc.) or as a reflection of historical events (cf. Hdt. 4.14 and 95).

8. The vagueness is highlighted in verse 414, well brought out in Kells' translation made to demonstrate the intensive force of the prefix *kata-* in *kat-oida*: 'I do not know it in exact detail.' *kathoran* is also used at 378 and 426: the verb highlights the difficulty of getting hold of an authorised account.

9. Compare *OC* 617-20: 'Infinite time as it goes gives birth to infinite days and nights in which men will scatter with war today's firm pledges *for a little word.*'

10. Herodotus too makes extraordinarily good narrative capital out of changing the addressee of a dream. In the sequence *Hdt.* 7.8-19 Xerxes, anxious because an authoritarian and recurrent dream figure insists that he should attack Greece just when he has accepted advice from his uncle Artabanus to the contrary, sends his uncle to sleep in his place. Beforehand, the wise uncle rationalises convincingly: 'dreams do not come from God. I ... will tell you what these visions are that float before our eyes in sleep: nearly always these drifting phantoms are the shadows of what we have been thinking about during the day ...' (7.16b2, Sélincourt's translation). But the last laugh is on Artabanus – who despite this admirable rationalisation dreams the same insistent dream. As a result, the fatal campaign against Greece gets under way.

11. Sophocles' shaping conforms to Near Eastern 'culture pattern' dreams, where anxiety for future prosperity is frequently symbolised in concrete terms relating to sexual potency/fertility (see Devereux, 1976, 229). There are several examples in Herodotus, eg. Hdt. 1.107: Astyages has two dreams about his daughter Mandane. In the first her urine floods the whole of Asia, in the second a vine grows out of her which envelops Asia. The same motif is used 7.19: Xerxes dreams of an olive branch on his head; branches extend from it over the whole earth: but afterwards, it vanished.' In the course of his complex narrative, Herodotus shows us that whatever action the dreamer takes, he cannot avoid the fulfilment of the dream.

12. See *Ag*. 1435 and Fraenkel ad loc. for the sexual connotations of *ephestion*, 'at the hearth'. The sceptre has obvious phallic significance (see Devereux, 1976, 239, who links the sceptre with Agamemnon's penis, cut off in *maschalismos*, and now separately entering Clytemnestra in her dream).

13. The symbolism here is assisted by the language of 98-9: Agamemnon's murderers had acted 'like woodcutters chopping an oak'.

14. See A.A. Long, *Language and thought in Sophocles*, London 1968, 136-7, also Kells and Kamerbeek ad loc., Dawe, *Gnomon* 48 (1976), 231 (review of

Kamerbeek's edition). The subject of *epeba* cannot be determined, and this gives Dawe's adoption of Blaydes' conjecture *epeban* (found in Codex R) an added attraction. But however it may be with the verb, *miaiphonôn gamôn* must refer to Clytemnestra's sexual activities.

15. A similar kind of subtle negating technique may be seen in the expression 'the dark night of stars has left off' (19), where the weakness of the verb and the notion of fading stars dampens the optimistic sense of dawn breaking (see Segal, 1966, 492).

16. Pelops was referred to just once before in line 10, in the sinister phrase *poluphthoron te dôma Pelopidôn*, 'The house of Pelops' descendants, rich in destruction'.

17. Another such movement away occurs briefly during the *kommos* between Electra and the chorus, where another similar, but ultimately less 'black' family story is recalled as consolation. The chorus refer to Amphiareus, who despite a fate somewhat similar to Agamemnon's (*chrusodetois herkesi kruphthenta gunaikôn*, 'destroyed by women's golden necklaces', 837f.) nonetheless 'reigns in full life', *pampsuchos anassei*, 841. Electra, of course, rejects the comparison (846-8).

18. Frequentative markers: *au*, 'again' 516; *aei*, 'always' 517, 525, 530; *thama*, 'frequently' 524. See also 552. One unarguable function of the epode has been to create the wearisome sense of the past unchanging into the present.

19. The prayer's addressee is Phoebus *prostatêrios*, 'who stands before the door' (637). This epithet, together with 1374f., makes it virtually certain that there was a statue of the god outside the entrance to the stage building throughout the course of the play, as in *OT* (not just some sort of altar on which to lay offerings, *thumata*, 634). Clytemnestra's prayer reawakens our awareness of his presence.

20. Unless we adopt T. von Wilamowitz's view: 'Naturally we know that Orestes is not dead, that later on there will be a reversal, but now the news of his death with its consequences for Electra is so vividly before us that we forget everything else and experience the following scenes from her point of view without thinking of anything else .... If one asks about the point of view of the spectator, then Chrysothemis must seem like a wild child next to Electra's rigid calm; ... like a child that is playing with empty illusions in light-hearted joy, and when exposed to reality has to abandon her dreams immediately and come to terms with Electra's description of what she has found out' (1917, 193-4). Kamerbeek (on 697) is nearer the mark: 'The spectator, here as elsewhere during this deceitful speech, will waver between being carried away by the splendid rhetoric and his awareness of the deceit.'

21. Borges writes, in *Partial magic in the Quixote*: 'Why does it disturb us that Don Quixote be a reader of the *Quixote* and Hamlet a spectator of *Hamlet*? I believe I have found the answer: these inversions suggest that if the characters of a fictional work can be readers or spectators, we, its readers or spectators, can be fictitious.'

22. Erlebendes Ich and erzählendes Ich (see de Jong, 1991, 30f.).

23. A particularly rich application of restriction is the messenger speech of *OC*. At first the messenger is able with anyone else (*sumpantes*, 1646) to see Oedipus leading Theseus and his daughters to the appointed spot, to see the ritual washing, hear the words of farewell and orders to Theseus (1587f., 1597f., 1611-21, 1631-35); even to hear the voice of god himself (1627-8). From 1641 onwards, however, the idea of sights and sounds which are not lawful, *mê themis* (1641) is raised. There is to be only one privileged witness (the appointed Theseus 1643-4); the daughters and the bystanders, of whom the messenger is one, begin to move away. When they look back (1648) Oedipus has already disappeared and it is Theseus' expressive gestures which are described. The messenger does not know what has happened exactly (1656f.), but he knows it was miraculous (*thaumastos*, 1665, see also *kapothaumasai prepon*, 'fitting to marvel at', 1586, framing the entire speech with the notion of the miraculous). Sophocles harnesses the first person restriction of the messenger to help build up the necessary feeling of distanced awe, and to reinforce the unknowable nature of Oedipus' death.

24. *tôi telei pistin ferôn*, 'putting his trust in the goal', 735. Kamerbeek notes that *telein*, 'to reach the goal' recurs frequently in the closing stages of the play (1062, 1344, 1399, 1417, 1510 and cf. 779).

25. For Sophoclean headlines or summary phrases elsewhere, see *Trach*. 181-3, 234-5, 739-40, 874-5; *OT* 939-44, perhaps 1180-1, 1234-5; *Ant*. 245-7, 384, 1173; *El*. 877; *Phil*. 561-2; *OC* 1579-80.

26.The full narrative may occur after fairly lengthy question-and-answer sequences. See *Ajax* 747; *Trach*. 246-7, 748, 878; *OT* 1236; *Phil*. 601-2; *OC* 1585. *Ant*. 237-48 is a near-comic exchange in which the ordinary convention is turned on its head: Creon asks questions to stimulate the guard's account, but the latter resolutely insists on talking about himself, 387, 406, 1172, 1281. In the case of Chrysothemis' narrative at *El*. 871ff. there is a notable *absence* of the usual question: Chrysothemis gives the good news of Orestes' return ('Orestes is here', 877), but Electra absolutely refuses to elicit the details her sister is burning to relate. It is only after grudging permission to speak is given at 891 that the detailed account is given. The pattern of delaying the important information in a scene follows that of the preceding scenes described earlier. As so often, Electra exercises control over the flow of words.

27. 'Declaration of intent to narrate' expressions also at *Ajax* 719; *Trach*. 181-2, 749, 899 *OT* 1240; *Ant*. 234, 245, 407, 1193; *El*. 892; *OC* 551-3.

28. Jebb, Kamerbeek and Kells' commentaries, together with Davidson 1988, have adequately noted the similarities of diction which create Homeric colouring. On the whole my remarks will be restricted to similarities at the level of narrative elements.

29. For direct speech see e.g. *Ajax* 288f., 293f.; *Trach*. 797f., 920-2; *Ant*. 1211f., 1228f.; *OC* 1611f., 1627f., 1640f. *OT* contains no direct speech but many verbs of utterance, ie. 1245, 1249, 1252, 1255, 1260, 1265, 1275, and reported speech 1271-4. (For Euripidean examples see de Jong, 1991, Appendix H.) Homer himself does not hesitate to report the words of racing charioteers (*Iliad* 23.409f., 426f., 439f.)

30. Note exemplifying *gar* at 698. For this *paradeigma oikeion* see Friis Johansen, 1959, 54ff.

31. For example at *Ag*. 120 the hare is described as *blabenta loisthiôn dromôn*, 'prevented from its remaining courses'; 1535-6 *Dika d'ep' allo pragma thêgetai blabas pros allais thêganaisi Moiras* 'Justice is being sharpened for another deed of injury against other of Destiny's whetstones'. At *Cho*. 328 Agamemnon himself (following Garvie) is *ho blaptôn*, 'the one who injures', and there is the difficult but interesting conjunction *adolôs dolia blaptomenan*, 955-6 (see Garvie *ad loc*). Sophocles too uses *blaptein* and *feet/escape* elsewhere in contexts of *atê*, e.g. Ajax 455: *ei de tis theôn blaptoi, phugoi tan chô kakos ton kreissona*, 'If one of the gods inflicts harm, even the coward may escape the stronger man'. Similarly in *Antigone* when the chorus urge Creon, now fearing *atê*, to yield to Teiresias, they say *suntemnousi gar theôn podôkeis tous kakophronas Blabai*, 'Swift-footed Inflictors of Harm cut off those who think wrongly' (1103-4). See also *OC* 252-4: *ou gar idois an athrôn brotôn hostis an, ei theos agoi, ekphugein dunaito*, 'However hard you look, you would not see a mortal who, if the god drives him, can escape'.

32. Two passages from *Cho.* (794ff. and 1022ff.) are possibly reactivated in the audience's mind: in the first, Orestes appears both as horse and hoped-for victor, but in the second, pursued by the Erinyes, he says that his mind is like bolting horses carrying away their charioteer (Garvie is helpful with the difficult text at this point). *Electra's* association of *blaptein* with both Erinyes and family members adds to Winnington-Ingram's view (1980, 219ff.) that Aeschylus' Erinyes are essential to understanding the play.

33. The striking horse simile (25-8) describing the Paedagogus, could be an allusive pointer to this scene. Similes are scarce in Sophocles.

34. His advice to his son Antilochus is positioned early on (*Il.* 23.306-48), and his response to the award of fifth prize, with the story of his own earlier exploits in games, 626-50, concludes the horse race section.

35. An *ololugê* is often a *women's* cry of *thanksgiving* (e.g. *Il.* 6.301 and *Med.* 1176 where an *ololugê* is contrasted with a *kôkutos*, a cry of lamentation). There is thus a hint of Clytemnestra's reaction at this point.

8. Euripides' narrative strategy

1. The appearance of greater narrative diversity in Euripides is of course in part a function of the fact that seventeen tragedies in his case survive, as opposed to only seven each for Aeschylus and Sophocles. For his 'untragic' group, Knox (*Word in Action*, 251) lists some of the elements which went on to form the staple of New Comedy: prevalence of domestic drama of manners and situations; family misunderstandings (between father and son, husband and wife); mistaken identity and recognition; lost children reclaimed; angry fathers reconciled. Among the 'hypertragic' group, *Supplices* (on Rehm's persuasive reading, 1992, 123-32), *Trojan Women* and *Phoenissae* would certainly be included.

2. Some narrative elements may be less unique to Euripides than we suppose. Sophocles *El.*, *Phil.* and *OC* contain many strategies and features normally considered Euripidean, and there is need for great caution in attributing originality to one or other. There is doubtless a dense web of allusions and cross-references running across all three playwrights, of which only a few threads are now visible. Euripides was producing plays between 455 and 406; Sophocles was his fellow competitor throughout this period. If more plays survived, we might be able to trace not a few specific instances in which Sophocles and Euripides were vying on an annual basis in their exploitation of similar elements. For example: (1) *Use of deus*: Sophocles' *deus* in *Phil.* (409) had already been used by Euripides to enforce a 'happy' conclusion in his three 'romances' (*IT, Ion* and *Hel.*), all dated to 412 or shortly before. Euripides used a *deus* in the same way again in 408 to resolve the action of *Or.* (2) *Complex recognition*: if we were able to date the two poets' Electra plays with greater precision, we would know which of the two first began to exploit the intricacies of complex, delayed recognition, which receives major treatment also in *IT, Ion* and *Hel.* Annual rivalry on this score between, say, 415-408 is a possibility. (3) *Theseus*: both Sophocles and Euripides inspire a patriotic response by using the benevolent figure of Athenian Theseus, who helps suppliants in *Supp.* (before 423), *Her.* (before 415) and *OC* (406).

3. Euripides' plays become increasingly rich in precisely patterned formal sequences which demand attention as discrete items. This tendency is manifest in extended iambic trimeter stichomythia (e.g. the dialogue between Ion and Creusa, *Ion* 264-368) or distichomythia (*Hel.* 1030-84; Helen and Menelaus plot their escape). Euripides re-uses the apparently abandoned trochaic trimeter meter, both in continuous form and, again, in dazzling stichomythia (e.g. *Ion* 934-1029, Creusa and Old Man; even in *antilabê, Ion* 1529-62, between Xuthus and a reluctant Ion, or *Phoen.* 603-24, between Polyneices and Eteocles). There is a general avoidance of 'free' dialogue. The invariable prologue *rhêsis* (which may or may not have been a regular feature of archaic tragedy; see Michelini, 1987, 102 nn. 36 & 37) often makes little attempt to incorporate itself into the body of the play. It moves smoothly and lucidly through the past to the present and stands out as a separable unit. Long iambic trimeter message narratives occur in all extant plays; *Phoenissae* contains no fewer than four. Where Sophoclean *agônes* are incorporated naturalistically within scenes (see Lloyd, 1992), Euripides marks them out by exits and entrances, formal announcements, agonistic terminology, balanced and symmetrical arguments, usually of considerable length. Nine out of the seventeen extant plays end with a *deus* proceeding along regular lines: the god gives a command to hear or stop; identifies him/herself; explains the situation; prophesies the future; establishes a cult (Mikalson, 1991, 64f.).

Choral odes may return to Aeschylean lengths. This was an area in which Euripides (like Aeschylus) was continuously experimenting. Monodies, or solo lyric – a genuinely new introduction to tragedy (see Webster 18f.) – invite admiration in their own right for their complexity and emotional power.

4. For example, Conacher's 1967 'declension' which (ignoring chronology) groups the plays as follows: (1) mythological tragedy: *Hipp., Bacch., Her.* (2) political tragedy: *Supp., Her.* (3) aftermath of war: *Tro., Hec., And.* (4) realistic tragedy: *Med., El., Or.* (5) tragédie manquée: *Phoen., IA* (6) romantic tragedy *Ion, Hel., IT,* (6) satyric and pro-satyric: *Cyc., Alc.* Webster's analysis (also 1967) includes lost tragedies and divides the poet's output into five chronological periods. By this means almost obsessional repetitions emerge; Webster (rather oddly) suggests, for example, that in the early period, each year's production included one play about a bad woman, one about an unhappy woman and one play of a different kind. Repeated motifs such as the narrowly averted murder of son by mother (*Cresphontes, Phrixus B, Alexandros, Ion*) also come into focus, or the exotic settings and rescues of *Andromeda, Hel.* and *IT.* Burnett's *Catastrophe Survived* (1971) studies the typology of plot and scene in a category of plays with 'mixed and multiple reversal', discussing *Alcestis, IT, Helen, Ion, Andromache, Heracles* and *Orestes.*

5. Dunn's major work on closure in Euripides (*Tragedy's end,* 1996) appeared shortly before my own research had been completed. I am indebted to him for kindly sending me the final chapter of his earlier thesis.

6. Euripidean characters are notoriously sceptical of prophecy (e.g. *Hel.* 744-60; *El.* 1299-400; *IT* 570-1; *Phoen.* 954-9; *Bacch.* 255-7; *IA* 955-9).

7. The fascinating 'narrative suppression' of the curse in *Hippolytus* seems Aeschylean, thought on a smaller scale. In the following scene between father and son, exile is substituted for curse as Hippolytus' fate; then at 895-8 both are set up as alternative possibilities – either Poseidon will kill Hippolytus or he will live in exile. We return to the curse at the moment when fulfilment is marked (1169-70). Theseus cries, 'By the gods and Poseidon, how truly then you were my father after all, since you heard my prayers!' (see p. 68 and n. 21).

8. See Hamilton, 1978.

9. Use of *mêchanê* or *theologeion*; expressions of awe; commands; prophecy; *aition*: see Mikalson, 1991, 64f. and Dunn, 1996, 29f.

10. In 'Parting Words', Roberts' important article on the often identical final anapaests at the end of Euripidean plays, a similar conclusion is reached. The closing lines are 'clearly conventional, almost formulaic and even verging on the self-referential ... but have significance both for our experience of the end as an end and for our recognition of its limitations' (63-4).

11. It goes without saying that no detailed analysis of these three plays would content itself with this very general statement.

12. Compare, for example, *Alc*. 837ff., *And*. 802ff, *Her*. 822ff., *Bacch*. 848ff.

13. Some defences of structure: for *Her*. see Barlow pp. 193-203 in McAuslan and Walcot, 1993, and Bond, 1981, xviii-xxii: for *Hec*. see Collard, 1991, 21-3, Mossman 1995, 61 and for *And*. see Mossman, again, 1996, 2, 143-56.

14. *Meros holon tragôidias to pro chorou parodou*, Aristotle *Po*. 1452b19. This is not a fourth-century definition: during the parodic 'drama competition' in *Frogs* between Euripides and Aeschylus, the two poets take up the subject of prologues (1119-248). Under the circumstances they restrict themselves to opening verses, but the chorus still explicitly give the prologue its proper definition of *to prôton tês tragôidias meros* (*Frogs* 1120), the first *section* of the tragedy, not merely its first speech.

Here is a list of Euripidean prologues arranged chronologically (dates in brackets): *Alcestis* (438) begins with Apollo 1-27, then Apollo and Thanatos argue 38-76; *Medea* (431) with Nurse 1-48, then in dialogue with the Tutor 49-130 (children enter with Tutor, and Medea herself heard lamenting inside 96-7 and 111-14). *Heraclidae* (430-28) begins with Iolaus 1-54, joined by Eurystheus' Herald 55-72. *Hippolytus* (428) is on a slightly different pattern, beginning with Aphrodite 1-57; she withdraws as Hippolytus approaches, singing, and only just ahead of the subsidiary chorus of Huntsmen. *Andromache* (?425) is the familiar pattern: Andromache speaks on her own 1-55 and is joined by an attendant 56-116. Uniquely she sings in elegaics 103-16. *Hecuba* (before 423) is slightly different. The play begins with Polydorus' ghost 1-58 and Hecuba sings a monody in lyric anapaests 59-97 before the chorus enter using regular or marching anapaests. *Supplices* (?423) is even more deviant: the chorus are already onstage for Aethra's *rhêsis* 1-41, which is followed immediately by their first song; *Heracles* (?before 415) begins with Amphitryon 1-59, followed by a dialogue with Megara 60-106.

The protagonist's monody becomes more pronounced in the next three plays, which also involve simultaneous entries and exits and a situation of solo lyric followed immediately by choral. The start of *Electra* (? before 415) is particularly complex: the Farmer sets the scene 1-53, followed by dialogue with Electra 54-81. The stage is then re-occupied by Orestes and Pylades 82-111; Electra sings a monody 112-66 and is only then joined by the chorus. *Trojan Women* (415) begins with Poseidon 1-47 joined by Athena 48-97; Hecabe then sings alone 98-152 until joined by the chorus. Hermes begins *Ion* (?before 412) 1-81 and, like Aphrodite in *Hippolytus*, gives way before the arrival of Ion, who sings alone 82-183.

The opening situation of *Iphigeneia in Tauris* (before 412) is similar to that of *Electra* in that Orestes and Pylades must be introduced to the audience and so must the sister – but not together. Iphigeneia delivers the opening speech 1-66, giving way to Orestes and Pylades who are presented in dialogue, 67-122. *Helen* (412) begins with Helen herself 1-67, joined by Teucer 68-163. After a brief transition she begins to sing and is joined in the antistrophe by the chorus at 179. *Phoenissae* (?411-09) begins with Jocasta 1-87; she gives way to Antigone and her Tutor in a lyric *teichoscopia* scene 88-201 (in fact framed by iambic trimeters from the Tutor at beginning and end). Electra opens *Orestes* (408) 1-70 beside Orestes' sick-bed and is joined by Helen in dialogue 71-139; she then joins the chorus in a lyric sequence. Dionysus opens *Bacchae* (after 406) 1-63, followed immediately by the chorus of Lydian maenads he has summoned. *Iphigeneia in Aulis* (after 406) may be an exception: the internal evidence does not make clear which of the two apparently competing openings should be subordinated or discarded, and we cannot be certain that Euripides was not attempting a different kind of beginning. See Page, 1934, 130ff., and more recently Neitzel 'Prolog und Spiel in der euripidischen *IA*', and Guenter, 'Textprobleme im Prolog der Aulischen Iph. des Eur.', *WJA* 13, 1987, 59-74.

15. All scenes preceding choral entry are analogous, in a proscenium arch theatre, to opening scenes performed in front of the curtain before it rises (the rising curtain marks the beginning of the play proper).

16. We have already observed a tendency in Aeschylus to open with a single, human prologue-speaker with a narrow, internal focalisation. Such figures indicate a future crisis and display hopes and fears which elicit an emotional response from the audience: the opening lines of *Supplices*, *Agamemnon*, *Choephoroe*, *Eumenides* are, typically, prayers. Aeschylus' formal structure is, of course, as fluid in the prologues as elsewhere: *Persians* and *Supplices* open straight away with the choral parodos without a preceding *rhêsis* – the chorus themselves are the emotional barometer; by contrast the prologue section of *Eumenides* is extraordinarily long and complex. Only *Prometheus Bound*, of doubtful authenticity, opens with a dialogue. All surviving plays of Sophocles, apart from *Trachiniae*, begin with a dialogue such as that between Antigone and Ismene in *Antigone* or Oedipus and Antigone in *Oedipus at Colonus*. The transmission of information is naturalistically motivated: Antigone wants to consult Ismene about Creon's decree of which, it turns out, she is as yet ignorant; Oedipus' blindness naturally evokes Antigone's description. Some future project is adumbrated all the while the essential background information is delineated. Twice in surviving plays Sophocles imaginatively includes a third figure into the dialogue – the 'peepshow' of Ajax, *Aj.* 91-117; Electra's one-line, offstage cry, *El.* 77. In *Oedipus Tyrannos* and *Oedipus at Colonus* a new figure appears (Creon and a *xenos*, respectively) to create a second dialogue. In *Electra*, Electra's monody precedes the *parodos* (a strategy perhaps borrowed from Euripides). Sophocles tends to plunge the audience straight into the demanding complexities of the fictive world by dramatic *showing*; the audience are immediately required to understand by 'overhearing', and he does not 'ease them in' with the suggestive *telling* of Aeschylean prologue speakers.

17. Euripides may have been affected by – and himself affected – the development of forensic and political rhetoric in Athens from *c*. 450: for a brief discussion of this area see Lloyd, 1992, ch. 2. We have insufficient evidence to know whether the formal prologue-*rhêsis* strategy was a conscious point of departure from tragic predecessors or the reinvestment of archaic practice: of surviving plays, only *Eum*. opens with a narrative prologue, and this is soon subverted by the Furies.

18. Yet though Reinhardt, 1979, 197ff. and Dunn, 1992, 3ff. can describe Sophoclean prologues as a microcosm of the whole, a miniature version of the entire drama, the statement probably does not hold true for Euripides – as we might expect from so chameleon-like a strategist.

19. The abundance of tragedy and tragic material and their prevalence in the second half of the fifth century society deserves noting. Up to about 440, the raw annual figure for tragedies at the Great Dionysia is nine. After this four more were introduced at the Lenaia festival, bringing the annual total to thirteen. Tragedies were also performed at the rural Dionysia festivals in different demes scattered throughout Attica (see Pickard-Cambridge, 1988, 42, 45-6, 79-82). Members of the *polis* served as *choreutae* (members of the chorus). Then too, satyr plays share many of the same myths and genre elements as tragedy. The frequency of para-tragedy in comedy in itself implies audience familiarity with tragedy – and of course, sharpens its critical awareness. The little lyric *Frogs* 1109ff. explicitly comments on the audience's familiarity with tragic conventions: 'they're seasoned campaigners'. A man sharing Euripides' lifespan (470-406) who, from the age of fifteen, regularly attended tragic performances in Athens alone, would have seen some 630 plays during his life.

20. This is a difficult area. See Taplin, 1986, and now Taplin with Gredley's reply, Silk, 1996, 188-243 for a nuanced discussion. The presence of para-tragedy in comedy is pervasive and unproblematic, the reverse movement much more elusive. Cartledge (1990, 20) interestingly suggests that a reason why Aristophanes parodied Euripides so repeatedly was that 'his art was ... in a word, too comic'.

21. Fowler, in 'The life and death of literary forms' (*New Directions in Literary Theory*, London 1974, 90f.) distinguishes three phases in the development of a genre which are suggestive for ancient tragedy. '(1) The genre-complex assembles until a formal type appears. (2) The author consciously bases his work on the earlier primary version. He then makes the latter an object of sophisticated imitation, varying its themes and motifs, perhaps adapting it to slightly different purposes, but retaining all its main features, including those of formal structure. (3) The author ... uses a form in a radically new way ... for burlesque or antithesis, or symbolic modulation. This is the phase when genre is understood abstractly and *consciously*.'

9. Recognition

1. In *Cho*. Orestes hides behind Agamemnon's tomb and passively watches his sister as she finds her own way via the tokens to his hiding place. The subsequent recognition between brother and sister is moving but brief and inessential to the narrative structure of *Oresteia* as a whole; the joyful effect of the recognition is soon replaced by the theme of revenge and Electra herself, whose tremulous emotion on finding the succession of tokens is so well conveyed, disappears for good at 584. By contrast, deceit and delayed recognition are the core of Sophocles *Electra* (see ch. 7) – arguably so much so that they supplant revenge (incomplete at the play's close) as the main area of interest.

2. Twentieth-century literature shows a tendency towards more inward forms of recognition, no doubt mirroring this century's fascination with psychoanalysis.

3. Cf. Cave, 1990, 46: 'in the Aristotlean tradition of antiquity, *anagnôrisis* is not only a structural feature of complex epic and tragic poems, it is also a focus for reflections on the way fictions as such are constituted, the way in which they play with and on the reader, their distinctive marks *as* fictions – untruth, disguise, trickery, "suspense" or deferment, the creation of effects of shock or amazement, and so on. The commentators are led to these reflections almost unwittingly by the imbrication into the *Odyssey* of instances of story telling, by the latent possibility of reading Odysseus as a surrogate – and no doubt cleverly disguised – narrator. And the stories that are told are constantly, in their content or their effect, recognition stories. It already seems that *anagnôrisis* can become, by means of an almost imperceptible emphasis, the figure of poetics as a whole.'

4. The recognition duets *IT* 827-99, *Hel.* 625-97, *Ion* 1437-509, delivered on final recognition, 'cap' the chain of narrative incidents to date. In the early scenes Euripides grants his female protagonists narrative reach and extent to explore their painful pasts and react to present woes. (Iphigeneia mourns the situation in which she was supposedly sacrificed, Helen the cruel fate that has overtaken her family and the deaths at Troy, all done in her name, Creusa returns again and again to her rape by Apollo and the abandonment of her baby in the Long Rocks, a pain which intensifies to the point of murder when she learns that Xuthus is to adopt an heir.) The recognition duets not only portray the emotions of the reunited, embracing couple ('O dearest ...'), together with apostrophes on the operation of chance, but also provide a new, joint locus for important proleptic and analeptic reflections. In *IT* the duet shifts to a consideration of the future; in *Ion* the following entry of Athena with her proleptic information brings the play to an end.

5. Plot: 'recognition is a change from ignorance to knowledge experienced by the protagonist and brought about by the events of the plot which results in a turning of the action' (*Poet*. 1452a4). *Mimêsis*: at *Poet*. 1448b6ff. Aristotle tells us that 'imitation is innate in human beings from childhood ... and pleasure in instances of imitation is equally general'. This is connected with a pleasure (shared equally by philosophers and everyone else): 'the reason that we enjoy looking at likeness is that we learn as we look and infer what each thing is, as for example, "that's so-and-so".' As Richardson comments (1983, 221), 'the pleasure which the reader or audience derives from a work of literature (such as epic or drama) is for Aristotle actually one of recognition'.

6. Richardson concludes: 'it is clear that behind the [discussion of recognition in] *Poetics* ... there lies a whole tradition of debate' (ibid., 220).

7. The transformation here is to be associated with Aristotle's *peripeteia*, which he defines as a change of situation into its opposite, at its best when it occurs *kata to eikos ê anagkaion*, 'according to probability or necessity' (*Poet*. 1452a). He cites the scene with the messenger from Corinth in *Oedipus Tyrannus* as an example of *peripeteia* achieved in this way. Greimas and Courtés (1976, 570) use the same play to exemplify their idea of transformation: 'The first part of his [Oedipus'] life is spent in ignorance (le non-savoir) the second part in knowledge about himself ... The passage from one part to another corresponds to a transformation on the level of knowledge (of the subject about himself) which puts the narrative off balance and triggers a new narrative sequence ... there can come a moment of recognition when certain but erroneous knowledge gives way to another knowledge (perhaps "true", but it may be in highly complex narrative, that it is only a movement to another kind of false knowledge.) ... The transformational power of narrative, usually marking the climax, is the most intense and satisfying moment as far as the audience is concerned.' For a difficult, highly abstract definition of 'transform' and 'transformational rule' see Prince, 1987.

8. One particularly affecting group are those occurring between mother and dead child, as in *Hecuba* and *Bacchae*: the same theme is handled more tangentially through dialogue in *Trojan Women* (*Hec*. 657-725; *Bacch*. 1233ff.; *Tro*. 39-40, 260-71, 622-9).

9. The recognition of Alcestis by Admetus is excluded since Alcestis herself is played by a non-speaking actor and the recognition is engineered exclusively through Heracles, a third party (giving the scene a resemblance to the 'psychotherapy' scene *Bacch*.1233ff. in which Cadmus carefully directs Agave into identifying Pentheus).

10. Cf. *Ion* 237-400 (Creusa and Ion meet and sympathise), 517-675 (Xuthus identifies Ion as his son). Final recognition between Creusa and Ion occurs 1369ff. In *Bacchae* too recognition, fused with revenge, is established in the prologue as the overall theme – though it is recognition of kin-god rather than mere kin. A similar series of partial/minor recognitions also takes place (first Cadmus and Teiresias, then Guard, Chorus, Herdsman, Messenger and finally Cadmus' family in their different ways successively come to recognise Dionysus.)

11. In *Ion* the news that Apollo has granted Xuthus, not Creusa a child, triggers her conviction that her own child is dead (902, 951-2).

12. At *Poet*. 1454d Aristotle categorises types of recognition with and without the use of tokens (*sêmeia*). His discussion is detailed but unsatisfactory, 'both too concerned with categorisation and yet also insufficiently discriminating' (Halliwell, 1987, 144). One takes the general point, however, that he finds recognition achieved by 'artificial tokens like necklaces' as well as natural body marks such as scars and birthmarks, inferior to recognition which comes about solely from the integral progression of the narrative plot (for which he cites *Oedipus Tyrannos*).

13. A contemporary debate reflected later in Aristotle and his discussion of *paralogismos*, fallacious proof (*Poet.* 1460a18), 'which Homer has taught the rest'. Richardson's important 1983 article examines the Homeric scholiasts' interest in recognition and their concern for plausibility, citing Eustathius, who tells us that Aristotle criticised Eurycleia's recognition of Odysseus by his scar (although he admires it in *Poetics*): 'according to the poet, by this reckoning everyone who has a scar is Odysseus'. It seems likely that had Aristotle's *Homeric Problems* survived we would possess an illuminating discussion of the recognitions in the second half of *Odyssey*, by which Euripides' recognitions seem so influenced.

14. Although in a corrupt passage (287-92 for which see Dale *ad loc.*) Helen appears to lament the fact that, with Menelaus dead, she could not use tokens (*xumbola*, 291) to get herself recognised in Sparta.

15. Of surviving Euripidean plays, only *Alcestis* takes the overall form of a 'literal' death, with the wife's return from Hades completing the narrative. But an averted 'literal' death also occurs in the first section of *Heracles*: Amphitryon and Megara gradually lose all hope that Heracles will return from his trip to Hades to save them, making of his eventual entry (*Her.* 513ff.) a splendid *peripeteia*. Bond (1981, xvii) compares the release of audience emotion on his entry to that 'experienced by the great national congregation of modern Athens at the midnight Mass on Easter Day: *Christos anestê*, "Christ is risen"'.

16. Sophocles'*Electra* is structured so that Electra is holding, as she thinks, her brother's funeral urn all the while her living brother stands facing her – the chthonic aspects of *Choephoroe* brilliantly re-employed to prepare for the dazzling movement back into life. The phrase *anodos* drama (*anodos* = return from Hades) has been coined as a generic term by J-P. Guépin (*The tragic paradox: myth and ritual in Greek tragedy*, Amsterdam, 1968, 142), and taken up by Foley, 1992, in an article which explores the possibility that the symbolic deaths of the female characters of *Alc.* and *Hel.* undermine a series of contemporary ideologies. For narrative purposes, the phrase is too vague to be useful: the senses in which Alcestis and Helen are 'symbolically dead' are too different to be conflated. Less problematic (although avoided here) might be a category of *'katodos'* recognitions to describe identification of dead kin. See n. 8.

17. Comparing this with earlier expressions – Sophocles *El.* 1417-18 for example, where the chorus sing, 'those buried under earth are alive', perhaps echoing *Cho.* 886, 'I say the dead are killing the living', it is possible to conclude that Euripides is deliberately undercutting a convention here.

18. The lyric also has strong thematic relevance to the entire play, one which has been constructed, as Burnett remarks (1971, 50), with 'an almost mathematical symmetry'. The lyric (like other stasima in the play) is suffused with reference to the sea which separates the singers from their homeland. Journey by sea is an image of the significant past as well as the focus of present hopes. Hartigan, 1986, compares Aulis on the Euripos with Tauris on the Euxine – both sites of deceitful sacrifice. From Aulis the Greek fleet were to travel east; the desired movement in this play is to the opposite compass point. The lyric refers too to the flawed past of the family, its *daimon* (156, 202, 203-4) and *poina Tantalidôn*, 'price paid by the descendants of Tantalus' (200), which the outcome of the play will see redeemed.

The ritual pouring of milk, wine and honey enacted in the *kommos* also has continuing relevance: in her dream, Iphigeneia had sprinkled water on the pillar which she took as an omen that Orestes was already dead: the current ritual confirms it. Later, she will promise such offerings to her unknown brother when she believes he must be sacrificed (630-5) and finally, ritual lustrations poured by sister onto brother are both an essential part of the deceit that enables their escape from Thoas and, symbolically, from the last of the Furies.

19. The first meeting between Creusa and Ion is perhaps the most striking example of this. *Ion* 237-451 is suffused with a mutuality of filial and maternal feeling. In the long passage of stichomythia, Ion is the first to ask the questions and, suppressing only the fact of her son's birth, Creusa satisfies all his warmly curious questions about her family background and present circumstances. Then the positions are reversed, the stichomythia pivoting on Ion's expression of sympathy for her childless state (307). Her response, 'I am sure your mother is a lucky women' (308) then produces all Ion can tell her about himself. His statement, 'I have never known the breast, but the woman who brought me up –' (319) produces the excited interjection, 'Who was it, you poor thing? You have suffered the same affliction as me' (320). But there is a projected missing mother for Creusa to pity too, and this makes her create a 'friend' seduced by Apollo whose child 'would be about your age' (354). Projection skates into reality: correctly guessing his own history, Ion conjectures that maybe the god has brought his son up secretly (357). This dangerously premature idea is then blocked first by Creusa's emphasis on the injustice done to the mother if this were so and then blocked again when Ion rejects her desire to ask Apollo whether the child survived. The second, full *anagnôrisis* will end by mirroring this angry appeal: Ion demands an answer from Apollo on his own behalf, which is blocked by the arrival of Athena.

The intuitive sympathies of mother and son displayed here recap the prologue in giving us an entire conspectus of the significant past of the play, this time from the two major characters' points of view. The space devoted to establishing the positive emotion flowing between the two operates later as a guarantee that neither will kill the other in ignorance. The display of Creusa's anger against Apollo and Ion's contrasting, naive belief in the god's purity indicate the future complications of the plot.

20. The Oedipal conclusion of a recognition sequence, that the waiting person in fact kills their *philos*, to recognise them only after death, is not the pattern of these plays, but was apparently the story of Sophocles *Odysseus Acanthoplex* or *Niptra* (Telegonus killed his father Odysseus). (Extant Sophocles in particular shows much overall kin-murder, but only in *OT* is the kin-murder effected through ignorance of identity. In *Trachiniae* Deianeira unwittingly engineers Heracles' death, in *Antigone* Creon's actions bring about the death of his son Haemon and his wife Eurydice – examples of ignorance of *consequences*, not identity.) Averted son-killing by mother is a feature of *Ion* (and, among fragmentary plays, *Cresphontes* and *Alexandros*). In *Ion* the motif is then used again in reverse, as son threatens the life of mother.

21. See 380-91 with the resonant conclusion, 'I do not believe that any of the gods is evil'.

22. Sophocles' *El.* 1217 according to Jebb *ad* 1209; the moment is not absolutely clear from the text. It is clearly marked in *Alcestis*: Heracles: 'Have you got her?' Admetus 'I have, yes.' (*Alc.* 1119).

23. *tuchê* language at 473, 475, 478, 489, 500, 501, 511, 560, 607, 616, 630, 647, 694, 722.

24. For the pre-existing alternative traditions see Herodotus 2.112-20 (episode in Egypt) and Stesichorus (Plato *Phaedr*. 243A (= *PMG* 192) and *Rep*. 9, 586C as well as *PMG* 193 (phantom)). See also Euripides *El*. 1280-83. As Segal comments (1971, 561) Euripides' originality consists in using the *eidôlon*, the phantom-Helen, to ask philosophical questions.

25. Helen had already been reviled in *Andromache, Hecuba* and *Electra* and appeared as a specious, fluent character in *Trojan Women*, insensitive to the desperate suffering around her. She continues to be mentioned with abhorrence in later plays (and is an unsympathetic character in *Orestes*).

26. See Weimann, 'Textual authority and performative agency: the uses of disguise in Shakespeare's theatre', *NLH* 25, 1994, 789-808.

27. See Foley, 1992.

28. For details of the philosophical background see e.g. Solmsen, 1934, *passim*; Pippin, 1960, 159ff.; Dunn, 1996, 155f.

29. Helen 'splits' with Teucer and Orestes with Electra. Similarly in *Ion*, Creusa describes her pregnancy as having happened to a 'friend'. This play projects a particularly abundant number of substitute *philoi*. Ion has many false parents: the Pythia who brought him up is 'dear mother, though not she who bore me' (1324, cf. 321), while his birth-mother is consistently imagined by all to be some seduced Delphian girl who abandoned her baby at the temple (1365 and many earlier refs.). Ion himself is first 'of Apollo' then 'of Xuthus', then 'of Apollo' again.

30. The *onoma/sôma* (name/body) split for which, thanks to Solmsen's article, *Helen* is famous is in some degree a regular feature of recognition. Cf. Ion to Creusa supplicating at the altar: 'the pity you claim would be better felt for myself and my mother – for her *onoma* is not absent, even if her *sôma* is' (*Ion* 1277-8; the irony here is that the reverse position is actually the case).

31. 'My love is of a birth as rare/ as 'tis for object strange and high:/ it was begotten by Despair/ Upon Impossibility. 'Magnanimous Despair alone/ Could show me so divine a thing,/ Where feeble Hope could ne'er have flown/ But vainly flapped its tinsel wing.' (Andrew Marvell, *The Definition of Love*).

32. Teucer is a doublet for Menelaus, but his fate also mirrors Helen's (Burnett, 1971, 76): like her, he is hated because he did not share his *philos'* fate (he did not protect Ajax from death, or die with him, 104); like her, he wishes to consult Theonoe. And he too is destined to reach home – a new Salamis on Cyprus. In this second prologue scene, Helen's ability to think on her feet despite bad news, to befriend and manipulate Teucer and offer him good advice, suggest a positive outcome. The two part on good terms, wishing each other well, and the play will end with these good wishes repeated on the divine level.

33. The narrative of his wanderings at sea is made strikingly Odyssean (see Eisner, 1980): since the fall of Troy a god prevents his return; when he nears home a breeze blows him away (cf. *Od*. 10.28-49); a recent shipwreck has deprived him of companions (*Od*. 12.417-9); he himself escaped on the keel, *tropis* (*Od*. 12.420-5). Now he does not know the name of the land nor the people (a Homeric formulation) and is little more than naked (like Odysseus in *Od*. 6, though the humour of this is developed differently). He is in search of food for himself and his men (as is typically Odysseus). By contrast, the door-keeper scene seems to borrow heavily from equivalent scenes in comedy (e.g. the later *Frogs*, 460ff.). As with Dionysus, the scene essentially shows 'collapse of stout party'. I find little essential seriousness in the portrayal of Menelaus at this point (*contra* Podlecki).

34. Schmiel's psychological interpretation (of the recognition duet) argues that Helen is 'simply a variation on the old Helen' who cares only for her reputation. But reputation. how a person seems or is seen, *doxa* or *dokêsis* is a vital theme of the play (and, *pace* Sansone's discussion of Theonoe, it is not a valid criticism of the prophetess' view of justice that her ultimate motivation is to protect her father's *doxa*).

35. Compare Helen's reaction here with Electra's similar response on first coming face to face with Orestes (*El*. 215f.) Both women are temporarily poised for flight: only Orestes' restraining grasp, only the protection of Proteus' tomb keeps them where they are.

36. In *IT* the tritagonist throughout the recognition sequence is Pylades, whereas in *Helen* he is liberated – to the play's great enrichment – to play Teucer and then the Slave (before tackling Theonoe and Theoclymenus).

37. In *Ion*, another unheralded character also arrives with unlikely timeliness, but her appearance is handled with more concern to create probability. The Pythia hands over the cradle saying that 'only now' does Apollo wish it (1353). Her arrival resolves the crisis in which Ion, it appears, is set on Oedipal crimes and Oedipal recognition: killing his mother on Apollo's altar would neatly combine paternal sacrilege and matricide. The Pythia's opening restraint 'Stop, child' closely resembles the opening commands of the *deus* at *IT* 1437, *Hel*. 1642 and *Or*. 1625; in fact there almost seems a risk that, given her prophetic authority, she might short circuit the recognition scene by telling all herself. Euripides overtly sidesteps the problem of the Pythia's potential omniscience by making her somewhat oddly state that she has acted 'uncommanded but merely following the will of Apollo, without knowing what that is' (1359-60). The cradle is then handed to Ion not yet as a token but as the starting point in his quest for his mother (1357ff.).

38. The play makes sudden changes – usually in the direction of wish-fulfilment.

39. See *Ion* 1445ff. for a similarly troubled duet.

40. Apart from Zuntz, critical responses here are negative. Dale (1967, *ad* 711ff.) ponders 'how much awkwardness and doddering irrelevance we must accept'; Segal, 1971, like most others, omits all reference to this section in his lengthy study. However, like the Attendant or the Nurse in *Hipp*., the Farmer in *El*., or the humble messengers in *Bacch*. the opinions of these figures must be treated seriously.

41. 'His speech points forward to the enlightenment which is to come with Theonoe; where her all-embracing mind seizes the right in spiritual contact with some impersonal, supramundane reality (the 'ether') he finds it safely in his breast' (Zuntz, 1960, 223).

42. At 36f. Helen tells us that Zeus brought the Trojan War about to lighten the earth of mortals (and to make Achilles famous – perhaps a comment on the *Iliad*). Zeus' Malthusian plan, which appears in the *Cypria* (fr. 1) early introduces the idea that human effort at Troy was utterly futile. At this stage in the play, the Slave is the only character who shows understanding of this (at 593, 707, 751).

43. But compare the equally overwhelming role of the Old Man, Euripides *El*. 512ff. in the recognition between Orestes and Electra.

44. Apart from the stream of figures who aquiesce in Dionysus worship throughout the play, I note the chorus' warnings at the end of the first stasimon (esp. 424ff.), urging acceptance of the ways of *to plêthos phauloteron*, the common people.

10. Gods as prologue-speakers

1. The use of Cassandra in *Tro*. and Teiresias in *Phoen*. is powerful but not essential to the structure. Teiresias in *Bacch*. has been absolutely deprived of his prophetic role. His long rhetorical speech (266-327) is shaped as a reply to Pentheus and resembles the second speech of an *agon*. He gives warnings, not predictions and, despite the chorus' approving comment which alludes to his powers of prophecy, 'you certainly bring no shame to Apollo' (328-9), he explicitly concludes 'It is *not* by prophecy that I say this, but by the facts' (368-9).

2. Burnett (1970, 28 n. 4) considers the presence of the prologue-speaking god in the light of the folk-tale motif of a disguised god seeking human reception. The disguise is a test of piety, and humans are rewarded or punished in proportion to their hospitality. The text for this idea comes at *Od*. 17.485-7:

For the gods, you know, disguising themselves as travellers
from foreign lands, roam our cities noting human arrogance
and human civility (*hubris* and *eunomia*).

Frequently behind this divine visitation seems to stand the figure of Zeus, whose punishment for insubordination on Olympus may take the form of a period of service to mortals. Poseidon and Apollo were sent by Zeus to serve Laomedon for a year (*Il*. 21.441ff.); Apollo's service to Admetus was also Zeus' punishment (*Alc*. 3-7). But in tragedy, only *Alc*. makes the idea of *servitude* explicit, and possibly underlies the unusually muted nature of Apollo. In *Tro*., Euripides has elided Homer's account of Poseidon's servitude to Laomedon (and anger at lack of payment). As for the presentation of Dionysus in *disguise* in *Bacch*., that is presumably better accounted for by the god's role in drama and his transvestite cult connections (see Seaford 1981) rather than by a folk-tale motif.

3. The great exception to the rule that divine prologue-speakers, having set the play in motion, do not appear again within the body of the play is *Bacchae*, where Dionysus moves readily from his explanatory external role to that of creator of, and major player in, every subsequent episode leading up to disaster (except the first), concluding with his manifestation as *deus*. More than any other prologue god, he is evident *didaskalos*. (For one of the many metatheatrical readings of the play, see Segal, 1985, 156ff.)

4. Evidence for the first lost version comes from a comment in Aristophanes of Byzantium's hypothesis to the extant version, nineteen brief fragments, two paraphrases of lines or scenes, and a recently discovered, very fragmentary hypothesis of the first version. For a full discussion of the evidence for Euripides' first *Hippolytus* as well as the little that is known of Sophocles' *Phaedra*, see Barrett, 1964, 10-12, 15-45 and now Halleran's excellent up-to-date and careful survey, 1988, 25-37.

5. Dunn (1992, 103f.) takes the phrase *katopsion tes ges* (30-1), 'overlooking this land' (i.e. overlooking Troezen from the Acropolis) and links it to the closing aetiology (*Hipp*. 1423-30) which describes the cult of Hippolytus in Troezen. Pausanias (2.32,1-4) tells us that Aphrodite's cult title there was *Kataskopia*, as she was worshipped above a stadium named after Hippolytus. Dunn believes that the earlier *Hipp*. may well have ended, as this play does, by giving an aetion for *this* site. The transference of the epithet from one place to another here would then have the delicate effect of 'closing off' the previous version. This view is somewhat affected by the fact that the fragmentary hypothesis seems to imply that the setting of the first *Hipp*. was also Troezen and not, as earlier assumed, Athens. An unchanged setting would account for the otherwise strange delay in mentioning place at all until 29. Zeitlin's exploration of *katopsion* (102 n. 107) also becomes less compelling.

6. Cf. Luschnig's sensitive study of knowledge in the play (1988, esp. 93-111): 'The audience is in the position of both knowing and coming to know. We know in advance the fates of the characters, but we do not know how or why these fates fit

them (97). In the space of three lines (40-2) [Aphrodite] moves without giving a clue about the progress of this knowledge, from absolute lack of knowledge to lethally effective knowledge .... We watch the mortal characters play out their tragedies not with the attitude of superior knowledge that they are dispensable puppets to be cut off one by one, but with keen interest in their doings .... Euripides opens his play by involving his audience in this fascinating question: how is knowledge reached; and in the even more basic question, what is there to know?' (98)

7. Halleran cites among others Bremer, *Mnemosyne* 28, 1975, 268-80. See also Goff, 1990, 58ff.

8. These key ideas (for which the English synonyms given here are only a weak approximation), have been extensively explored by many critics (for a recent review see Halleran 1988, 43-9), so I do no more than list them here: *semnos*, already defined; *aidos* (78), 'respect' or 'reverence'; *sophia*, 'wisdom' (cf. *sophôterous*, 'wiser', 120) and, most important of all, *to sôphronein* (80), 'moderation', 'self-control', 'chastity' – all these moral/religious/societal concepts tightly packed into a play about sexual passion. As just one example of the dense use of concepts initiated in the prologue which recur, in the rhetoric of the *agôn*, Theseus strikingly inverts all Hippolytus' apparently unassailable attributes of innocence; being *sôphrôn* (80), consorting with gods (17,85), purity (73,76), *semnotês*, even hunting (18, 52). To Theseus they become, precisely, the properties which prove his guilt. For example Theseus taunts him (948-9):

Do you then *consort with the gods* as someone
special, are you *sophron* and *pure* of base actions?

He continues his attack 956-7:

(people like you) *hunt* with *arrogant* phrases,
all the while contriving disgraceful deeds.

The hunting image fits Hippolytus exactly (cf. *theras*, 18, 52) here coupled with a debased use of *semnos*. At 1064 Theseus says his son's *semnotês* will be the death of him. The innocence of all these prologue phrases has now been turned inside out, taken on sexual implications and become a source of furious hatred. Hippolytus' protestations of *sôphrosune* are deprived of conviction; as Theseus says of himself, he cannot tell true from false (925ff.; cf. Hippolytus on the same theme 616ff.). Aphrodite wins a victory totally appropriate to her sexual nature.

9. The ode compares interestingly with the Nurse, 443-58, who on learning that Phaedra was in love launched into a similar account of Aphrodite's universal power. Her concluding advice was acquiescence to it (as Zeus loved Semele and Eos, Cephalus); a good example of Euripides' technique of putting problematically good advice into the mouth of an unacceptable character.

10. *Sphallein* is another key word, cf. 183, 262, 671, 871 and – used literally of Hippolytus – 1232. See Knox, 1952, 109-10.

11. Consequently I think Dunn is too negative when he writes (1996, 100) that the 'lifeless and repetitive action replicates suffering without transforming it, enacting *pathos* without *mathos*'.

12. These are listed by Seaford, 1996, 26 n. 9.

13. The information here comes from Lloyd-Jones *Aeschylus* vol. 2. (1) Dionysus' costume: Aeschylus *Edones* fr. 29 (59). (2) Capture and release: Apoll. *Library* iii.5.i; probably an element in at least a proportion of Aeschylus *Bacch.*, *Penth.*, Sophocles *Bacch.*, Xenocles *Bacch.*, Iophon *Bacch./ Penth.* (3) Palace shaking: Aeschylus *Ed.* fr. 28 (58). (4) Madness (sometimes personified) and *sparagmos*: in Aeschylus *Ed.* – according to Apoll.– Lycurgus chops off his son's extremities with an axe and wild horses tear him apart, in Aeschylus *Bassarids* – according to Eratos. 24 p. 140 Roberts – the Bassarids tear Pentheus apart; in Aeschylus

Xantriae – see Lloyd-Jones' conjecture pp. 435-6 – Dionysus drives mad the three daughters of Minyas, Leucippe, Arsippe and Alcithoe so that they tear Leucippe's son apart; for this they are pursued by Maenads. Other plays presumably treated this. (5) Mountain: Mt. Cithaeron if play concerns Pentheus, Mt. Pangaeus if Lycurgus or Orpheus. (6) Hera's disguise: Aeschylus *Semele/Hydrophoroi*; *Xantriae*; Spintharos *Semele Keraunoumene*.

14. March's article (1989) develops a persuasive argument, on the basis of vase-paintings and a close reading of the text, that the play shows three distinct innovations: (1) the maddening of Pentheus, (2) his journey in womens' clothes to Cithaeron, (3) the killing of Pentheus by his mother. For a response see Seaford, 1996, 27 and *ad* 50-2.

15. Burnett refers to the Attic myths of Eleuther, Semachus and Amphictyon, humans who welcomed Dionysus and received no punishment. She suggests that during the play Dionysus offers Pentheus a real chance to accept him. I think this possibility has disappeared by 42.

16. His reaction is not staged at this point perhaps because it would detract from the scenes of mad delusion developed after 810.

17. Foley (1985, 246f.) writes perceptively of the changing idea of the god's identity controlled by his unchanging smiling mask throughout the action of the play.... 'The mask in the epiphany can be understood only as a sign that represents forces that are in fact not directly accessible to the eye ... [the mask becomes] the central mocking image of what human beings understand about divinity' (253-4).

Bibliography

Alexiou, M. (1974) *The ritual lament in Greek tradition*, Cambridge
Almansi, G. (1975) *The writer as liar: narrative techniques in The Decameron*, London
Arnott, W.G. (1973) 'Euripides and the unexpected' in McAuslan and Walcot (eds), 138-52
Arnott, W.G. (1981) 'Double the vision: a reading of Euripides' *Electra*' in McAuslan and Walcot (eds), 204-15
Austin, N. (1994) *Helen of Troy and her shameless phantom*, Ithaca and London
Bain, D. (1987) 'Some reflections on the illusion in Greek tragedy', in *Essays on Greek Drama* ed. B. Gredley, *BICS* 34, 1-14
Bal, M. (1981) 'The laughing mice or: On focalisation', *Poetics Today* 2.2, 202-10
Bal, M. (1985) *Narratology: introduction to the theory of narrative*, trans. C. van Boheemen, Toronto [first published as *De theorie van vertellen en verhalen*, Coutinho, 1980]
Barlow, S. (1971) *The Imagery of Euripides*, London
Barlow, S. (1986) *Euripides: Troades*, Warminster
Barrett, W.S. (1964) *Euripides: Hippolytus*, Oxford
Barthes, R. (1974) *S/Z*, trans. R. Miller, New York [first published Paris, 1973]
Barthes, R. (1975) 'An Introduction to the structural analysis of narrative', *NLH* 6, 2, 237-72, trans. L. Diusit [first published in *Communications* 8, 1966]
Blundell, M.W. (1989) *Helping friends and harming enemies, a study in Sophocles and Greek ethics*, Cambridge
Bond, G.W. (1981) *Euripides: Heracles*, Oxford
Bowra, M. (1944) *Sophoclean tragedy*, Oxford
Brann, E. (1957) 'A Note on the structure of Sophocles' *Electra*', *CPh* 52, 103-4
Bremer, J.M. (1976) 'Why messenger speeches?' in *Miscellanea tragica in honorem J.C. Kamerbeek*, ed. Bremer, Radt and Ruigh, Amsterdam, 29-48
Bremond, C. (1973) *Logique du recit*, Paris
Broadhead, H.D. (1960) *The Persae of Aeschylus*, Cambridge
Brody, J. (1985) *'Fate' in Oedipus Tyrannos: a textual approach*, New York
Brown, A.L. (1976) 'The end of the *Seven Against Thebes*', *CQ* n.s. 26, 206ff.
Brown, A.L. (1984) 'Eumenides in Greek tragedy', *CQ* n.s. 34 (ii) 260-81
Burian, P. (ed.) (1985) *Directions in Euripidean criticism: a collection of essays*, Durham
Burkert, W. (1985) *Greek religion*, trans. J. Raffan, Oxford [first published as *Griechische Religion der archaischen und klassischen Epoche* in the series *Die Religionen der Menschheit*, 15, Stuttgart, 1977]
Burkert, W. (1991) 'Oedipus, oracles and meaning: from Sophocles to Umberto Eco', Samuel James Stubbs lecture, University College, Toronto

Burnett, A.P. (1965) 'The Virtues of Admetus', *CP* 60, 240-55 (reprinted in E. Segal (ed.), *Euripides*)

Burnett, A.P. (1970) 'Pentheus and Dionysus: host and guest', *CP* 65, 15-29

Burnett, A.P. (1971) *Catastrophe survived*, Oxford

Burnett, A.P. (1977) 'Trojan Women and the Ganymede ode', *YClS* 25, 291-316

Burton, R.W.B. (1980) *The Chorus in Sophocles' tragedies*, Oxford

Buxton, R. (1982) *Persuasion in Greek tragedy: a study in peitho*, Cambridge

Buxton, R. (1991) 'News from Cithaeron: narrators and narratives in the *Bacchae*', *Pallas* 37, 39-48

Buxton, R. (1996) 'What can you rely on in *Oedipus Rex*? Response to Calame', in Silk (ed.), 38-48

Cameron, H.D. (1970) 'The power of words in the *Seven Against Thebes*', *TAPhA* 101, 95ff.

Cartledge, P. (1990) *Aristophanes and his theatre of the absurd*, London

Cave, T. (1990) *Recognition: a study in poetics*, Oxford

Chamberlain, D.F. (1990) *Narrative perspective in fiction: a phenomenological mediation of reader, text and word*, Toronto

Chambers, R. (1984) *Story and situation: narrative seduction and the power of fiction*, Manchester and Minnesota

Chatman, S.B. (1978) *Story and discourse: narrative structure in fiction and film*, Ithaca and London

Collard, C. (1973) *Euripides: Supplices*, 2 vols., Groningen

Collard, C. (1991) *Euripides: Hecuba*, Warminster

Conacher, D.J. (1967) *Euripidean drama: myth, theme and structure*, Toronto and London

Conacher, D.J. (1988) *Euripides: Alcestis*, Warminster

Craik, E. (1988) *Euripides: Phoenician Women*, Warminster

Croally, N.T. (1994) *Euripidean polemic*, Cambridge

Cropp, M., Fantham, E. and Scully, S.E. (eds.) (1986) *Greek tragedy and its legacy: essays presented to D.J.Conacher*, Calgary

Cropp, M. (1986) 'Heracles, Electra and the *Odyssey*', in Cropp, Fantham and Scully (eds.), 187-99

Cropp, M.J. (1988) *Euripides: Electra*, Warminster

Culler, J. (1975) *Structuralist poetics*, London

Culler, J. (1981) *The pursuit of signs: semiotics, literature, deconstruction*, Ithaca

Dale, A.M. (1954) *Euripides: Alcestis*, Oxford

Dale, A.M. (1967) *Euripides: Helen*, Oxford

Davidson, J.F. (1988) 'Homer and Sophocles' *Electra*', *BICS* 35, 45-72

Davies, M. (1988) *Epicorum graecorum fragmenta*, Göttingen

Davies, M. (1991) *Sophocles: Trachiniae*, Oxford

Dawe, R.D. (1963) 'Inconsistency of plot and character in Aeschylus', *PCPhS* 189 (n.s. 9) 21-62

Dawe, R.D. (1978) 'The end of the *Seven Against Thebes* yet again', in Dawe, Diggle and Easterling (eds.) *Dionysiaca: nine studies by former pupils presented to Sir Denys Page on his seventieth birthday*, Cambridge, 87-104

Dawe, R.D. (1982) *Sophocles: Oedipus Rex*, Cambridge

de Hoz, J. (1979) *Aeschylean composition I*, Salamanca

de Jong, I.J.F. (1987) *Narrators and focalisers: the presentation of the story in the Iliad*, Netherlands

de Jong, I.J.F. (1991) *Narrative in drama: the art of the Euripidean messenger speech*, Netherlands

de Romilly, J. (1968) *Time in Greek tragedy*, Ithaca

Denniston, J.D. *Euripides: Electra*, Oxford, 1939

Denniston, J.D. & Page, D. (1957) *Aeschylus: Agamemnon*, Oxford

Detienne M. & Vernant, J-P (1991) *Cunning intelligence in Greek culture and society*, trans. J. Lloyd, Chicago and London [first published as *Les Ruses de l'intelligence: la Métis des grecs*, Paris, 1974]

Devereux, G. (1976) *Dreams in Greek tragedy: an ethno-psycho-analytical study*, Oxford

Dietrich, D.C. (1967) *Death, fate and the gods*, London

Dodds, E.R. (1944) *Euripides: Bacchae*, Oxford

Dodds, E.R. (1951) *The Greeks and the irrational*, Berkeley

Dover, K. (1993) *Aristophanes: Frogs*, Oxford

Dunn, F. (1992) 'Fearful symmetry: the two tombs of Hippolytus', *MD* 28, 103-11

Dunn, F. (1996) *Tragedy's end*, New York and Oxford

Eagleton, T. (1983) *Literary theory: an introduction*, Oxford

Easterling, P.E. (1968) 'Sophocles *Trachiniae*', *BICS* 15, 58-69

Easterling, P.E. (1977) 'Character in Sophocles', *G&R* 24, 121-9, reprinted in *Oxford readings in Greek tragedy*, ed. E. Segal, 1983

Easterling, P.E. (1978) '*Philoctetes* and modern criticism', *ICS* 3, 27-39

Easterling, P.E. (1981) 'The end of the *Trachiniae*', *ICS*, 56-74, 6ff.

Easterling, P.E. (1982) *Sophocles: Trachiniae*, Cambridge

Easterling, P.E. (1984) 'The tragic Homer', *BICS* 31, 1-8

Easterling, P.E. (1985) 'Anachronism in Greek tragedy', *JHS* 105, 1-10

Easterling, P.E. (1988) 'Tragedy and ritual', *Metis* 3, 89-109

Easterling, P.E. (1989) 'Agamemnon's *skeptron* in the *Iliad*', in *Images of authority: papers presented to J.Reynolds*, *PCPhS* 60, supp. 16, 104-32

Easterling, P.E. (1990) 'Constructing character in Greek tragedy', in C.B.R. Pelling (ed.) *Characterisation and individuality in Greek literature*, Oxford, 83-99

Easterling, P.E. (1991) 'Euripides in the theatre', *Pallas* 37, 49-59

Easterling, P.E. (1993) 'Gods on stage in Greek tragedy', in *Gräzer Beiträge* supp. 5 für Walter Potscher, Horn, 77-86

Easterling, P.E. and Knox, B.M.W. (eds.) (1985) *The Cambridge history of classical literature*, vol. 1, Cambridge

Easterling, P.E. (ed.) (1997) *The Cambridge companion to Greek tragedy*, Cambridge

Ehrenberg, V. (1950) 'Origins of democracy', *Historia* 1, 515-48

Eisner, R. (1980) 'Echoes of the *Odyssey* in Euripides' *Helen*', *Maia*, 31-7

Elam, K. (1980) *The semiotics of theatre and drama*, London

Else, G.F. (1967) *The origin and early form of Greek tragedy*, Cambridge Mass.

Erbse, H. (1984) *Studien zum Prolog der euripideischen Tragoedie*, Berlin and New York

Esslin, M. (1976) *An anatomy of drama*, London

Esslin, M. (1987) *The field of drama*, London

Euben, J.P. (ed.) (1986) *Greek tragedy and political theory*, Los Angeles and London

Finley, M.I. and Pleket, H.W. (1976) *The Olympic Games*, London

Foley, H.P. (1980) 'The Masque of Dionysus', *TAPhA*, 110, 107-33

Foley, H.P. (1985) *Ritual irony: poetry and sacrifice in Euripides*, Ithaca

Foley, H.P. (1992) 'Anodos dramas: Euripides' *Alcestis* and *Helen*', in Hexter and Selden (eds.) *Innovations of antiquity*, New York and London, 133-60

Fowler, D.P. (1991) 'Narrate and describe: the problems of ekphrasis', *JRS* 81, 25-35

Fraenkel, E. (1950) *Aeschylus: Agamemnon* vols. 1-3, Oxford

Friis Johansen, H. (1959) *General reflections on tragic rhesis: a study of form*, Copenhagen

Friis Johansen, H. (1984) 'Die Elektra des Sophokles: versuch einer neuen Deutung', *C&M* 25-6, 9-32

Garvie, A.F. (1969) *Aeschylus' Supplices play and trilogy*, Cambridge

Garvie, A.F. (1970) 'The opening of the *Choephori*', *BICS* 17, 79-81

Garvie, A.F. (1972) 'Deceit, violence and persuasion in the *Philoctetes*', *Studi classici in onore di Quintino Cataudella*, vol. 1, Catania, 213-26

Garvie, A.F. (1978) 'Aeschylus' simple plots', in Dawe, Diggle and Easterling (eds.) 63-86.

Garvie, A.F. (1986) *Aeschylus: Choephori*, Oxford

Gellie, G.H. (1972) *Sophocles: a reading*, Melbourne

Genette, G. (1980) *Narrative discourse*, trans. J. Lewin, Ithaca [first published as 'Discours du récit', a portion of *Figures III*, Paris 1972]

Genette, G. (1988) *Literary discourse revisited*, trans. J. Lewin, Ithaca [first published as *Nouveau discours du récit*, Paris, 1983]

Goff, B. (1990) *The noose of words: readings of desire, violence and language in Euripides' Hippolytus*, Cambridge

Goffman, E. (1974) *Frame analysis: an essay on the organisation of experience*, London and New York

Goldhill, S.D. (1984) *Language, sexuality, narrative: the Oresteia*, London

Goldhill, S.D. (1986) *Reading Greek tragedy*, Cambridge

Goldhill, S.D. (1987) 'The Great Dionysia and civic ideology', *JHS* 107, 58-76

Goldhill, S.D. (1988) 'Battle narrative and politics in Aeschylus' *Persae*', *JHS* 108, 189-92

Goldhill, S.D. (1988) 'Language in Sophocles' *Electra*', *CA Proceedings* 85, 33-4

Goldhill, S.D. (1991) *The poet's voice: essays on poetics and Greek literature*, Cambridge

Gould, J. (1973) 'Hiketeia', *JHS* 93, 74-103

Gredley, B. (1996) 'Comedy and tragedy – inevitable distinctions', in Silk (ed.) 203-16

Greengard, C. (1987) *Sophocles' reconstruction of genre and politics in Philoctetes*, Nederlands

Gregorio, L. di (1967) *Le Scene d'annuncio della tragedia greca*, Milan

Gregory, J. (1991) *Euripides and the instruction of the Athenians*, Michigan, 1991

Greimas, A.J. (1983) *Structural semantics: an attempt at a method*, trans. McDowell, Schliefer and Velie, Lincoln and London [first published in Paris, 1966]

Greimas A.J. and Courtés J. (1976) 'The cognitive dimension of narrative discourse', *NLH* 7, 433-7 [reprinted *NLH* 20.3, 1989, 563-79]

Greimas A.J. and Ricoeur, P. (1989) 'On narrativity', *NLH* 20.3, 551-62

Griffith, J.G. (1953) 'Some thoughts on the *Helena* of Euripides', *JHS* 73, 36-41

Griffith, M. (1977) *The authenticity of the Prometheus Bound*, Cambridge

Griffith, M. (1983) *Aeschylus: Prometheus Bound*, Cambridge

Griffith, M. (1984) 'The vocabulary of *Prometheus Bound*', *CQ* 34 (ii), 282-91

Griffiths, A. (ed.) (1995) *Stage directions: essays in ancient drama in honour of E.W. Handley*, ICS

Hall, E. (1989) *Inventing the barbarian*, Oxford

Hall, E. (1993) 'Political and cosmic turbulence in Euripides' *Orestes*', in Sommerstein, Halliwell, Henderson, Zimmerman (eds.), 1993

Halleran, M.R. (1988) *Euripides: Hippolytus*, Warminster

Halliwell, S. (1986) *Aristotle's Poetics*, London & Chapel Hill

Halliwell, S. (1987) *The Poetics of Aristotle: translation and commentary*, London

Hamilton, R. (1974) '*Bacchae* 47-52: Dionysus' plan', *TAPhA* 104, 139-50
Hamilton, R. (1978) 'Prologue, prophecy and plot in four plays of Euripides', *AJPh* 99, 277-302
Hartigan, L.V. (1986) 'A new look at the *Iphigeneia in Tauris*', *Eranos* 84, 119-25
Herington, J. (1970) *The author of the Prometheus Bound*, Austin and London
Herington, J. (1985) *Poetry into drama: early Greek tragedy and the Greek poetic tradition*, Berkeley
Herrnstein Smith, B. (1986) *Poetic closure: a study of how poems end*, Chicago and London
Hester, D. (1979) ' "Either ... or" versus "both ... and": a dramatic device in Sophocles', *Antichthon* 13, 12-18
Holloway, J. (1979) *Narrative and structure*, Cambridge
Holt, P. (1989) 'The end of *Trachiniae* and the fate of Herakles', *JHS* 109, 69-80
Hutchinson, G.O. (1989) *Aeschylus: Septem contra Thebas*, Oxford
Iser, W. (1978) *The act of reading: a theory of aesthetic response*, London [first published as *Der Akt des Lesens*, Munich, 1976]
Jakobson, R. (1960) 'Closing statement: linguistics and poetics', in T.A. Sebeok (ed.) *Style in Language*, New York & London, 350-85
Jebb, R.C. (1883-96) *Sophocles, the plays and fragments with critical notes, commentary and translations in English prose*, 7 vols., Cambridge
Kamerbeek, J.C. (1974) *The plays of Sophocles: commentaries: part 5: Electra*, Leiden
Kells, J.H. (1973) *Sophocles: Electra*, Cambridge
Kessels, A.H.M. (1978) *Studies on the dream in Greek literature*, Utrecht
Kirkwood, G.M. (1942) 'Two structural features of Sophocles' *Electra*', *TAPhA* 73, 86-95
Kirkwood, G.M. (1958) *A Study of Sophoclean drama*, Ithaca
Kitto, H.D.F. (1939) *Greek tragedy: a literary study*, London [3rd edn. 1961]
Kitto, H.D.F. (1958) *Sophocles, dramatist and philosopher*, Oxford
Knox, B.M.W. (1952) 'The *Hippolytus* of Euripides', *YClS*, 13, 3-31, reprinted in E. Segal (ed.) 1968
Knox, B.M.W. (1964) *The heroic temper: studies in Sophoclean tragedy*, Berkeley
Knox, B.M.W. (1971) review of Ronnet's *Sophocle, poète tragique* in *AJPh* 92, 692-701
Knox, B.M.W. (1979) *Word and action: essays on the ancient theater*, Baltimore
Kraus, C.S. (1991) 'LOGOS MEN EST ARCHAIOS: stories and story-telling in Sophocles' *Trachiniae*', *TAPhA* 121, 75-98
Lattimore, R. (1964) *Story patterns in Greek tragedy*, London
Lattimore, R. (1973) *Iphigeneia in Tauris*, Oxford
Lebeck, A. (1971) *The Oresteia: a study in language and structure*, Washington
Lee, K.H. (1976) *Euripides: Troades*, Basingstoke and London
Lee, K.H. (1997) *Euripides: Ion*, Warminster
Ley G. and Ewans, M. (1985) 'The Orchestra as acting area in Greek tragedy', *Ramus* 14, 75-84
Lloyd, M. (1985) 'Euripides *Alcestis*', *G&R*, 32, 2
Lloyd, M. (1992) *The agon in Euripides*, Oxford
Lloyd, M. (1994) *Euripides: Andromache*, Warminster
Lloyd-Jones, H. (1959) 'The end of the *Seven Against Thebes*', *CQ* n.s. 9, 80ff.
Lloyd-Jones, H. & Wilson, N. (1990) *Sophoclea*, Oxford
Long, A.A. (1968) *Language and thought in Sophocles*, London
Longo, O. (1978) 'Tecniche della comunicazione e ideologie sociali nel Grecia antica', *QUCC* 27, 63-92

Loraux, N. (1986) *The invention of Athens: the funeral oration in the classical city*, trans. A. Sheridan, Cambridge Mass. & London [first published Paris, 1981]

Luschnig, C.A.E. (1988) 'Time holds the mirror', *Mnemosyne* supp. 102, Leiden

Luschnig, C.A.E. (1995) 'The Gorgon's severed head', *Mnemosyne* supp. 153, Leiden

Machin, A. (1991) 'Electre, ou le triomphe maitrisé', *Pallas* 37, 25-37

Maclean, M. (1988) *Narrative as performance: the Baudelairean experiment*, London and New York

Macleod, C. (1975) 'Clothing in the *Oresteia*', *Maia* n.s. 27, 201-3A.

March, J.R. (1987) 'The creative poet: studies on the treatment of myths in Greek poetry', *BICS* supp. 49

March, J.R. (1989) 'Euripides' *Bacchae*: a reconsideration in the light of vase-paintings', *BICS* 36, 33-66

March, J.R. (1991-2) 'Sophocles' *Ajax*: the rehabilitation of a dishonoured hero', *BICS* 38, 1-33

Masaracchia, A. (1964) 'La Scena dell' EMPOROS nel Filottete di Sofocle', *Maia* 16, 79-98

Masaracchia, A. (1978) 'Sul racconto della falsa morte di Oreste nell'*Elletra* di Sofocle', *RCCM* 20 in memoria di Marino Barchiesi, 1027-44

McAuslan, I. and Walcot, P. (eds.) (1993) *Greek tragedy*, *G&R* studies vol. 2, Oxford

Meier, C. (1993) *The political art of Greek tragedy*, trans. A. Webber, Cambridge [first published as *Die politische Kunst der Griechischen Tragoedie*, Munich, 1988]

Mette, H.J. (1959) *Die Fragmente der Tragoedien des Aischylos*, Berlin

Michelini, A.N (1987) *Euripides and the tragic tradition*, Wisconsin

Mikalson, J.D. (1991) *Honor thy gods*, Chapel Hill and London

Minadeo, R.W. (1967) 'Plot, theme and meaning in Sophocles' *Electra*', *C&M* 28, 114-42

Moore, J. (1977) 'The dissembling speech of Ajax', *YClS* 25, 47-66

Mossman, J. (1995) *Wild justice*, Oxford

Mossman, J. (1996) 'Waiting for Neoptolemus: the unity of Euripides' *Andromache*', *G&R* xliii, 2, 143-56

Murnaghan, S. (1987) *Disguise and recognition in the Odyssey*, Princeton and Guildford

O'Higgins, D. (1991) 'Narrators and narrative in the *Philoctetes* of Sophocles', *Ramus* 20 1, 37-52

Oranje, H. (1984) 'Euripides' *Bacchae*: the play and its audience', *Mnemosyne* supp. 78, Leiden

Osterud, S. (1973) 'The Intermezzo with the false merchant in Sophocles' *Philoctetes*', in O.S. Due et al. (eds.) *C&M* Francisco Blatt septuagenario dedicata, Copenhagen, 542-627

Owen, A.S. (1939) *Euripides: Ion*, Oxford

Padel, R. (1990) 'Making space speak', in Winkler and Zeitlin (eds.), 336-65

Page, D.L. (1934) *Actors' interpolations in Greek tragedy*, Oxford

Parlavantza-Friedrich, U. (1969) *Taüschungsszenen in den Tragödien des Sophokles*, Berlin

Pearson, A.C. (1917) *The fragments of Sophocles* (ed. with additional notes from the papers of Jebb and Headlam), 3 vols, Cambridge

Peradotto, J. (1969) 'Cledonomancy in the *Oresteia*', *AJPh* 90, 1-22A.

Peradotto, J. (1990) *Man in the middle voice: name and narration in the Odyssey*, Princeton

Peretti, A. (1939) *Epirrema e tragedia: studio sul dramma attico archaico*, Florence

Perron, P. (1989) 'Introduction: A.J. Greimas', *NLH* 20.3, 523-38

Perry, M. (1979) 'Literary dynamics: how the order of a text creates its meanings', *Poetics Today* 1, 35ff.

Pfeiffer, R. (1968) *History of classical scholarship from the beginnings to the Hellenistic age*, Oxford

Pfister, M. (1988) *The theory and analysis of drama*, trans. J. Halliday, Cambridge [first published as *Das Drama*, Munich, 1977]

Pickard-Cambridge, A. (1988) *The dramatic festivals of Athens*, 2nd. edn. revised by Gould and Lewis, reissued with supplement and corrections, Oxford

Pippin, A.N. (1960) 'Euripides' *Helen*: a comedy of ideas', *CP* 55 no. 3, 151-63

Platnauer, M. (1938) *Iphigeneia in Tauris*, Oxford

Podlecki, A.J. (1970) 'The basic seriousness of Euripides' *Helen*', *TAPhA* 101, 401-18

Podlecki, A.J. (1989) *Aeschylus: Eumenides*, Warminster

Post, L.A. (1953) 'Sophocles, strategy and the *Electra*', *CW* 46, 150-3

Prag, A.J.N.W. (1985) *The Oresteia*: iconographic and narrative tradition, Warminster

Prince, G. (1982) *Narratology: the form and functioning of narrative*, Berlin, New York and Amsterdam

Prince, G. (1987) *Dictionary of narratology*, Nebraska

Propp, V. (1968) *Morphology of the folktale*, 2nd. ed., Austin and London [first published as *Morfologiia Skazki*, 1927]

Rabinowitz, P. (1977) 'Truth in fiction: a reexamination of audiences', *Critical Inquiry* 4, 121-42

Rabinowitz, P. (1980) 'What's Hecuba to us? The audience's experience of literary borrowings,' in Suleiman and Crossman (eds.) *The reader in the text*, Princeton, 241-63

Rehm, R. (1992) *Greek tragic theatre*, London and New York

Rehm, R. (1994) *Marriage to death: the conflation of wedding and funeral rites in Greek tragedy*, New Jersey

Reid, I. (1992) *Narrative exchanges*, London

Reinhardt, K. (1979) *Sophocles*, trans. H. & D. Harvey, Oxford [first published 1933]

Richardson, N.J. (1983) 'Recognition scenes in the *Odyssey* and ancient literary criticism', *Papers of the Liverpool Latin Seminar* 4, 219-35

Richardson, S. (1990) *The Homeric narrator*, Nashville

Rimmon-Kenan, S. (1983) *Narrative fiction: contemporary poetics*, London

Roberts, D.H. (1984) *Apollo and his oracle in the Oresteia*, Göttingen

Roberts, D.H. (1987) 'Parting words: final lines in Sophocles and Euripides', *CQ* n.s. 37 1, 51-64

Roberts, D.H. (1988) 'Sophoclean endings: another story', *Arethusa* 21 2, 177-94

Roberts, D.H. (1989) 'Different stories: Sophoclean narrative(s) in the *Philoctetes*', *TAPhA* 119, 161-76

Romilly, J. de (1968) *Time in Greek tragedy*, Ithaca

Rosenmeyer, T.G. (1962) *The Art of Aeschylus*, Los Angeles and London

Rutherford, R.B. (1992) *Homer: Odyssey 19 and 20*, Cambridge

Sandbach, F.H. (1977) 'Sophocles, *Electra* 77-85', *PCPhS* 23, 71-3

Sansone, D. (1985) 'Theonoe and Theoclymenus', *Symbolae Osloenses* 60, 17-36

Schmiel, R. (1972) 'The recognition duo in Euripides' *Helen*', *Hermes* 100, 274-94

Scodel, R. (1984) *Sophocles*, Boston

Seaford, R. (1981) 'Dionysiac drama and the Dionysiac mysteries', *CQ* 31(ii), 252-75

Seaford, R. (1985) 'The destruction of limits in Sophocles' *Electra*', *CQ* n.s. 35, 315-23

Seaford, R. (1996) *Euripides' Bacchae*, Warminster

Seale, D. (1982) *Vision and stagecraft in Sophocles*, London

Segal, C. (1966) 'The *Electra* of Sophocles', *TAPhA* 97, 473-545

Segal, C. (1971) 'The two worlds of Euripides' *Helen*', *TAPhA* 102, 553-614

Segal, C. (1981) *Tragedy and civilisation*, Cambridge and London

Segal, C. (1985) 'Tragedy, corporeality and the texture of language: matricide in the three Electra plays', *CW* 79 1, 7-23

Segal, C. (1986) *Interpreting Greek tragedy: myth, poetry, text*, Ithaca

Segal, C. (1989-90) 'Drama, narrative and perspective in Sophocles' *Ajax*', *Sacris Erudiri* 31, 398-404

Segal, C. (1992) 'Tragic beginnings: narration, voice and authority in the prologues of Greek drama', *YClS* 29, 85-112

Segal, C. (1996) 'Catharsis, audience and closure in Greek tragedy', in Silk (ed.) 149-72

Segal, E. (ed.) (1968) *Euripides: a collection of critical essays*, New Jersey

Segal, E. (1995) ' "The Comic catastrophe" – an essay on Euripidean comedy', in A. Griffiths (ed.), 46-55

Segré, C. (1980) 'A contribution to the semiotics of the theatre', *Poetics Today*, 1, 3-4, 40-38

Silk, M.S. (1974) *Interaction in poetic imagery, with special reference to early Greek poetry*, Cambridge

Silk, M.S. (1993) 'Heracles and Greek tragedy', in McAuslan and Walcot (eds.) 116-37

Silk, M.S. (ed.) (1996) *Tragedy and the tragic: Greek theatre and beyond*, Oxford

Smethurst, J. (1989) *The artistry of Aeschylus and Zeami*, New Jersey

Solmsen, F. (1934) '*Onoma* and *pragma* in Euripides' *Helen*', *CR* 48, 119-21

Solmsen, F. (1949) *Hesiod and Aeschylus*, New York

Solmsen, F. (1967) 'Electra and Orestes: three recognitions in Greek tragedy', *MAWBL* 30.2, Amsterdam, 31-62

Sommerstein, A.H. (1989) *Aeschylus: Eumenides*, Cambridge

Sommerstein, Halliwell, Henderson, Zimmerman (eds.) (1993) *Tragedy, comedy and the polis*: papers from the Greek drama conference, Nottingham 1990, Bari

Souriau, E. (1950) *Les 200,000 situations dramatiques*, Paris

Stanford, W.B. (1963) *Sophocles: Ajax*, London

Stanley-Porter, D.P. (1968) *Messenger scenes in Euripides*, Ph.D. thesis, London

Stanzel, F.K. (1984) *A theory of narrative*, trans. C. Goedsche, Cambridge [first published as *Theorie des Erzählens*, Göttingen, 1979]

Stevens, P.T. (1986) 'Ajax in the Trugrede', *CQ* n.s. 36 (ii), 327-36

Stinton, T.C.W. (1986) 'The scope and limits of allusion in Greek tragedy', in Cropp, Fantham, Scully (eds.), 67-91

Styan, J.L. (1985) *Drama, stage and audience*, Cambridge

Taplin, O. (1972) 'Aeschylean silences and silences in Aeschylus', *HSPh* 76, 57-97

Taplin, O. (1977) *The stagecraft of Aeschylus: the dramatic use of exits and entrances in Greek tragedy*, Oxford

Taplin, O. (1978) *Greek tragedy in action*, London

Taplin, O. (1982) 'Sophocles in his theatre', *Hardt Sophocle* 29, 155-74

Taplin, O. (1986) 'Tragedy and comedy: a *synkrisis*', *JHS* 106, 163-74

Taplin, O. (1996) 'Comedy and the tragic', in Silk (ed.) 188-202

Thalmann, W.G. (1978) *Dramatic art in Aeschylus' Seven Against Thebes*, New Haven and London

Thalmann, W.G. (1986) 'Aeschylus' physiology of the emotions', *AJPh* 107, 489-511

Torrance, R.M. (1965) 'Sophocles: some bearings', *HSPh* 69, 269-322

Trendall, A.D. and Cambitoglou, A. (1978-82) *The red-figured vases of Apulia*, 3 vols, Oxford

Trendall A.D. and Webster, T.B.L. (1971) *Illustrations of Greek drama*, London

Turner, V.S. (1975) *Dramas, fields and metaphors: symbolic actions in human society*, New York and London

van Gennep, A. (1960) *The rites of passage*, trans. M.B. Vizedom et al., London [first published Paris, 1908]

van Lieshout, R.G.A. (1980) *Greeks on dreams*, Utrecht

Vernant, J.P. and Vidal-Naquet, P. (1988) *Tragedy and myth in ancient Greece*, trans. J. Lloyd, New York [first published as *Mythe et Tragédie en Grèce Ancienne*, Paris, 1986]

Vidal-Nacquet, P. (1988) 'Ajax ou le mort du héros', Académie Royale de Belgique, *Bulletin de la Classe des lettres et des sciences morales et politiques* 5, 74, 463-86

von Wilamowitz-Moellendorf, T. (1917) *Die dramatische Technik des Sophokles*, Berlin

Walton, J.M. (1980) *Greek theatre practice*, Connecticut and London

Webster, T.B.L. (1967) *The Tragedies of Euripides*, London

West, M.L. (1966) *Hesiod: Theogony*, Oxford

West, M.L. (1974) *Studies in Greek elegy and iambus*, Berlin and New York

West, M.L. (1986) *Euripides: Orestes*, Warminster

West, M.L. (1990) *Studies in Aeschylus*, Stuttgart

White, R.J. (1980) *The interpretation of dreams: Oneirocritica by Artemidorus, translation and commentary*, Netherlands

Whitman, C.H. (1957) *Sophocles: a study of heroic humanism*, Cambridge

Whitman, C.H. (1974) *Euripides and the full circle of myth*, Cambridge, Mass.

Wiles, D. (1991) *The masks of Menander: sign and meaning in Greek and Roman performance*, Cambridge

Wiles, D. (1993) 'The seven gates of Aechylus', *Drama* 2, 180-93

Wilkins, J. (1993) *Euripides: Heraclidae*, Oxford

Willink, C.W. (1996) 'Some problems in the *Bacchae* 1', *CQ* 16, 27-50

Wilson, E. (1929) *The wound and the bow: seven studies in literature*, Cambridge

Winkler J.J. and Zeitlin, F.I. (eds.) (1990) *Nothing to do with Dionysos? Athenian drama in its social context*, Princeton

Winnington-Ingram, R.P. (1943) 'The role of Apollo in the *Oresteia*', *CR* 47, 97-104

Winnington-Ingram, R.P. (1948) 'Clytemnestra and the vote of Athena', *JHS* 68, 130-47

Winnington-Ingram, R.P. (1948) *Euripides and Dionysus*, Cambridge

Winnington-Ingram, R.P. (1954-5) 'The *Electra*: prolegomena to an interpretation', *PCPhS* 183, 20-6

Winnington-Ingram, R.P. (1969) 'Euripides: *poietes sophos*', *Arethusa* 2.1, 127-42

Winnington-Ingram, R.P. (1969a) 'Tragica', *BICS* 16, 44-7

Winnington-Ingram, R.P. (1980) *Sophocles: an interpretation*, Cambridge

Winnington-Ingram, R.P. (1983) *Studies in Aeschylus*, Cambridge

Wolff, C. (1973) 'On Euripides' *Helen*', *HSCPh* 77, 61-84

Woodard, T.M. (1964, 1965) '*Electra* by Sophocles: the dialectical design', *HSPh* 68, 163-205; 70, 195-227

Zeitlin, F.I. (1982) *Under the sign of the shield: semiotics and Aeschylus' Septem*, Rome

Zeitlin, F.I. (1985) 'The power of Aphrodite: Eros and the boundaries of self in the *Hippolytus*', in Burian (ed.) 52-111

Zuntz, G. (1955) *The political plays of Euripides*, Manchester

Zuntz, G. (1960) 'On Euripides' *Helena*: theology and irony', in *Entretiens sur l'Antiquité Classique* 6.1, Geneva, 199-241

Index

Numbers in italics refer to line numbers in the plays.